THE

D1323940

General Editor
R.B. Kennedy

Additional notes and editing
Mike Gould

HENRY IV PART I
& PART II

William Shakespeare

COLLINS
CLASSICS

Harper Press
An imprint of HarperCollins*Publishers*
77–85 Fulham Palace Road
Hammersmith
London W6 8JB

This Harper Press paperback edition published 2011

A catalogue record for this book is available from the British Library

ISBN-13: 978-0-00-790230-9

Printed and bound in Great Britain by Clays Ltd, St Ives plc

MIX
Paper from
responsible sources
FSC™ C007454

FSC™ is a non-profit international organisation established to promote
the responsible management of the world's forests. Products carrying the
FSC label are independently certified to assure consumers that they come
from forests that are managed to meet the social, economic and
ecological needs of present and future generations,
and other controlled sources.

Find out more about HarperCollins and the environment at
www.harpercollins.co.uk/green

Life & Times section © Gerard Cheshire
Introductions by Alec Yearling and Donald MacKenzie
Shakespeare: Words and Phrases adapted from
Collins English Dictionary
Typesetting in Kalix by Palimpsest Book Production Limited,
Falkirk, Stirlingshire

10 9 8 7 6 5 4 3 2 1

Prefatory Note

This Shakespeare play uses the full Alexander text. By keeping in mind the fact that the language has changed considerably in four hundred years, as have customs, jokes, and stage conventions, the editors have aimed at helping the modern reader – whether English is their mother tongue or not – to grasp the full significance of the play. The Notes, intended primarily for examination candidates, are presented in a simple, direct style. The needs of those unfamiliar with British culture have been specially considered.

Since quiet study of the printed word is unlikely to bring fully to life plays that were written directly for the public theatre, attention has been drawn to dramatic effects which are important in performance. The editors see Shakespeare's plays as living works of art which can be enjoyed today on stage, film and television in many parts of the world.

CONTENTS

An Elizabethan playhouse. Note the apron stage protruding into the auditorium, the space below it, the inner room at the rear of the stage, the gallery above the inner stage, the canopy over the main stage, and the absence of a roof over the audience.

The Theatre in Shakespeare's Day

On the face of it, the conditions in the Elizabethan theatre were not such as to encourage great writers. The public playhouse itself was not very different from an ordinary inn-yard; it was open to the weather; among the spectators were often louts, pickpockets and prostitutes; some of the actors played up to the rowdy elements in the audience by inserting their own jokes into the authors' lines, while others spoke their words loudly but unfeelingly; the presentation was often rough and noisy, with fireworks to represent storms and battles, and a table and a few chairs to represent a tavern; there were no actresses, so boys took the parts of women, even such subtle and mature ones as Cleopatra and Lady Macbeth; there was rarely any scenery at all in the modern sense. In fact, a quick inspection of the English theatre in the reign of Elizabeth I by a time-traveller from the twentieth century might well produce only one positive reaction: the costumes were often elaborate and beautiful.

Shakespeare himself makes frequent comments in his plays about the limitations of the playhouse and the actors of his time, often apologizing for them. At the beginning of *Henry V* the Prologue refers to the stage as 'this unworthy scaffold' and to the theatre building (the Globe, probably) as 'this wooden O', and emphasizes the urgent need for imagination in making up for all the deficiencies of presentation. In introducing Act IV the Chorus goes so far as to say:

> . . . we shall much disgrace
> With four or five most vile and ragged foils,
> Right ill-dispos'd in brawl ridiculous,
> The name of Agincourt, (lines 49–52)

In *A Midsummer Night's Dream* (Act V, Scene i) he seems to dismiss actors with the words:

The best in this kind are but shadows.

Yet Elizabeth's theatre, with all its faults, stimulated dramatists to a variety of achievement that has never been equalled and, in Shakespeare, produced one of the greatest writers in history. In spite of all his grumbles he seems to have been fascinated by the challenge that it presented him with. It is necessary to re-examine his theatre carefully in order to understand how he was able to achieve so much with the materials he chose to use. What sort of place was the Elizabethan playhouse in reality? What sort of people were these criticized actors? And what sort of audiences gave them their living?

The Development of the Theatre up to Shakespeare's Time

For centuries in England noblemen had employed groups of skilled people to entertain them when required. Under Tudor rule, as England became more secure and united, actors such as these were given more freedom, and they often performed in public, while still acknowledging their 'overlords' (in the 1570s, for example, when Shakespeare was still a schoolboy at Stratford, one famous company was called 'Lord Leicester's Men'). London was rapidly becoming larger and more important in the second half of the sixteenth century, and many of the companies of actors took the opportunities offered to establish themselves at inns on the main roads leading to the City (for example, the Boar's Head in Whitechapel and the Tabard in South-wark) or in the City itself. These groups of actors would come to an agreement with the inn-keeper which would give them the use of the yard for their performances after people had eaten and drunk well in the middle of the day. Before long, some inns were taken over completely by companies of players and thus became the first public theatres. In 1574 the officials of the City of London issued an order which shows clearly that these theatres were both popular and also offensive to some respectable people, because the order complains about 'the inordinate haunting of great multitudes of people, specially youth, to plays interludes and shows; namely occasion of frays and quarrels, evil practices of incontinency in great inns . . .' There is evidence that, on public holidays, the theatres on the banks of the Thames were crowded with noisy apprentices and tradesmen, but it would be wrong to think that audiences were always undiscriminating and loudmouthed. In spite of the disapproval of Puritans and the more staid members of society, by the 1590s, when Shakespeare's plays were beginning to be performed, audiences consisted of a good cross-section of English society, nobility as well as workers, intellectuals as well as simple people out for a laugh; also (and in this respect English theatres were unique in Europe), it was quite normal for respectable women to attend plays. So Shakespeare had to write plays which would appeal to people of widely different kinds. He had to provide 'something for everyone' but at the same time to take care to unify the material so that it would not seem to fall into separate pieces as they watched it. A speech like that of the drunken porter in *Macbeth* could provide the 'groundlings' with a belly-laugh, but also held a deeper significance for those who could appreciate it. The audience he wrote for was one of a number of apparent drawbacks which Shakespeare was able to turn to his and our advantage.

Shakespeare's Actors

Nor were all the actors of the time mere 'rogues, vagabonds and sturdy beggars' as some were described in a Statute of 1572. It is true that many of them had a hard life and earned very little money, but leading actors could become partners in the ownership of the theatres in which they acted: Shakespeare was a shareholder in the Globe and the Blackfriars theatres when he was an actor as well as a playwright. In any case, the attacks made on Elizabethan actors were usually directed at their morals and not at their acting ability; it is clear that many of them must have been good at their trade if they were able to interpret complex works like the great tragedies in such a way as to attract enthusiastic audiences. Undoubtedly some of the boys took the women's parts with skill and confidence, since a man called Coryate, visiting Venice in 1611, expressed surprise that women could act as well as they: 'I saw women act, a thing that I never saw before . . . and they performed it with as good a grace, action, gesture . . . as ever I saw any masculine actor.' The quality of most of the actors who first presented Shakespeare's plays is probably accurately summed up by Fynes Moryson, who wrote, '. . . as there be, in my opinion, more plays in London than in all the parts of the world I have seen, so do these players or comedians excel all other in the world.'

The Structure of the Public Theatre

Although the 'purpose-built' theatres were based on the inn-yards which had been used for play-acting, most of them were circular. The walls contained galleries on three storeys from which the wealthier patrons watched, they must have been something like the 'boxes' in a modern theatre, except that they held much larger numbers – as many as 1500. The 'groundlings' stood on the floor of the building, facing a raised stage which projected from the 'stage-wall', the main features of which were:

1 a small room opening on to the back of the main stage and on the same level as it (rear stage),
2 a gallery above this inner stage (upper stage),
3 canopy projecting from above the gallery over the main stage, to protect the actors from the weather (the 700 or 800 members of the audience who occupied the yard, or 'pit' as we call it today, had the sky above them).

In addition to these features there were dressing-rooms behind the stage and a space underneath it from which entrances could be made through trap-doors. All the acting areas – main stage, rear stage, upper stage and under stage – could be entered by actors directly from their dressing rooms, and all of them were used in productions of Shakespeare's plays. For example, the inner stage, an almost cavelike structure, would have been where Ferdinand and Miranda are 'discovered' playing chess in the last act of *The Tempest*, while the upper stage was certainly the balcony from which Romeo climbs down in Act III of *Romeo and Juliet*.

It can be seen that such a building, simple but adaptable, was not really unsuited to the presentation of plays like Shakespeare's. On the contrary, its simplicity guaranteed the minimum of distraction, while its shape and construction must have produced a sense of involvement on the part of the audience that modern producers would envy.

Other Resources of the Elizabethan Theatre

Although there were few attempts at scenery in the public theatre (painted backcloths were occasionally used in court performances), Shakespeare and his fellow playwrights were able to make use of a fair variety of 'properties', lists of such articles have survived: they include beds, tables, thrones, and also trees, walls, a gallows, a Trojan horse and a 'Mouth of Hell'; in a list of properties belonging to the manager, Philip Henslowe, the curious item 'two mossy banks' appears. Possibly one of them was used for the

> bank whereon the wild thyme blows,
> Where oxlips and the nodding violet grows

in *A Midsummer Night's Dream* (Act II, Scene i). Once again, imagination must have been required of the audience.

Costumes were the one aspect of stage production in which

trouble and expense were hardly ever spared to obtain a magnificent effect. Only occasionally did they attempt any historical accuracy (almost all Elizabethan productions were what we should call 'modern-dress' ones), but they were appropriate to the characters who wore them: kings were seen to be kings and beggars were similarly unmistakable. It is an odd fact that there was usually no attempt at illusion in the costuming: if a costume looked fine and rich it probably was. Indeed, some of the costumes were almost unbelievably expensive. Henslowe lent his company £19 to buy a cloak, and the Alleyn brothers, well-known actors, gave £20 for a 'black velvet cloak, with sleeves embroidered all with silver and gold, lined with black satin striped with gold'.

With the one exception of the costumes, the 'machinery' of the playhouse was economical and uncomplicated rather than crude and rough, as we can see from this second and more leisurely look at it. This meant that playwrights were stimulated to produce the imaginative effects that they wanted from the language that they used. In the case of a really great writer like Shakespeare, when he had learned his trade in the theatre as an actor, it seems that he received quite enough assistance of a mechanical and structural kind without having irksome restrictions and conventions imposed on him; it is interesting to try to guess what he would have done with the highly complex apparatus of a modern television studio. We can see when we look back to his time that he used his instrument, the Elizabethan theatre, to the full, but placed his ultimate reliance on the communication between his imagination and that of his audience through the medium of words. It is, above all, his rich and wonderful use of language that must have made play-going at that time a memorable experience for people of widely different kinds. Fortunately, the deep satisfaction of appreciating and enjoying Shakespeare's work can be ours also, if we are willing to overcome the language difficulty produced by the passing of time.

Shakespeare: A Timeline

Very little indeed is known about Shakespeare's private life; the facts included here are almost the only indisputable ones. The dates of Shakespeare's plays are those on which they were first produced.

1558	Queen Elizabeth crowned.	
1561	Francis Bacon born.	
1564	Christopher Marlowe born.	William Shakespeare born, April 23rd, baptized April 26th.
1566		Shakespeare's brother, Gilbert, born.
1567	Mary, Queen of Scots, deposed. James VI (later James I of England) crowned King of Scotland.	
1572	Ben Jonson born. Lord Leicester's Company (of players) licensed; later called Lord Strange's, then the Lord Chamberlain's and finally (under James) the King's Men.	
1573	John Donne born.	
1574	The Common Council of London directs that all plays and playhouses in London must be licensed.	
1576	James Burbage builds the first public playhouse, The Theatre, at Shoreditch, outside the walls of the City.	
1577	Francis Drake begins his voyage round the world (completed 1580). *Holinshed's Chronicles of England, Scotland and Ireland* published (which	

Shakespeare later used extensively).

1582		Shakespeare married to Anne Hathaway.
1583	The Queen's Company founded by royal warrant.	Shakespeare's daughter, Susanna, born.
1585		Shakespeare's twins, Hamnet and Judith, born.
1586	Sir Philip Sidney, the Elizabethan ideal 'Christian knight', poet, patron, soldier, killed at Zutphen in the Low Countries.	
1587	Mary, Queen of Scots, beheaded. Marlowe's *Tamburlaine (Part I)* first staged.	
1588	Defeat of the Spanish Armada. Marlowe's *Tamburlaine (Part II)* first staged.	
1589	Marlowe's *Jew of Malta* and Kyd's *Spanish Tragedy* (a 'revenge tragedy' and one of the most popular plays of Elizabethan times).	
1590	Spenser's *Faerie Queene* (Books I–III) published.	
1592	Marlowe's *Doctor Faustus* and *Edward II* first staged. Witchcraft trials in Scotland. Robert Greene, a rival playwright, refers to Shakespeare as 'an upstart crow' and 'the only Shake-scene in a country'.	*Titus Andronicus* *Henry VI, Parts I, II and III* *Richard III*
1593	London theatres closed by the plague. Christopher Marlowe killed in a Deptford tavern.	*Two Gentlemen of Verona* *Comedy of Errors* *The Taming of the Shrew* *Love's Labour's Lost*
1594	Shakespeare's company becomes The Lord Chamberlain's Men.	*Romeo and Juliet*

1595	Raleigh's first expedition to Guiana. Last expedition of Drake and Hawkins (both died).	*Richard II* *A Midsummer Night's Dream*
1596	Spenser's *Faerie Queene* (Books IV–VI) published. James Burbage buys rooms at Blackfriars and begins to convert them into a theatre.	*King John* *The Merchant of Venice* Shakespeare's son Hamnet dies. Shakespeare's father is granted a coat of arms.
1597	James Burbage dies, his son Richard, a famous actor, turns the Blackfriars Theatre into a private playhouse.	*Henry IV (Part I)* Shakespeare buys and redecorates New Place at Stratford.
1598	Death of Philip II of Spain	*Henry IV (Part II)* *Much Ado About Nothing*
1599	Death of Edmund Spenser. The Globe Theatre completed at Bankside by Richard and Cuthbert Burbage.	*Henry V* *Julius Caesar* *As You Like It*
1600	Fortune Theatre built at Cripplegate. East India Company founded for the extension of English trade and influence in the East. The Children of the Chapel begin to use the hall at Blackfriars.	*Merry Wives of Windsor* *Troilus and Cressida*
1601		*Hamlet*
1602	Sir Thomas Bodley's library opened at Oxford.	*Twelfth Night*
1603	Death of Queen Elizabeth. James I comes to the throne. Shakespeare's company becomes The King's Men. Raleigh tried, condemned and sent to the Tower	
1604	Treaty of peace with Spain	*Measure for Measure* *Othello* *All's Well that Ends Well*
1605	The Gunpowder Plot: an attempt by a group of Catholics to blow up the Houses of Parliament.	

1606	Guy Fawkes and other plotters executed.	*Macbeth* *King Lear*
1607	Virginia, in America, colonized. A great frost in England.	*Antony and Cleopatra* *Timon of Athens* *Coriolanus* Shakespeare's daughter, Susanna, married to Dr. John Hall.
1608	The company of the Children of the Chapel Royal (who had performed at Blackfriars for ten years) is disbanded. John Milton born. Notorious pirates executed in London.	Richard Burbage leases the Black-friars Theatre to six of his fellow actors, including Shakespeare. *Pericles, Prince of Tyre*
1609		Shakespeare's Sonnets published.
1610	A great drought in England	*Cymbeline*
1611	Chapman completes his great translation of the *Iliad*, the story of Troy. Authorized Version of the Bible published.	*A Winter's Tale* *The Tempest*
1612	Webster's *The White Devil* first staged.	Shakespeare's brother, Gilbert, dies.
1613	Globe theatre burnt down during a performance of *Henry VIII* (the firing of small cannon set fire to the thatched roof). Webster's *Duchess of Malfi* first staged.	*Henry VIII* *Two Noble Kinsmen* Shakespeare buys a house at Blackfriars.
1614	Globe Theatre rebuilt in 'far finer manner than before'.	
1616	Ben Jonson publishes his plays in one volume. Raleigh released from the Tower in order to prepare an expedition to the gold mines of Guiana.	Shakespeare's daughter, Judith, marries Thomas Quiney. Death of Shakespeare on his birthday, April 23rd.
1618	Raleigh returns to England and is executed on the charge for which he was imprisoned in 1603.	
1623	Publication of the Folio edition of Shakespeare's plays	Death of Anne Shakespeare (née Hathaway).

Life & Times

William Shakespeare the Playwright

There exists a curious paradox when it comes to the life of William Shakespeare. He easily has more words written about him than any other famous English writer, yet we know the least about him. This inevitably means that most of what is written about him is either fabrication or speculation. The reason why so little is known about Shakespeare is that he wasn't a novelist or a historian or a man of letters. He was a playwright, and playwrights were considered fairly low on the social pecking order in Elizabethan society. Writing plays was about providing entertainment for the masses – the great unwashed. It was the equivalent to being a journalist for a tabloid newspaper.

In fact, we only know of Shakespeare's work because two of his friends had the foresight to collect his plays together following his death and have them printed. The only reason they did so was apparently because they rated his talent and thought it would be a shame if his words were lost.

Consequently his body of work has ever since been assessed and reassessed as the greatest contribution to English literature. That is despite the fact that we know that different printers took it upon themselves to heavily edit the material they worked from. We also know that Elizabethan plays were worked and reworked frequently, so that they evolved over time until they were honed to perfection, which means that many different hands played their part in the active writing process. It would therefore be fair to say that any play attributed to Shakespeare is unlikely to contain a great deal of original input. Even the plots were based on well known historical events, so it would be hard to know what fragments of any Shakespeare play came from that single mind.

One might draw a comparison with the Christian bible, which remains such a compelling read because it came from the collaboration of many contributors and translators over centuries, who each adjusted the stories until they could no longer be improved. As virtually nothing is known of Shakespeare's life and even less about his method of working, we shall never know the truth about his plays. They certainly contain some very elegant phrasing, clever plot devices and plenty of words never before seen in print, but as to whether Shakespeare invented them from a unique imagination or whether he simply took them from others around him is anyone's guess.

The best bet seems to be that Shakespeare probably took the lead role in devising the original drafts of the plays, but was open to collaboration from any source when it came to developing them into workable scripts for effective performances. He would have had to work closely with his fellow actors in rehearsals, thereby finding out where to edit, abridge, alter, reword and so on.

In turn, similar adjustments would have occurred in his absence, so that definitive versions of his plays never really existed. In effect Shakespeare was only responsible for providing the framework of plays, upon which others took liberties over time. This wasn't helped by the fact that the English language itself was not definitive at that time either. The consequence was that people took it upon themselves to spell words however they pleased or to completely change words and phrasing to suit their own preferences.

It is easy to see then, that Shakespeare's plays were always going to have lives of their own, mutating and distorting in detail like Chinese whispers. The culture of creative preservation was simply not established in Elizabethan England. Creative ownership of Shakespeare's plays was lost to him as soon as he released them into the consciousness of others. They saw nothing wrong with taking his ideas and running with them, because no one had ever suggested that one shouldn't, and Shakespeare probably regarded his work in the same way. His plays weren't sacrosanct works of art, they were templates for theatre folk to make their livings from, so they had every right to mould them into productions that drew in the crowds as effectively as possible. Shakespeare was like the helmsman of a sailing ship, steering the vessel but wholly reliant on the team work of his crew to arrive at the desired destination.

It seems that Shakespeare certainly had a natural gift, but the genius of his plays may be attributable to the collective efforts of Shakespeare and others. It is a rather satisfying notion to think that *his* plays might actually be the creative outpourings of the Elizabethan milieu in which Shakespeare immersed himself. That makes them important social documents as well as seminal works of the English language.

Money in Shakespeare's Day

It is extremely difficult, if not impossible, to relate the value of money in our time to its value in another age and to compare prices of commodities today and in the past. Many items *are* simply not comparable on grounds of quality or serviceability.

There was a bewildering variety of coins in use in Elizabethan England. As nearly all English and European coins were gold or silver, they had intrinsic value apart from their official value. This meant that foreign coins circulated freely in England and were officially recognized, for example the French crown (écu) worth about 30p (72 cents), and the Spanish ducat worth about 33p (79 cents). The following table shows some of the coins mentioned by Shakespeare and their relation to one another.

GOLD	British	American	SILVER	British	American
sovereign (heavy type)	£1.50	$3.60	shilling	10p	24c
sovereign (light type)	66p–£1	$1.58–$2.40	groat	1.5p	4c
angel royal	33p–50p	79c–$1.20			
noble	50p	$1.20			
crown	25p	60c			

A comparison of the following prices in Shakespeare's time with the prices of the same items today will give some idea of the change in the value of money.

ITEM	PRICE British	American	ITEM	PRICE British	American
beef, per lb.	0.5p	1c	cherries (lb.)	1p	2c
mutton, leg	7.5p	18c	7 oranges	1p	2c
rabbit	3.5p	9c	1 lemon	1p	2c
chicken	3p	8c	cream (quart)	2.5p	6c
potatoes (lb)	10p	24c	sugar (lb.)	£1	$2.40
carrots (bunch)	1p	2c	sack (wine) (gallon)	14p	34c
8 artichokes	4p	9c	tobacco (oz.)	25p	60c
1 cucumber	1p	2c	biscuits (lb.)	12.5p	30c

INTRODUCTION TO PART 1

by Alec Yearling

This play differs notably from its predecessor *Richard II* (apparently written several years before), which had been lyrical in manner and largely single-minded in chronicling its protagonist's downfall. Events in the later play largely stem from that traumatic deposition; but here the approach is prismatic and disjunct. We see manoeuvres of statecraft and rebellion, glimpse common life, hear idealistic and cynical voices; and centrally, we contemplate the prince who will be Henry V and his association with Sir John Falstaff.

The result is the first of those dramas in which Shakespeare perfects the art of fruitful confusion. We are beset by contrarieties in a continually self-modifying text where no statement can be taken as absolute. 'Thus ever did rebellion find rebuke' says the finally victorious monarch who gained his position by successful revolt against his anointed liege.

It is magnificent to be a king; also a barely tolerable burden, as Henry's opening words indicate. Shakespeare's interest is in how, by what codes, rulers rule. The rebel allies are doomed to failure because they are factious, with traits either ridiculous (Glendower's sorcery) or unrealistic (Hotspur's pursuit of honour). None of them has any idea of what it means to unite a kingdom. Their shallowness is far from the spiritual dimension – manifest in guilt – which is a marked feature of King Henry's part, and it is into this deeper awareness that Prince Hal must be initiated. Shakespeare was bold with the details of his source-chronicles, but he followed their insistence that God's providential scheme required atonement for the overthrow and murder of King Richard: Hal will eventually accept his burden (in *Part Two*) and glorify it (in

Henry V), but for the moment father and son are caught in a primal tragic situation. We see Hal finding his way, accessible to our gaze as the king rarely is. He is repeatedly paralleled with Hotspur, and given contrasting father-figures in Falstaff and the king. Schematically, his role is to learn through observation and experience so as finally to perfectly blend humanity and royalty. A difficulty arises in that this is not quite what the play delivers. In Act 1 Scene 2 the prince reveals himself only superficially involved in the Eastcheap world which, epitomised in Falstaff, signifies the pleasures and miseries of carnal frailty. He pretends to be errant so as to impress his people with an eventual appearance of reform. (His father in Act 3 Scene 2 is similarly dedicated to the manipulation of public opinion.) This is the world of *Realpolitik*; the danger is that it will render Hal unsympathetic and cripple the dramatic potential of his relationship with Falstaff. In popular tradition Hal was genuinely errant: Shakespeare sanitises him. He becomes a virtuous trickster in the Gadshill robbery, with potentially anarchic moments like the assault on the Lord Chief Justice confined to passing reported references.

Whereas Hal is thematically central, with the climactic battle at Shrewsbury showing his maturity in vanquishing Hotspur and his magnanimity in condoning Falstaff's outrageous lies, Falstaff himself is at the human heart of the drama. Essentially his is a simple character-type: the Braggart Soldier, with limitless entertainment-potential in the chasm between words and actualities. Some see him as a version of the traditional Vice, a gleeful tempter to sin. But a rich vitality overruns the stereotypes. Falstaff is a Vice only as Shylock, a contemporary creation, is a Wicked Jew. Unlike the Vice, he neither delights in wickedness for its own sake, nor rejoices in misleading youth. Compounded of the seven sins, he will eventually be cast out and punished: but as with Shylock, we need to consider causes and effects, and the human complexity that blurs moral judgements. Shylock the humanised monster fits indifferently into his conventional plot; Falstaff gains from being featured rather in a series of incidents, and is the superior creation because a degree of irony is suggested in his portrayal. So keen on citing scriptural and moral tags, so blatant at denying the truth about himself, and yet so clearly not an idiot, he comes across as self-constructed. A role-playing Falstaff confronts a Hal locked in a public-relations exercise:

> – Banish plump Jack, and banish all the world.
> – I do, I will. [2.4.462–464]

And if we find ourselves deeply uneasy at the implications of that, then we are attuned to this disturbing, equivocal play.

LIST OF CHARACTERS FOR PART 1

King Henry The Fourth

Henry, Prince Of Wales,
Prince John Of Lancaster } sons of Henry IV

Earl Of Westmoreland,
Sir Walter Blunt } friends of the King

Thomas Percy, Earl Of Worcester

Henry Percy, Earl Of Northumberland

Henry Percy,   his son
surnamed *Hotspur*

Edmund Mortimer, Earl Of March

Archibald, Earl Of Douglas

Scroop, Archbishop Of York

Sir Michael   friend of the Archbishop

Owen Glendower

Sir Richard Vernon

Sir John Falstaff
Poins
Bardolph   } irregular humorists
Peto
Gadshill

Francis   a drawer

Lady Percy   wife of Hotspur and sister of
                          Mortimer

Lady Mortimer   wife of Mortimer and daughter
                             of Glendower

Hostess Quickly   of the Boar's Head, Eastcheap

Lords, Officers, Attendants, an Ostler, a Servant, a Messenger, a Sheriff, a Vintner, a Chamberlain, Drawers, Carriers, and Travellers.

The Scene: England And Wales

ACT ONE
SCENE I

London. The palace.

[*Enter the* KING, LORD JOHN OF LANCASTER, EARL OF
WESTMORELAND, SIR WALTER BLUNT, *and Others.*]

King
    So shaken as we are, so wan with care,
    Find we a time for frightened peace to pant
    And breathe short-winded accents of new broils
    To be commenc'd in strands afar remote.
    No more the thirsty entrance of this soil   5
    Shall daub her lips with her own children's blood;
    No more shall trenching war channel her fields,
    Nor bruise her flow'rets with the armed hoofs
    Of hostile paces. Those opposed eyes
    Which, like the meteors of a troubled heaven,   10
    All of one nature, of one substance bred,
    Did lately meet in the intestine shock
    And furious close of civil butchery,
    Shall now in mutual well-beseeming ranks
    March all one way, and be no more oppos'd   15
    Against acquaintance, kindred, and allies.
    The edge of war, like an ill-sheathed knife,
    No more shall cut his master. Therefore, friends,
    As far as to the sepulchre of Christ –
    Whose soldier now, under whose blessed cross   20
    We are impressed and engag'd to fight –
    Forthwith a power of English shall we levy,
    Whose arms were moulded in their mothers' womb
    To chase these pagans in those holy fields
    Over whose acres walk'd those blessed feet   25
    Which fourteen hundred years ago were nail'd
    For our advantage on the bitter cross.

But this our purpose now is twelvemonth old,
And bootless 'tis to tell you we will go;
30   Therefore we meet not now. Then let me hear
Of you, my gentle cousin Westmoreland,
What yesternight our Council did decree
In forwarding this dear expedience.

Westmoreland

My liege, this haste was hot in question
35   And many limits of the charge set down
But yesternight, when all athwart there came
A post from Wales loaden with heavy news;
Whose worst was that the noble Mortimer,
Leading the men of Herefordshire to fight
40   Against the irregular and wild Glendower,
Was by the rude hands of that Welshman taken,
A thousand of his people butchered;
Upon whose dead corpse there was such misuse,
Such beastly shameless transformation,
45   By those Welshwomen done, as may not be
Without much shame re-told or spoken of.

King

It seems then that the tidings of this broil
Brake off our business for the Holy Land.

Westmoreland

This match'd with other did, my gracious Lord;
50   For more uneven and unwelcome news
Came from the north, and thus it did import:
On Holy-rood day, the gallant Hotspur there,
Young Harry Percy, and brave Archibald,
That ever-valiant and approved Scot,
55   At Holmedon met,
Where they did spend a sad and bloody hour;
As by discharge of their artillery
And shape of likelihood the news was told;
For he that brought them, in the very heat
60   And pride of their contention did take horse,
Uncertain of the issue any way.

King
> Here is a dear, a true industrious friend,
> Sir Walter Blunt, new lighted from his horse,
> Stain'd with the variation of each soil
> Betwixt that Holmedon and this seat of ours;   65
> And he hath brought us smooth and welcome news.
> The Earl of Douglas is discomfited:
> Ten thousand bold Scots, two and twenty knights,
> Balk'd in their own blood, did Sir Walter see
> On Holmedon's plains; of prisoners, Hotspur took   70
> Mordake, Earl of Fife and eldest son
> To beaten Douglas; and the Earl of Athol,
> Of Murray, Angus, and Menteith.
> And is not this an honourable spoil?
> A gallant prize? Ha, cousin, is it not?   75

Westmoreland
> In faith,
> It is a conquest for a prince to boast of.

King
> Yea, there thou mak'st me sad and mak'st me sin
> In envy that my Lord Northumberland
> Should be the father to so blest a son –   80
> A son who is the theme of honour's tongue;
> Amongst a grove, the very straightest plant;
> Who is sweet Fortune's minion and her pride;
> Whilst I, by looking on the praise of him,
> See riot and dishonour stain the brow   85
> Of my young Harry. O that it could be prov'd
> That some night-tripping fairy had exchang'd
> In cradle-clothes our children where they lay,
> And call'd mine Percy, his Plantagenet!
> Then would I have his Harry, and he mine.   90
> But let him from my thoughts. What think you, coz,
> Of this young Percy's pride? The prisoners
> Which he in this adventure hath surpris'd
> To his own use he keeps; and sends me word,
> I shall have none but Mordake Earl of Fife.   95

Westmoreland
    This is his uncle's teaching, this is Worcester,
    Malevolent to you in all aspects;
    Which makes him prune himself, and bristle up
    The crest of youth against your dignity.
King
100   But I have sent for him to answer this;
    And for this cause awhile we must neglect
    Our holy purpose to Jerusalem.
    Cousin, on Wednesday next our council we
    Will hold at Windsor – so inform the lords;
105   But come yourself with speed to us again,
    For more is to be said and to be done
    Than out of anger can be uttered.
Westmoreland
    I will, my liege.

[Exeunt.]

SCENE II

London. The Prince's lodging.

[Enter the PRINCE OF WALES *and* SIR JOHN FALSTAFF.*]*

Falstaff
Now, Hal, what time of day is it, lad?
Prince
Thou art so fat-witted with drinking of old sack, and
unbuttoning thee after supper, and sleeping upon
benches after noon, that thou hast forgotten to demand
that truly which thou wouldest truly know. What a   5
devil hast thou to do with the time of the day? Unless
hours were cups of sack, and minutes capons, and
clocks the tongues of bawds, and dials the signs of
leaping-houses, and the blessed sun himself a fair hot
wench in flame-coloured taffeta, I see no reason why   10
thou shouldst be so superfluous to demand the time
of the day.
Falstaff
Indeed, you come near me now, Hal; for we that take
purses go by the moon and the seven stars, and not
by Phœbus, he 'that wand'ring knight so fair'. And, I   15
prithee, sweet wag, when thou art a king, as, God save
thy Grace – Majesty, I should say; for grace thou wilt
have none –
Prince
What, none?
Falstaff
No, by my troth; not so much as will serve to be   20
prologue to an egg and butter.
Prince
Well, how then? Come, roundly, roundly.
Falstaff
Marry, then, sweet wag, when thou art king, let not
us that are squires of the night's body be called thieves
of the day's beauty; let us be Diana's foresters,   25

gentlemen of the shade, minions of the moon; and let men say we be men of good government, being governed, as the sea is, by our noble and chaste mistress the moon, under whose Countenance we steal.

Prince

30   Thou sayest well, and it holds well too; for the fortune of us that are the moon's men doth ebb and flow like the sea, being governed, as the sea is, by the moon. As, for proof, now: a purse of gold most resolutely snatch'd on Monday night, and most dissolutely spent

35   on Tuesday morning; got with swearing 'Lay by' and spent with crying 'Bring in'; now in as low an ebb as the foot of the ladder, and by and by in as high a flow as the ridge of the gallows.

Falstaff

By the Lord, thou say'st true, lad. And is not my hostess

40   of the tavern a most sweet wench?

Prince

As the honey of Hybla, my old lad of the castle. And is not a buff jerkin a most sweet robe of durance?

Falstaff

How now, how now, mad wag!
What, in thy quips and thy quiddities?

45   What a plague have I to do with a buff jerkin?

Prince

Why, what a pox have I to do with my hostess of the tavern?

Falstaff

Well, thou hast call'd her to a reckoning many a time and oft.

Prince

50   Did I ever call for thee to pay thy part?

Falstaff

No; I'll give thee thy due, thou hast paid all there.

Prince

Yea, and elsewhere, so far as my coin would stretch; and where it would not, I have used my credit.

Falstaff

Yea, and so us'd it that, were it not here apparent that
thou art heir apparent – but, I prithee, sweet wag, shall   55
there be gallows standing in England when thou art
king, and resolution thus fubb'd as it is with the rusty
curb of old father antic the law? Do not thou, when
thou art king, hang a thief.

Prince

No; thou shalt.   60

Falstaff

Shall I? O rare! By the Lord, I'll be a brave judge!

Prince

Thou judgest false already: I mean thou shalt have the
hanging of the thieves, and so become a rare hangman.

Falstaff

Well, Hal, well; and in some sort it jumps with my
humour as well as waiting in the court, I can tell you.   65

Prince

For obtaining of suits?

Falstaff

Yea, for obtaining of suits, whereof the hangman hath
no lean wardrobe. 'Sblood, I am as melancholy as a
gib cat or a lugg'd bear.

Prince

Or an old lion, or a lover's lute.   70

Falstaff

Yea, or the drone of a Lincolnshire bagpipe.

Prince

What sayest thou to a hare, or the melancholy of Moor
Ditch?

Falstaff

Thou hast the most unsavoury similes, and art indeed
the most comparative, rascalliest, sweet young prince.   75
But, Hal, I prithee, trouble me no more with vanity. I
would to God thou and I knew where a commodity
of good names were to be bought. An old lord of the
Council rated me the other day in the street about

80   you, sir, but I mark'd him not; and yet he talk'd very
wisely, but I regarded him not; and yet he talk'd wisely,
and in the street too.

Prince

Thou didst well; for wisdom cries out in the streets,
and no man regards it.

Falstaff

85   O, thou hast damnable iteration, and art indeed able
to corrupt a saint. Thou hast done much harm upon
me, Hal – God forgive thee for it! Before I knew thee,
Hal, I knew nothing; and now am I, if a man should
speak truly, little better than one of the wicked. I must

90   give over this life, and I will give it over. By the Lord,
an I do not I am a villain! I'll be damn'd for never a
king's son in Christendom.

Prince

Where shall we take a purse to-morrow, Jack?

Falstaff

Zounds, where thou wilt, lad: I'll make one. An I do

95   not, call me villain and baffle me.

Prince

I see a good amendment of life in thee – from praying
to purse-taking.

Falstaff

Why, Hal, 'tis my vocation, Hal; 'tis no sin for a man
to labour in his vocation.

[Enter POINS.]

100   Poins! – Now shall we know if Gadshill have set a
match. O, if men were to be saved by merit, what hole
in hell were hot enough for him? This is the most
omnipotent villain that ever cried 'Stand' to a true
man.

Prince

105   Good morrow, Ned.

Poins

Good morrow, sweet Hal. What says Monsieur Remorse?

What says Sir John Sack and Sugar? Jack, how agrees
the devil and thee about thy soul, that thou soldest
him on Good Friday last for a cup of Madeira and a
cold capon's leg? 110

Prince

Sir John stands to his word – the devil shall have his
bargain; for he was never yet a breaker of proverbs; he
will give the devil his due.

Poins

Then art thou damn'd for keeping thy word with the
devil. 115

Prince

Else he had been damn'd for cozening the devil.

Poins

But, my lads, my lads, to-morrow morning, by four
o'clock early, at Gadshill! There are pilgrims going to
Canterbury with rich offerings, and traders riding to
London with fat purses. I have vizards for you all; you 120
have horses for yourselves. Gadshill lies to-night in
Rochester; I have bespoke supper to-morrow night in
Eastcheap. We may do it as secure as sleep. If you will
go, I will stuff your purses full of crowns; if you will
not, tarry at home and be hang'd. 125

Falstaff

Hear ye, Yedward: if I tarry at home and go not, I'll
hang you for going.

Poins

You will, chops?

Falstaff

Hal, wilt thou make one?

Prince

Who? – I rob, I a thief? Not I, by my faith. 130

Falstaff

There's neither honesty, manhood, nor good fellowship
in thee, nor thou cam'st not of the blood royal, if thou
darest not stand for ten shillings.

Prince

Well then, once in my days I'll be a madcap.

Falstaff

135 Why, that's well said.

Prince

Well, come what will, I'll tarry at home.

Falstaff

By the lord, I'll be a traitor then, when thou art king.

Prince

I care not.

Poins

Sir John, I prithee, leave the Prince and me alone: I
140 will lay him down such reasons for this adventure that
he shall go.

Falstaff

Well, God give thee the spirit of persuasion, and him
the ears of profiting, that what thou speakest may
move, and what he hears may be believed; that the
145 true prince may, for recreation sake, prove a false thief;
for the poor abuses of the time want countenance.
Farewell; you shall find me in Eastcheap.

Prince

Farewell, thou latter spring! Farewell, All-hallown
summer! *[Exit* FALSTAFF.*]*

Poins

150 Now, my good sweet honey lord, ride with us
to-morrow. I have a jest to execute that I cannot
manage alone. Falstaff, Bardolph, Peto, and Gadshill,
shall rob those men that we have already waylaid;
yourself and I will not be there; and when they have
155 the booty, if you and I do not rob them, cut this head
off from my shoulders.

Prince

How shall we part with them in setting forth?

Poins

Why, we will set forth before or after them, and appoint
them a place of meeting, wherein it is at our pleasure

to fail; and then will they adventure upon the exploit 160
themselves; which they shall have no sooner achieved
but we'll set upon them.

Prince

Yea, but 'tis like that they will know us by our horses,
by our habits, and by every other appointment, to be
ourselves. 165

Poins

Tut! our horses they shall not see – I'll tie them in the
wood; our vizards we will change after we leave them;
and, sirrah, I have cases of buckram for the nonce, to
immask our noted outward garments.

Prince

Yea, but I doubt they will be too hard for us. 170

Poins

Well, for two of them, I know them to be as true-bred
cowards as ever turn'd back; and for the third, if he
fight longer than he sees reason, I'll forswear arms.
The virtue of this jest will be the incomprehensible
lies that this same fat rogue will tell us when we meet 175
at supper: how thirty, at least, he fought with; what
wards, what blows, what extremities he endured; and
in the reproof of this lives the jest.

Prince

Well, I'll go with thee. Provide us all things necessary,
and meet me to-morrow night in Eastcheap; there I'll 180
sup. Farewell.

Poins

Farewell, my lord. *[Exit Poins.]*

Prince

I know you all, and will awhile uphold
The unyok'd humour of your idleness;
Yet herein will I imitate the sun, 185
Who doth permit the base contagious clouds
To smother up his beauty from the world,
That, when he please again to be himself,
Being wanted, he may be more wond'red at

190   By breaking through the foul and ugly mists
Of vapours that did seem to strangle him.
If all the year were playing holidays,
To sport would be as tedious as to work;
But when they seldom come, they wish'd-for come,
195   And nothing pleaseth but rare accidents.
So, when this loose behaviour I throw off
And pay the debt I never promised,
By how much better than my word I am,
By so much shall I falsify men's hopes;
200   And, like bright metal on a sullen ground,
My reformation, glitt'ring o'er my fault,
Shall show more goodly and attract more eyes
Than that which hath no foil to set it off.
I'll so offend to make offence a skill,
205   Redeeming time when men think least I will.

[Exit.]

SCENE III

London. The palace.

[Enter the KING, NORTHUMBERLAND, WORCESTER,
HOTSPUR, SIR WALTER BLUNT, *with Others.]*

King
    My blood hath been too cold and temperate,
    Unapt to stir at these indignities,
    And you have found me; for accordingly
    You tread upon my patience. But be sure
    I will from henceforth rather be myself,   5
    Mighty and to be fear'd, than my condition,
    Which hath been smooth as oil, soft as young
       down,
    And therefore lost that title of respect
    Which the proud soul ne'er pays but to the proud.
Worcester
    Our house, my sovereign liege, little deserves   10
    The scourge of greatness to be us'd on it –
    And that same greatness too which our own hands
    Have holp to make so portly.
Northumberland
    My lord –
King
    Worcester, get thee gone; for I do see   15
    Danger and disobedience in thine eye.
    O, sir, your presence is too bold and peremptory,
    And majesty might never yet endure
    The moody frontier of a servant brow.
    You have good leave to leave us; when we need   20
    Your use and counsel, we shall send for you.

[Exit WORCESTER.*]*

    You were about to speak.
Northumberland
               Yea, my good lord.

Those prisoners in your Highness' name demanded,
Which Harry Percy here at Holmedon took,
25 Were, as he says, not with such strength denied
As is delivered to your Majesty.
Either envy, therefore, or misprision
Is guilty of this fault, and not my son.

Hotspur

My liege, I did deny no prisoners.
30 But I remember when the fight was done,
When I was dry with rage and extreme toil,
Breathless and faint, leaning upon my sword,
Came there a certain lord, neat, and trimly dress'd,
Fresh as a bridegroom, and his chin new reap'd
35 Show'd like a stubble-land at harvest-home.
He was perfumed like a milliner,
And 'twixt his finger and his thumb he held
A pouncet-box, which ever and anon
He gave his nose and took't away again;
40 Who therewith angry, when it next came there,
Took it in snuff – and still he smil'd and talk'd –
And as the soldiers bore dead bodies by,
He call'd them untaught knaves, unmannerly,
To bring a slovenly unhandsome corse
45 Betwixt the wind and his nobility.
With many holiday and lady terms
He questioned me: amongst the rest, demanded
My prisoners in your Majesty's behalf.
I then, all smarting with my wounds being cold,
50 To be so pest'red with a popinjay,
Out of my grief and my impatience
Answer'd neglectingly I know not what –
He should, or he should not – for he made me mad
To see him shine so brisk, and smell so sweet,
55 And talk so like a waiting-gentlewoman
Of guns, and drums, and wounds – God save the
      mark! –
And telling me the sovereignest thing on earth

Was parmaceti for an inward bruise;
And that it was great pity, so it was,
This villainous saltpetre should be digg'd   60
Out of the bowels of the harmless earth,
Which many a good tall fellow had destroy'd
So cowardly; and but for these vile guns
He would himself have been a soldier.
This bald unjointed chat of his, my lord,   65
I answered indirectly, as I said;
And I beseech you, let not his report
Come current for an accusation
Betwixt my love and your high Majesty.

Blunt

The circumstance considered, good my lord,   70
Whate'er Lord Harry Percy then had said
To such a person, and in such a place,
At such a time, with all the rest re-told,
May reasonably die, and never rise
To do him wrong, or any way impeach   75
What then he said, so he unsay it now.

King

Why, yet he doth deny his prisoners,
But with proviso and exception –
That we at our own charge shall ransom straight
His brother-in-law, the foolish Mortimer;   80
Who, on my soul, hath wilfully betray'd
The lives of those that he did lead to fight
Against that great magician, damn'd Glendower,
Whose daughter, as we hear, that Earl of March
Hath lately married. Shall our coffers, then,   85
Be emptied to redeem a traitor home?
Shall we buy treason, and indent with fears,
When they have lost and forfeited themselves?
No, on the barren mountains let him starve;
For I shall never hold that man my friend   90
Whose tongue shall ask me for one penny cost
To ransom home revolted Mortimer.

Hotspur
Revolted Mortimer!
He never did fall off, my sovereign liege,
95   But by the chance of war; to prove that true,
Needs no more but one tongue for all those wounds,
Those mouthed wounds, which valiantly he took
When on the gentle Severn's sedgy bank,
In single opposition hand to hand,
100 He did confound the best part of an hour
In changing hardiment with great Glendower.
Three times they breath'd, and three times did they
     drink,
Upon agreement, of swift Severn's flood;
Who then, affrighted with their bloody looks,
105 Ran fearfully among the trembling reeds
And hid his crisp head in the hollow bank
Bloodstained with these valiant combatants.
Never did base and rotten policy
Colour her working with such deadly wounds;
110 Nor never could the noble Mortimer
Receive so many, and all willingly.
Then let him not be slandered with revolt.
King
Thou dost belie him, Percy, thou dost belie him;
He never did encounter with Glendower.
115 I tell thee
He durst as well have met the devil alone
As Owen Glendower for an enemy.
Art thou not asham'd? But, sirrah, henceforth
Let me not hear you speak of Mortimer;
120 Send me your prisoners with the speediest means,
Or you shall hear in such a kind from me
As will displease you. My Lord Northumberland,
We license your departure with your son.
Send us your prisoners, or you will hear of it.

[Exeunt KING HENRY, BLUNT, *and* TRAIN.*]*

Hotspur

An if the devil come and roar for them, 125
I will not send them. I will after straight
And tell him so; for I will ease my heart,
Albeit I make a hazard of my head.

Northumberland

What, drunk with choler? Stay and pause awhile.
Here comes your uncle.

[Re-enter WORCESTER.]

Hotspur

     Speak of Mortimer! 130
Zounds, I will speak of him; and let my soul
Want mercy if I do not join with him.
Yea, on his part I'll empty all these veins
And shed my dear blood drop by drop in the dust,
But I will lift the down-trod Mortimer 135
As high in the air as this unthankful king,
As this ingrate and cank'red Bolingbroke.

Northumberland

Brother, the King hath made your nephew mad.

Worcester

Who struck this heat up after I was gone?

Hotspur

He will, forsooth, have all my prisoners; 140
And when I urg'd the ransom once again
Of my wife's brother, then his cheek look'd pale,
And on my face he turn'd an eye of death,
Trembling even at the name of Mortimer.

Worcester

I cannot blame him: was not he proclaim'd 145
By Richard that dead is the next of blood?

Northumberland

He was: I heard the proclamation;
And then it was when the unhappy King –
Whose wrongs in us God pardon! – did set forth
Upon his Irish expedition; 150

From whence he intercepted did return
To be depos'd, and shortly murdered.

Worcester

And for whose death we in the world's wide mouth
Live scandaliz'd and foully spoken of.

Hotspur

155 But soft, I pray you: did King Richard then
Proclaim my brother, Edmund Mortimer,
Heir to the crown?

Northumberland

He did: myself did hear it.

Hotspur

Nay, then I cannot blame his cousin king,
That wish'd him on the barren mountains starve.

160 But shall it be that you that set the crown
Upon the head of this forgetful man,
And for his sake wear the detested blot
Of murderous subornation – shall it be
That you a world of curses undergo,

165 Being the agents or base second means,
The cords, the ladder, or the hangman rather?
O, pardon me that I descend so low
To show the line and the predicament
Wherein you range under this subtle king!

170 Shall it, for shame, be spoken in these days
Or fill up chronicles in time to come,
That men of your nobility and power
Did gage them both in an unjust behalf –
As both of you, God pardon it! have done –

175 To put down Richard, that sweet lovely rose,
And plant this thorn, this canker, Bolingbroke?
And shall it, in more shame, be further spoken
That you are fool'd, discarded, and shook off,
By him for whom these shames ye underwent?

180 No; yet time serves wherein you may redeem
Your banish'd honours, and restore yourselves
Into the good thoughts of the world again;

Revenge the jeering and disdain'd contempt
Of this proud king, who studies day and night
To answer all the debt he owes to you   185
Even with the bloody payment of your deaths.
Therefore I say –

Worcester
                    Peace, cousin, say no more.
And now I will unclasp a secret book,
And to your quick-conceiving discontents
I'll read you matter deep and dangerous,   190
As full of peril and adventurous spirit
As to o'er-walk a current roaring loud
On the unsteadfast footing of a spear.

Hotspur
If he fall in, good night, or sink or swim.
Send danger from the east unto the west,   195
So honour cross it from the north to south,
And let them grapple. O, the blood more stirs
To rouse a lion than to start a hare!

Northumberland
Imagination of some great exploit
Drives him beyond the bounds of patience.   200

Hotspur
By heaven, methinks it were an easy leap
To pluck bright honour from the pale-fac'd moon;
Or dive into the bottom of the deep,
Where fathom-line could never touch the ground,
And pluck up drowned honour by the locks;   205
So he that doth redeem her thence might wear
Without corrival all her dignities.
But out upon this half-fac'd fellowship!

Worcester
He apprehends a world of figures here,
But not the form of what he should attend.   210
Good cousin, give me audience for a while.

Hotspur
I cry you mercy.

Worcester
       Those same noble Scots
 That are your prisoners –
Hotspur
          I'll keep them all;
 By God, he shall not have a Scot of them;
215 No, if a Scot would save his soul, he shall not.
 I'll keep them, by this hand.
Worcester
         You start away,
 And lend no ear unto my purposes.
 Those prisoners you shall keep.
Hotspur
           Nay, I will; that's flat.
 He said he would not ransom Mortimer;
220 Forbad my tongue to speak of Mortimer;
 But I will find him when he lies asleep,
 And in his ear I'll holla 'Mortimer!'
 Nay,
 I'll have a starling shall be taught to speak
225 Nothing but 'Mortimer', and give it him
 To keep his anger still in motion.
Worcester
 Hear you, cousin; a word.
Hotspur
 All studies here I solemnly defy,
 Save how to gall and pinch this Bolingbroke.
230 And that same sword-and-buckler Prince of Wales –
 But that I think his father loves him not
 And would be glad he met with some mischance –
 I would have him poison'd with a pot of ale.
Worcester
 Farewell, kinsman: I'll talk to you
235 When you are better temper'd to attend.
Northumberland
 Why, what a wasp-stung and impatient fool
 Art thou to break into this woman's mood,

Tying thine ear to no tongue but thine own!

Hotspur

Why, look you, I am whipt and scourg'd with rods,
Nettled, and stung with pismires, when I hear   240
Of this vile politician, Bolingbroke.
In Richard's time – what do you call the place? –
A plague upon it, it is in Gloucestershire –
'Twas where the madcap duke his uncle kept –
His uncle York – where I first bow'd my knee   245
Unto this king of smiles, this Bolingbroke –
'Sblood!
When you and he came back from Ravenspurgh –

Northumberland

At Berkeley Castle.

Hotspur

You say true.   250
Why, what a candy deal of courtesy
This fawning greyhound then did proffer me!
'Look when his infant fortune came to age'
And 'gentle Harry Percy' and 'kind cousin' –
O, the devil take such cozeners! God forgive me!   255
Good uncle, tell your tale – I have done.

Worcester

Nay, if you have not, to it again;
We will stay your leisure.

Hotspur

                              I have done, i' faith.

Worcester

Then once more to your Scottish prisoners:
Deliver them up without their ransom straight,   260
And make the Douglas' son your only mean
For powers in Scotland; which, for divers reasons
Which I shall send you written, be assur'd
Will easily be granted. *[To* NORTHUMBERLAND*]* You,
    my lord,
Your son in Scotland being thus employ'd,   265
Shall secretly into the bosom creep
Of that same noble prelate, well belov'd,

The Archbishop.

Hotspur

Of York, is it not?

Worcester

270　True; who bears hard
His brother's death at Bristow, the Lord Scroop.
I speak not this in estimation,
As what I think might be, but what I know
Is ruminated, plotted, and set down,

275　And only stays but to behold the face
Of that occasion that shall bring it on.

Hotspur

I smell it. Upon my life, it will do well.

Northumberland

Before the game is afoot thou still let'st slip.

Hotspur

Why, it cannot choose but be a noble plot.

280　And then the power of Scotland and of York
To join with Mortimer, ha?

Worcester

　　　　　　　　　　　And so they shall.

Hotspur

In faith, it is exceedingly well aim'd.

Worcester

And 'tis no little reason bids us speed,
To save our heads by raising of a head;

285　For, bear ourselves as even as we can,
The King will always think him in our debt,
And think we think ourselves unsatisfied,
Till he hath found a time to pay us home.
And see already how he doth begin

290　To make us strangers to his looks of love.

Hotspur

He does, he does. We'll be reveng'd on him.

Worcester

Cousin, farewell. No further go in this
Than I by letters shall direct your course.

When time is ripe, which will be suddenly,
I'll steal to Glendower and Lord Mortimer; 295
Where you and Douglas and our pow'rs at once,
As I will fashion it, shall happily meet,
To bear our fortunes in our own strong arms,
Which now we hold at much uncertainty.

Northumberland

Farewell, good brother. We shall thrive, I trust. 300

Hotspur

Uncle, adieu. O, let the hours be short
Till fields and blows and groans applaud our sport!

[Exeunt.]

ACT TWO
SCENE I

Rochester. An inn yard.

[Enter a Carrier with a lantern in his hand.]

First Carrier
Heigh-ho! an it be not four by the day, I'll be hang'd;
Charles' wain is over the new chimney, and yet our
horse not pack'd. What, ostler!

Ostler
[Within] Anon, anon.

First Carrier
5   I prithee, Tom, beat Cut's saddle; put a few flocks in the
point; poor jade is wrung in the withers out of all cess.

[Enter another Carrier.]

Second Carrier
Peas and beans are as dank here as a dog, and that is
the next way to give poor jades the bots; this house
is turned upside down since Robin Ostler died.

First Carrier
10   Poor fellow never joyed since the price of oats rose; it
was the death of him.

Second Carrier
I think this be the most villainous house in all London
road for fleas; I am stung like a tench.

First Carrier
Like a tench! By the mass, there is ne'er a king christen
15   could be better bit than I have been since the first
cock.

Second Carrier
Why, they will allow us ne'er a jordan; and then we
leak in your chimney; and your chamber-lye breeds
fleas like a loach.

First Carrier

What, ostler! come away, and be hang'd; come away. 20

Second Carrier

I have a gammon of bacon and two razes of ginger,
to be delivered as far as Charing Cross.

First Carrier

God's body! the turkeys in my pannier are quite starved.
What, ostler! A plague on thee! hast thou never an eye
in thy head? Canst not hear? An 'twere not as good 25
deed as drink to break the pate on thee, I am a very
villain. Come, and be hang'd! Hast no faith in thee?

[Enter GADSHILL.]

Gadshill

Good morrow, carries. What's o'clock?

First Carrier

I think it be two o'clock.

Gadshill

I prithee lend me thy lantern to see my gelding in the 30
stable.

First Carrier

Nay, by God! Soft! I know a trick worth two of that,
i' faith.

Gadshill

I pray thee lend me thine.

Second Carrier

Ay, when, canst tell? Lend me thy lantern, quoth 'a? 35
Marry, I'll see thee hang'd first.

Gadshill

Sirrah carrier, what time do you mean to come to
London?

Second Carrier

Time enough to go to bed with a candle, I warrant
thee. Come, neighbour Mugs, we'll call up the 40
gentlemen; they will along with company, for they
have great charge.

[Exeunt Carriers.]

Gadshill
What, ho! chamberlain!

Chamberlain
[Within] At hand, quoth pick-purse.

Gadshill
45 That's even as fair as – at hand, quoth the chamberlain;
for thou variest no more from picking of purses than
giving direction doth from labouring; thou layest the
plot how.

[Enter CHAMBERLAIN.]

Chamberlain
Good morrow, Master Gadshill. It holds current that
50 I told you yesternight: there's a franklin in the Wild
of Kent hath brought three hundred marks with him
in gold; I heard him tell it to one of his company last
night at supper, a kind of auditor; one that hath abundance of charge too – God knows what. They are up
55 already and call for eggs and butter; they will away
presently.

Gadshill
Sirrah, if they meet not with Saint Nicholas' clerks, I'll
give thee this neck.

Chamberlain
No, I'll none of it; I pray thee keep that for the
60 hangman; for I know thou worshippest Saint Nicholas
as truly as a man of falsehood may.

Gadshill
What talkest thou to me of the hangman? If I hang,
I'll make a fat pair of gallows; for if I hang, old Sir
John hangs with me; and thou knowest he is no
65 starveling. Tut! there are other Troyans that thou
dream'st not of, the which for sport sake are content
to do the profession some grace; that would, if matters
should be look'd into, for their own credit sake, make
all whole. I am joined with no foot landrakers, no
70 long-staff six-penny strikers, none of these mad

mustachio purple-hu'd malt-worms; but with nobility
and tranquility, burgomasters and great oneyers, such
as can hold in, such as will strike sooner than speak,
and speak sooner than drink, and drink sooner than
pray. And yet, zounds, I lie; for they pray continually   75
to their saint, the commonwealth; or, rather, not pray
to her, but prey on her; for they ride up and down on
her, and make her their boots.

Chamberlain

What, the commonwealth their boots? Will she hold
out water in foul way?   80

Gadshill

She will, she will; justice hath liquor'd her. We steal
as in a castle, cocksure; we have the receipt of fern-
seed, we walk invisible.

Chamberlain

Nay, by my faith, I think you are more beholding to
the night than to fern-seed for your walking   85
invisible.

Gadshill

Give me thy hand: thou shalt have a share in our
purchase, as I am a true man.

Chamberlain

Nay, rather let me have it, as you are a false thief.

Gadshill

Go to; 'homo' is a common name to all men. Bid the   90
ostler bring my gelding out of the stable. Farewell, you
muddy knave.

[Exeunt.]

SCENE II

The highway, near Gadshill.

[Enter the PRINCE OF WALES *and* POINS.*]*

Poins

Come, shelter, shelter, I have remov'd Falstaff's horse, and he frets like a gumm'd velvet.

Prince

Stand close.

[Enter FALSTAFF.*]*

Falstaff

Poins! Poins! And be hang'd! Poins!

Prince

5 Peace, ye fat-kidney'd rascal; what a brawling dost thou keep!

Falstaff

Where's Poins, Hal?

Prince

He is walk'd up to the top of the hill; I'll go seek him.

Falstaff

I am accurs'd to rob in that thief's company; the rascal
10 hath removed my horse, and tied him I know not where. If I travel but four foot by the squier further afoot, I shall break my wind. Well, I doubt not but to die a fair death for all this, if I scape hanging for killing that rogue. I have forsworn his company hourly
15 any time this two and twenty years, and yet I am bewitch'd with the rogue's company. If the rascal have not given me medicines to make me love him, I'll be hang'd. It could not be else: I have drunk medicines. Poins! Hal! A plague upon you both! Bardolph! Peto!
20 I'll starve ere I'll rob a foot further. An 'twere not as good a deed as drink to turn true man, and to leave these rogues, I am the veriest varlet that ever chewed with a tooth. Eight yards of uneven ground is

three-score and ten miles afoot with me; and the
stony-hearted villains know it well enough. A plague 25
upon it, when thieves cannot be true one to another!
[They whistle] Whew! A plague upon you all! Give me
my horse, you rogues; give me my horse, and be
hang'd.

Prince

Peace, ye fat-guts! lie down; lay thine ear close to the 30
ground, and list if thou canst hear the tread of
travellers.

Falstaff

Have you any levers to lift me up again, being down?
'Sblood, I'll not bear mine own flesh so far afoot again
for all the coin in thy father's exchequer. What a plague 35
mean ye to colt me thus?

Prince

Thou liest: thou art not colted, thou art uncolted.

Falstaff

I prithee, good Prince Hal, help me to my horse, good
king's son.

Prince

Out, ye rogue! shall I be your ostler? 40

Falstaff

Hang thyself in thine own heir-apparent garters. If I
be ta'en, I'll peach for this. An I have not ballads made
on you all, and sung to filthy tunes, let a cup of sack
be my poinson. When a jest is so forward, and afoot
too! – I hate it. 45

[Enter GADSHILL, BARDOLPH *and* PETO *with him.]*

Gadshill

Stand!

Falstaff

So I do, against my will.

Poins

O, 'tis our setter: I know his voice.
Bardolph, what news?

Bardolph

50   Case ye, case ye; on with your vizards: there's money
        of the King's coming down the hill; 'tis going to the
        King's exhequer.

Falstaff

        You lie, ye rogue; 'tis going to the King's tavern.

Gadshill

        There's enough to make us all.

Falstaff

55   To be hang'd.

Prince

        Sirs, you four shall front them in the narrow lane; Ned
        Poins and I will walk lower; if they scape from your
        encounter, then they light on us.

Peto

        How many be there of them?

Gadshill

60   Some eight or ten.

Falstaff

        Zounds, will they not rob us?

Prince

        What, a coward, Sir John Paunch?

Falstaff

        Indeed, I am not John of Gaunt, your grandfather; but
        yet no coward, Hal.

Prince

65   Well, we leave that to the proof.

Poins

        Sirrah Jack, thy horse stands behind the hedge: when
        thou need'st him, there thous shalt find him. Farewell,
        and stand fast.

Falstaff

        Now cannot I strike him, if I should be hang'd.

Prince

70   *[Aside to Poins]* Ned, where are our disguises?

Poins

        [Aside] Here, hard by; stand close.

[Exeunt the PRINCE and POINS.]

Falstaff
    Now, my masters, happy man be his dole, say I; every
    man to his business.

[Enter the Travellers.]

First Traveller
    Come, neighbour; the boy shall lead our horses down
    the hill; we'll walk afoot awhile, and ease our legs.   75
Thieves
    Stand!
Travellers
    Jesus bless us!
Falstaff
    Strike; down with them; cut the villains' throats. Ah,
    whoreson caterpillars! bacon-fed knaves! They hate us
    youth. Down with them; fleece them.   80
Traveller
    O, we are undone, both we and ours for ever!
Falstaff
    Hang ye, gorbellied knaves, are ye undone? No, ye fat
    chuffs; I would your store were here. On, bacons, on!
    What, ye knaves! young men must live. You are grand-
    jurors, are ye? we'll jure ye, faith.   85

[Here they rob them and bind them. Exeunt.]

[Re-enter the PRINCE and POINS in buckram.]

Prince
    The thieves have bound the true men. Now, could
    thou and I rob the thieves and go merrily to London,
    it would be argument for a week, laughter for a month,
    and a good jest for ever.
Poins
    Stand close; I hear them coming.   90

[Enter the Thieves again.]

Falstaff

Come, my masters, let us share, and then to horse
before day. An the Prince and Poins be not two arrant
cowards, there's no equity stirring. There's no more
valour in that Poins than in a wild duck.

[As they are sharing, the PRINCE *and* POINS *set upon
them.]*

Prince

95   Your money!

Poins

Villains!

[They all run away, and FALSTAFF, *after a blow or two,
runs away too, leaving the booty behind them.]*

Prince

Got with much ease. Now merrily to horse.
The thieves are all scattered, and possess'd with fear
So strongly that they dare not meet each other;
100   Each takes his fellow for an officer.
Away, good Ned. Falstaff sweats to death
And lards the lean earth as he walks along.
Were't not for laughing, I should pity him.

Poins

How the fat rogue roar'd!

[Exeunt.]

SCENE III

Warkworth Castle.

[Enter HOTSPUR *solus, reading a letter.]*

Hotspur

'But, for mine own part, my lord, I could be well
contented to be there, in respect of the love I bear
your house.' He could be contented – why is he not,
then? In respect of the love he bears our house – he
shows in this he loves his own barn better than he   5
loves our house. Let me see some more. 'The purpose
you undertake is dangerous' – why, that's certain: 'tis
dangerous to take a cold, to sleep, to drink; but I tell
you, my lord fool, out of this nettle, danger, we pluck
this flower, safety. 'The purpose you undertake is   10
dangerous; the friends you have named uncertain; the
time itself unsorted; and your whole plot too light for
the counterpoise of so great an opposition.' Say you
so, say you so? I say unto you again, you are a shallow,
cowardly hind, and you lie. What a lack-brain is this!   15
By the Lord, our plot is a good plot as ever was laid;
our friends true and constant – a good plot, good
friends, and full of expectation; an excellent plot, very
good friends. What a frosty-spirited rogue is this! Why,
my Lord of York commends the plot and the general   20
course of the action. Zounds, an I were now by this
rascal, I could brain him with his lady's fan. Is there
not my father, my uncle, and myself; Lord Edmund
Mortimer, my Lord of York, and Owen Glendower? Is
there not, besides, the Douglas? Have I not all their   25
letters to meet me in arms by the ninth of the next
month, and are they not some of them set forward
already? What a pagan rascal is this! an infidel! Ha!
you shall see now, in very sincerity of fear and cold
heart, will he to the King and lay open all our proceed-   30
ings. O, I could divide myself and go to buffets for

moving such a dish of skim milk with so honourable
an action! Hang him; let him tell the King: we are
prepared. I will set forward to-night.

[Enter LADY PERCY.]

35 How now, Kate! I must leave you within these two
hours.

Lady Percy
O my good lord, why are you thus alone?
For what offence have I this fortnight been
A banish'd woman from my Harry's bed?
40 Tell me, sweet lord, what is't that takes from thee
Thy stomach, pleasure, and thy golden sleep?
Why dost thou bend thine eyes upon the earth,
And start so often when thou sit'st alone?
Why hast thou lost the fresh blood in thy cheeks,
45 And given my treasures and my rights of thee
To thick-ey'd musing and curs'd melancholy?
In thy faint slumbers I by thee have watch'd,
And heard thee murmur tales of iron wars;
Speak terms of manage to thy bounding steed;
50 Cry 'Courage! To the field!' And thou hast talk'd
Of sallies and retires, of trenches, tents,
Of palisadoes, frontiers, parapets,
Of basilisks, of cannon, culverin,
Of prisoners' ransom, and of soldiers slain,
55 And all the currents of a heady fight.
Thy spirit within thee hath been so at war,
And thus hath so bestirr'd thee in thy sleep,
That beads of sweat have stood upon thy brow
Like bubbles in a late disturbed stream;
60 And in thy face strange motions have appear'd,
Such as we see when men restrain their breath
On some great sudden hest. O, what portents are
    these?
Some heavy business hath my lord in hand,
And I must know it, else he loves me not.

Hotspur
What, ho!

[Enter a Servant.]

Is Gilliams with the packet gone?   65
Servant
He is, my lord, an hour ago.
Hotspur
Hath Butler brought those horses from the sheriff?
Servant
One horse, my lord, he brought even now.
Hotspur
What horse? A roan, a crop-ear, is it not?
Servant
It is, my lord.
Hotspur
                    That roan shall be my throne.   70
Well, I will back him straight. O esperance!
Bid Butler lead him forth into the park.

[Exit Servant.]

Lady Percy
But hear you, my lord.
Hotspur
What say'st thou, my lady?
Lady Percy
What is it carries you away?   75
Hotspur
Why, my horse, my love, my horse.
Lady Percy
Out, you mad-headed ape!
A weasel hath not such a deal of spleen
As you are toss'd with. In faith,
I'll know your business, Harry, that I will.   80
I fear my brother Mortimer doth stir
About his title and hath sent for you
To line his enterprise; but if you go –

Hotspur
So far afoot, I shall be weary, love.
Lady Percy
85   Come, come, you paraquito, answer me
Directly unto this question that I ask.
In faith, I'll break thy little finger, Harry,
An if thou wilt not tell me all things true.
Hotspur
Away.
90   Away, you trifler! Love, I love thee not,
I care not for thee, Kate; this is no world
To play with mammets and to tilt with lips:
We must have bloody noses and crack'd crowns,
And pass them current too. God's me, my horse!
What say'st thou, Kate? what wouldst thou have
95   with me?
Lady Percy
Do you not love me? Do you not, indeed?
Well, do not, then; for since you love me not,
I will not love myself. Do you not love me?
Nay, tell me if you speak in jest or no.
Hotspur
100   Come, wilt thou see me ride?
And when I am o' horseback, I will swear
I love thee infinitely. But hark you, Kate:
I must not have you henceforth question me
Whither I go, nor reason whereabout.
105   Whither I must, I must; and, to conclude,
This evening must I leave you, gentle Kate.
I know you wise, but yet no farther wise
Than Harry Percy's wife; constant you are,
But yet a woman; and for secrecy,
110   No lady closer; for I well believe
Thou wilt not utter what thou dost not know,
And so far will I trust thee, gentle Kate.
Lady Percy
How, so far?

Hotspur

    Not an inch further. But hark you, Kate:

    Whither I go, thither shall you go too;   115

    To-day will I set forth, to-morrow you.

    Will this content you, Kate?

Lady Percy

    It must, of force.

[Exeunt.]

SCENE IV

Eastcheap. The Boar's Head Tavern.

[Enter the PRINCE, and POINS.]

Prince

Ned, prithee, come out of that fat room and lend me
thy hand to laugh a little.

Poins

Where hast been, Hal?

Prince

With three or four loggerheads amongst three or four-
5   score hogsheads. I have sounded the very base-string
of humility. Sirrah, I am sworn brother to a leash of
drawers and can call them all by their christen names,
as Tom, Dick, and Francis. They take it already upon
their salvation that though I be but Prince of Wales
10   yet I am the king of courtesy; and tell me flatly I am
no proud Jack, like Falstaff, but a Corinthian, a lad of
mettle, a good boy – by the Lord, so they call me – and
when I am King of England I shall command all the
good lads in Eastcheap. They call drinking deep, dyeing
15   scarlet; and when you breathe in your watering, they
cry 'hem!' and bid you play it off. To conclude, I am
so good a proficient in one quarter of an hour that I
can drink with any tinker in his own language during
my life. I tell thee, Ned, thou hast lost much honour
20   that thou wert not with me in this action. But, sweet
Ned – to sweeten which name of Ned, I give thee this
pennyworth of sugar, clapp'd even now into my hand
by an under-skinker, one that never spake other English
in his life than 'Eight shillings and sixpence' and 'You
25   are welcome' with this shrill addition, 'Anon, anon,
sir! Score a pint of bastard in the Half-moon' or so.
But, Ned, to drive away the time till Falstaff come, I
prithee, do thou stand in some by-room, while I question my puny drawer to what end he gave me the

sugar; and do thou never leave calling 'Francis!' that   30
his tale to me may be nothing but 'Anon'. Step aside,
and I'll show thee a precedent.

[Exit POINS.]

Poins
   [Within] Francis!
Prince
   Thou are perfect.
Poins
   [Within] Francis!   35

[Enter FRANCIS.]

Francis
   Anon, anon, sir. Look down into the Pomgarnet, Ralph.
Prince
   Come hither, Francis.
Francis
   My lord?
Prince
   How long has thou to serve, Francis?
Francis
   Forsooth, five years, and as much as to –   40
Poins
   [Within] Francis!
Francis
   Anon, anon, sir.
Prince
   Five year! by'r lady, a long lease for the clinking of
   pewter. But, Francis, darest thou be so valiant as to
   play the coward with thy indenture and show it a fair   45
   pair of heels and run from it?
Francis
   O Lord, sir, I'll be sworn upon all the books in England,
   I could find in my heart –
Poins
   [Within] Francis!

Francis
50   Anon, sir.
Prince
     How old art thou, Francis?
Francis
     Let me see, about Michaelmas next I shall be –
Poins
     [Within] Francis!
Francis
     Anon, sir. Pray stay a little, my lord.
Prince
55   Nay, but hark you, Francis: for the sugar thou gavest
     me – 'twas a penny-worth, was't not?
Francis
     O Lord, I would it had been two!
Prince
     I will give thee for it a thousand pound; ask me when
     thou wilt, and thou shalt have it.
Poins
60   *[Within]* Francis!
Francis
     Anon, anon.
Prince
     Anon, Francis? No, Francis; but tomorrow, Francis; or,
     Francis, o' Thursday; or indeed, Francis, when thou
     wilt. But, Francis –
Francis
65   My lord?
Prince
     Wilt thou rob this leathern jerkin, crystal-button, knot-
     pated, agatering, puke stocking, caddis-garter,
     smooth-tongue, Spanish-pouch –
Francis
     O Lord, sir, who do you mean?
Prince
70   Why, then, your brown bastard is your only drink; for,
     look you, Francis, your white canvas doublet will sully.
     In Barbary, sir, it cannot come to so much.

Francis

    What, sir?

Poins

    [Within] Francis!

Prince

    Away, you rogue! Dost thou not hear them call?   75

    [Here they both call him; FRANCIS *stands amazed, not knowing which way to go.]*

    [Enter VINTNER.*]*

Vintner

    What, stand'st thou still, and hear'st such a calling? Look to the guests within. *[Exit Francis]* My lord, old Sir John, with half-a-dozen more, are at the door. Shall I let them in?

Prince

    Let them alone awhile, and then open the door. *[Exit*   80
    VINTNER*]* Poins!

    [Re-enter POINS.*]*

Poins

    Anon, anon, sir.

Prince

    Sirrah, Falstaff and the rest of the thieves are at the door. Shall we be merry?

Poins

    As merry as crickets, my lad. But hark ye: what cunning   85 match have you made with this jest of the drawer? Come, what's the issue?

Prince

    I am now of all humours that have showed themselves humours since the old days of goodman Adam to the pupil-age of this present twelve o'clock at midnight.   90

    [Re-enter FRANCIS.*]*

    What's o'clock, Francis?

Francis

Anon, anon, sir. *[Exit.]*

Prince

That ever this fellow should have fewer words than a parrot, and yet the son of a woman! His industry is
95   upstairs and downstairs; his eloquence the parcel of a reckoning. I am not yet of Percy's mind, the Hotspur of the north; he that kills me some six or seven dozen of Scots at a breakfast, washes his hands, and says to his wife 'Fie upon this quiet life! I want work'. 'O my
100   sweet Harry,' says she 'how many hast thou kill'd to-day?' 'Give my roan horse a drench' says he; and answers 'Some fourteen,' an hour after, 'a trifle, a trifle'. I prithee call in Falstaff; I'll play Percy, and that damn'd brawn shall play Dame Mortimer his wife. 'Rivo!' says
105   the drunkard. Call in ribs, call in tallow.

[Enter FALSTAFF, GADSHILL, BARDOLPH, and PETO;
followed by FRANCIS with wine.]

Poins

Welcome, Jack. Where hast thou been?

Falstaff

A plague of all cowards, I say, and a vengeance too! Marry and amen! Give me a cup of sack, boy. Ere I lead this life long, I'll sew nether-stocks, and mend
110   them and foot them too. A plague of all cowards! Give me a cup of sack, rogue. Is there no virtue extant?

[He drinks.]

Prince

Didst thou never see Titan kiss a dish of butter, pitiful-hearted Titan, that melted at the sweet tale of the sun's? If thou didst, then behold that compound.

Falstaff

115   You rogue, here's lime in this sack too! There is nothing but roguery to be found in villainous man; yet a coward is worse than a cup of sack with lime in it. A villainous

coward! Go thy ways, old Jack; die when thou wilt; if
manhood, good manhood, be not forgot upon the
face of the earth, then am I a shotten herring. There 120
lives not three good men unhang'd in England, and
one of them is fat and grows old. God help the while!
A bad world, I say. I would I were a weaver; I could
sing psalms or anything. A plague of all cowards, I
say still.   125

Prince

How now, woolsack! What mutter you?

Falstaff

A king's son! If I do not beat thee out of thy kingdom
with a dagger of lath, and drive all thy subjects afore
thee like a flock of wild geese, I'll never wear hair on
my face more. You Prince of Wales!   130

Prince

Why, you whoreson round man, what's the matter?

Falstaff

Are not you a coward? Answer me to that – and Poins
there?

Poins

Zounds, ye fat paunch, an ye call me coward, by the
Lord, I'll stab thee.   135

Falstaff

I call thee coward! I'll see thee damn'd ere I call thee
coward; but I would give a thousand pound I could
run as fast as thou canst. You are straight enough in
the shoulders – you care not who sees your back. Call
you that backing of your friends? A plague upon such 140
backing! Give me them that will face me. Give me a
cup of sack; I am a rogue if I drunk to-day.

Prince

O villain! thy lips are scarce wip'd since thou drunk'st
last.

Falstaff

All is one for that. *[He drinks]* A plague of all cowards, 145
still say I.

Prince

What's the matter?

Falstaff

What's the matter! There be four of us here have ta'en a thousand pound this day morning.

Prince

150   Where is it, Jack? Where is it?

Falstaff

Where is it! taken from us it is: a hundred upon poor four of us.

Prince

What, a hundred, man?

Falstaff

I am a rogue if I were not at halfsword with a dozen
155   of them two hours together. I have scap'd by miracle. I am eight times thrust through the doublet, four through the hose; my buckler cut through and through; my sword hack'd like a hand-saw – ecce signum! I never dealt better since I was a man – all would not
160   do. A plague of all cowards! Let them speak; if they speak more or less than truth, they are villains and the sons of darkness.

Prince

Speak, sirs; how was it?

Gadshill

We four set upon some dozen –

Falstaff

165   Sixteen at least, my lord.

Gadshill

And bound them.

Peto

No, no, they were not bound.

Falstaff

You rogue, they were bound, every man of them; or I am a Jew else, an Ebrew Jew.

Gadshill

170   As we were sharing, some six or seven fresh men set upon us –

Falstaff

And unbound the rest, and then come in the other.

Prince

What, fought you with them all?

Falstaff

All! I know not what you call all, but if I fought not
with fifty of them, I am a bunch of radish. If there 175
were not two or three and fifty upon poor old Jack,
then am I no two-legg'd creature.

Prince

Pray God you have not murd'red some of them.

Falstaff

Nay, that's past praying for: I have pepper'd two of
them; two I am sure I have paid – two rogues in 180
buckram suits. I tell thee what, Hal, if I tell thee a lie,
spit in my face, call me horse. Thou knowest my old
ward: here I lay, and thus I bore my point. Four rogues
in buckram let drive at me –

Prince

What, four? Thou saidst but two even now. 185

Falstaff

Four, Hal; I told thee four.

Poins

Ay, ay, he said four.

Falstaff

These four came all afront, and mainly thrust at me.
I made me no more ado but took all their seven points
in my target, thus. 190

Prince

Seven? Why, there were but four even now.

Falstaff

In buckram.

Poins

Ay, four, in buckram suits.

Falstaff

Seven, by these hilts, or I am a villain else.

Prince

195   [*Aside to* POINS] Prithee, let him alone; we shall have
        more anon.

Falstaff

        Dost thou hear me, Hal?

Prince

        Ay, and mark thee too, Jack.

Falstaff

        Do so, for it is worth the list'ning to. These nine in
200   buckram that I told thee of –

Prince

        So, two more already.

Falstaff

        Their points being broken –

Poins

        Down fell their hose.

Falstaff

        Began to give me ground; but I followed me close,
205   came in foot and hand, and with a thought seven of
        the eleven I paid.

Prince

        O monstrous! eleven buckram men grown out of two!

Falstaff

        But, as the devil would have it, three misbegotten
        knaves in Kendal green came at my back and let drive
210   at me – for it was so dark, Hal, that thou couldest not
        see thy hand.

Prince

        These lies are like their father that begets them – gross
        as a mountain, open, palpable. Why, thou clay-brain'd
        guts, thou knotty-pated fool, thou whoreson, obscene,
215   greasy tallow-catch –

Falstaff

        What, art thou mad? art thou mad? Is not the truth
        the truth?

Prince

        Why, how couldst thou know these men in Kendal

green, when it was so dark thou couldst not see thy
hand? Come, tell us your reason; what sayest thou to 220
this?

Poins

Come, your reason, Jack, your reason.

Falstaff

What, upon compulsion? Zounds, an I were at the
strappado, or all the racks in the world, I would not
tell you on compulsion. Give you a reason on compul- 225
sion! If reasons were as plentiful as blackberries, I would
give no man a reason upon compulsion, I.

Prince

I'll be no longer guilty of this sin; this sanguine coward,
this bed-presser, this horse-back-breaker, this huge hill
of flesh –   230

Falstaff

'Sblood, you starveling, you eel-skin, you dried neat's-
tongue, you bull's pizzle, you stock-fish – O for breath
to utter what is like thee! – you tailor's yard, you sheath,
you bow-case, you vile standing tuck!

Prince

Well, breathe awhile, and then to it again; and when 235
thou hast tired thyself in base comparisons, hear me
speak but this.

Poins

Mark, Jack.

Prince

We two saw you four set on four, and bound them
and were masters of their wealth. Mark now, how a 240
plain tale shall put you down. Then did we two set on
you four; and, with a word, out-fac'd you from your
prize, and have it; yea, and can show it you here in
the house. And, Falstaff, you carried your guts away
as nimbly, with as quick dexterity, and roar'd for mercy, 245
and still run and roar'd, as ever I heard bull-calf. What
a slave art thou to hack thy sword as thou hast done,
and then say it was in fight! What trick, what device,

250 what starting-hole, canst thou now find out to hide thee from this open and apparent shame?

Poins

Come, let's hear, Jack; what trick hast thou now?

Falstaff

By the Lord, I knew ye as well as he that made ye. Why, hear you, my masters: was it for me to kill the heir-apparent? Should I turn upon the true prince?

255 Why, thou knowest I am as valiant as Hercules; but beware instinct – the lion will not touch the true prince. Instinct is a great matter: I was now a coward on instinct. I shall think the better of myself and thee during my life – I for a valiant lion, and thou

260 for a true prince. But, by the Lord, lads, I am glad you have the money. Hostess, clap to the doors. Watch to-night, pray to-morrow. Gallants, lads, boys, hearts of gold, all the titles of good fellowship come to you! What, shall we be merry? Shall we have a

265 play extempore?

Prince

Content – and the argument shall be thy running away.

Falstaff

Ah, no more of that, Hal, an thou lovest me!

[Enter Hostess.]

Hostess

O Jesu, my lord the Prince!

Prince

How now, my lady the hostess!

270 What say'st thou to me?

Hostess

Marry, my lord, there is a nobleman of the court at door would speak with you; he says he comes from your father.

Prince

Give him as much as will make him a royal man, and

275 send him back again to my mother.

Falstaff

What manner of man is he?

Hostess

An old man.

Falstaff

What doth gravity out of his bed at midnight? Shall I
give him his answer?

Prince

Prithee do, Jack.   280

Falstaff

Faith, and I'll send him packing. *[Exit.]*

Prince

Now, sirs: by'r lady, you fought fair; so did you, Peto;
so did you, Bardolph. You are lions too: you ran away
upon instinct; you will not touch the true prince; no,
fie!

Bardolph   285

Faith, I ran when I saw others run.

Prince

Faith, tell me now in earnest, how came Falstaff's sword
so hack'd?

Peto

Why, he hack'd it with his dagger, and said he would
swear truth out of England but he would make you   290
believe it was done in fight; and persuaded us to do
the like.

Bardolph

Yea, and to tickle our noses with spear-grass to make
them bleed, and then to beslubber our garments with
it, and swear it was the blood of true men. I did that 295
I did not this seven year before – I blush'd to hear his
monstrous devices.

Prince

O villain! Thou stolest a cup of sack eighteen years
ago, and wert taken with the manner, and ever since
thou hast blush'd extempore. Thou hadst fire and 300
sword on thy side, and yet thou ran'st away; what
instinct hadst thou for it?

Bardolph

My lord, do you see these meteors? do you behold these exhalations?

Prince

305 I do.

Bardolph

What think you they portend?

Prince

Hot livers and cold purses.

Bardolph

Choler, my lord, if rightly taken.

Prince

No, if rightly taken, halter.

[Re-enter FALSTAFF.]

310 Here comes lean Jack, here comes barebone.
How now, my sweet creature of bombast! How long
is't ago, Jack, since thou sawest thine own knee?

Falstaff

My own knee! When I was about thy years, Hal, I was
not an eagle's talon in the waist: I could have crept
315 into any alderman's thumb-ring. A plague of sighing
and grief! it blows a man up like a bladder. There's
villainous news abroad. Here was Sir John Bracy from
your father: you must to the court in the morning.
That same mad fellow of the north, Percy, and he of
320 Wales that gave Amaimon the bastinado, and made
Lucifer cuckold, and swore the devil his true liegeman
upon the cross of a Welsh hook – what a plague call
you him?

Poins

O, Glendower.

Falstaff

325 Owen, Owen – the same; and his son-in-law Mortimer,
and old Northumberland, and that sprightly Scot of
Scots, Douglas, that runs o' horseback up a hill perpen-
dicular –

Prince

He that rides at high speed and with his pistol kills a
sparrow flying?   330

Falstaff

You have hit it.

Prince

So did he never the sparrow.

Falstaff

Well, that rascal hath good mettle in him; he will not
run.

Prince

Why, what a rascal art thou, then, to praise him so 335
for running!

Falstaff

O' horseback, ye cuckoo; but afoot he will not budge
a foot.

Prince

Yes, Jack, upon instinct.

Falstaff

I grant ye, upon instinct. Well, he is there too, and 340
one Mordake, and a thousand blue-caps more.
Worcester is stol'n away to-night; thy father's beard is
turn'd white with the news; you may buy land now
as cheap as stinking mack'rel.

Prince

Why, then, it is like, if there come a hot June, and 345
this civil buffeting hold, we shall buy maidenheads as
they buy hob-nails, by the hundreds.

Falstaff

By the mass, lad, thou sayest true: it is like we shall
have good trading that way. But tell me, Hal, art not
thou horrible afeard. Thou being heir-apparent, could 350
the world pick thee out three such enemies again as
that fiend Douglas, that spirit Percy, and that devil
Glendower? Art thou not horribly afraid? Doth not
thy blood thrill at it?

Prince

355   Not a whit, i' faith; I lack some of thy instinct.

Falstaff

Well, thou wilt be horribly chid tomorrow when thou
comest to thy father. If thou love me, practise an answer.

Prince

Do thou stand for my father, and examine me upon
the particulars of my life.

Falstaff

360   Shall I? Content! This chair shall be my state, this
dagger my sceptre, and this cushion my crown.

Prince

Thy state is taken for a join'd-stool, thy golden sceptre
for a leaden dagger, and thy precious rich crown for
a pitiful bald crown!

Falstaff

365   Well, an the fire of grace be not quite out of thee, now
shalt thou be moved. Give me a cup of sack to make
my eyes look red, that it may be thought I have wept;
for I must speak in passion, and I will do it in King
Cambyses' vein.

Prince

370   Well, here is my leg.

Falstaff

And here is my speech. Stand aside, nobility.

Hostess

O Jesu, this is excellent sport, i' faith!

Falstaff

Weep not, sweet queen, for trickling tears are vain.

Hostess

O, the father, how he holds his countenance!

Falstaff

375   For God's sake, lords, convey my tristful queen;
For tears do stop the floodgates of her eyes.

Hostess

O Jesu, he doth it as like one of these harlotry players
as ever I see!

Falstaff

Peace, good pint-pot; peace, good tickle-brain. – Harry,
I do not only marvel where thou spendest thy time, 380
but also how thou art accompanied; for though the
camomile, the more it is trodden on the faster it grows,
yet youth, the more it is wasted the sooner it wears.
That thou art my son I have partly thy mother's word,
partly my own opinion, but chiefly a villainous trick 385
of thine eye, and a foolish hanging of thy nether lip,
that doth warrant me. If then thou be son to me, here
lies the point: why, being son to me, art thou so pointed
at? Shall the blessed sun of heaven prove a micher and
eat blackberries? A question not to be ask'd. Shall the 390
son of England prove a thief and take purses? A question to be ask'd. There is a thing, Harry, which thou
hast often heard of, and it is known to many in our
land by the name of pitch. This pitch, as ancient writers
do report, doth defile; so doth the company thou 395
keepest; for, Harry, now I do not speak to thee in drink,
but in tears; not in pleasure, but in passion; not in
words only, but in woes also. And yet there is a virtuous
man whom I have often noted in thy company, but I
know not his name. 400

Prince

What manner of man, an it like your Majesty?

Falstaff

A goodly portly man, i' faith, and a corpulent; of a
cheerful look, a pleasing eye, and a most noble carriage;
and, as I think, his age some fifty, or, by'r lady, inclining
to three-score. And now I remember me, his name is 405
Falstaff. If that man should be lewdly given, he
deceiveth me; for, Harry, I see virtue in his looks. If
then the tree may be known by the fruit, as the fruit
by the tree, then peremptorily I speak it, there is virtue
in that Falstaff: him keep with, the rest banish. And 410
tell me now, thou naughty varlet, tell me, where hast
thou been this month?

Prince
> Dost thou speak like a king? Do thou stand for me, and I'll play my father.

Falstaff
415   Depose me? If thou dost it half so gravely, so majestically, both in word and matter, hang me up by the heels for a rabbit-sucker or a poulter's hare.

Prince
> Well, here I am set.

Falstaff
> And here I stand. Judge, my masters.

Prince
420   Now, Harry, whence come you?

Falstaff
> My noble lord, from Eastcheap.

Prince
> The complaints I hear of thee are grievous.

Falstaff
> 'Sblood, my lord, they are false. Nay, I'll tickle ye for a young prince, i' faith.

Prince
425   Swearest thou, ungracious boy?
> Henceforth ne'er look on me. Thou art violently carried away from grace; there is a devil haunts thee in the likeness of an old fat man; a tun of man is thy companion. Why dost thou converse with that trunk
430   of humours, that bolting-hutch of beastliness, that swoll'n parcel of dropsies, that huge bombard of sack, that stuff'd cloak-bag of guts, that roasted Manningtree ox with the pudding in his belly, that reverend vice, that grey iniquity, that father ruffian, that vanity in
435   years? Wherein is he good, but to taste sack and drink it? wherein neat and cleanly, but to carve a capon and eat it? wherein cunning, but in craft? wherein crafty, but in villainy? wherein villainous, but in all things? wherein worthy, but in nothing?

Falstaff

I would your Grace would take me with you; whom 440
means your Grace?

Prince

That villainous abominable misleader of youth, Falstaff,
that old white-bearded Satan.

Falstaff

My lord, the man I know.

Prince

I know thou dost. 445

Falstaff

But to say I know more harm in him than in myself
were to say more than I know. That he is old – the
more the pity – his white hairs do witness it; but that
he is – saving your reverence – a whoremaster, that I
utterly deny. If sack and sugar be a fault, God help the 450
wicked! If to be old and merry be a sin, then many an
old host that I know is damn'd; if to be fat be to be
hated, then Pharaoh's lean kine are to be loved. No,
my good lord: banish Peto, banish Bardolph, banish
Poins; but, for sweet Jack Falstaff, kind Jack Falstaff, true 455
Jack Falstaff, valiant Jack Falstaff – and therefore more
valiant, being, as he is, old Jack Falstaff – banish not
him thy Harry's company, banish not him thy Harry's
company. Banish plump Jack, and banish all the world.

Prince

I do, I will. *[A knocking heard.]* 460

[Exeunt Hostess, FRANCIS, and BARDOLPH.]

[Re-enter BARDOLPH, running.]

Bardolph

O, my lord, my lord! the sheriff with a most monstrous
watch is at the door.

Falstaff

Out, ye rogue! Play out the play: I have much to say
in the behalf of that Falstaff.

[Re-enter the Hostess.]

Hostess
465   O Jesu, my lord, my lord!
Prince
    Heigh, heigh! the devil rides upon a fiddle-stick; what's
    the matter?
Hostess
    The sheriff and all the watch are at the door; they are
    come to search the house. Shall I let them in?
Falstaff
470   Dost thou hear, Hal? Never call a true piece of gold a
    counterfeit. Thou art essentially made, without seeming
    so.
Prince
    And thou a natural coward, without instinct.
Falstaff
    I deny your major. If you will deny the sheriff, so; if
475   not, let him enter. If I become not a cart as well as
    another man, a plague on my bringing up! I hope I
    shall as soon be strangled with a halter as another.
Prince
    Go, hide thee behind the arras; the rest walk up above.
    Now, my masters, for a true face and good conscience.
Falstaff
480   Both which I have had; but their date is out, and
    therefore I'll hide me.

[Exeunt all but the PRINCE *and* PETO.*]*

Prince
    Call in the sheriff.

[Enter SHERIFF *and the* CARRIER.*]*

    Now, master sheriff, what is your will with me?
Sheriff
    First, pardon me, my lord. A hue and cry
485   Hath followed certain men unto this house.

Prince

What men?

Sheriff

One of them is well known, my gracious lord –
A gross fat man.

Carrier

As fat as butter.

Prince

The man, I do assure you, is not here,   490
For I myself at this time have employ'd him.
And, sheriff, I will engage my word to thee
That I will, by to-morrow dinner-time,
Send him to answer thee, or any man,
For any thing he shall be charg'd withal;   495
And so let me entreat you leave the house.

Sheriff

I will, my lord. There are two gentlemen
Have in this robbery lost three hundred marks.

Prince

It may be so; if he have robb'd these men
He shall be answerable; and so, farewell.   500

Sheriff

Good night, my noble lord.

Prince

I think it is good morrow, is it not?

Sheriff

Indeed, my lord, I think it be two o'clock. *[Exeunt*
SHERIFF *and* CARRIER.*]*

Prince

This oily rascal is known as well as Paul's. Go, call him
forth.   505

Peto

Falstaff! Fast asleep behind the arras, and snorting like
a horse.

Prince

Hark how hard he fetches breath. Search his pockets.
[He searcheth his pocket, and findeth certain papers] What
hast thou found?   510

Peto

Nothing but papers, my lord.

Prince

Let's see what they be: read them.

Peto

[Reads]

Item, A capon 2s. 2d.

Item, Sauce 4d.

515 Item, Sack, two gallons 5s. 8d.

Item, Anchovies and sack after supper 2s. 6d.

Item, Bread ob.

Prince

O monstrous! but one halfpenny-worth of bread to this intolerable deal of sack! What there is else, keep
520 close; we'll read it at more advantage. There let him sleep till day. I'll to the court in the morning. We must all to the wars, and thy place shall be honourable. I'll procure this fat rogue a charge of foot; and I know his death will be a march of twelve-score. The money shall
525 be paid back again with advantage. Be with me betimes in the morning; and so, good morrow, Peto.

Peto

Good morrow, good my lord.

[Exeunt.]

ACT THREE

SCENE I

Wales. Glendower's Castle.

[*Enter* HOTSPUR, WORCESTER, MORTIMER, *and*
GLENDOWER.]

Mortimer
    These promises are fair, the parties sure,
    And our induction full of prosperous hope.
Hotspur
    Lord Mortimer, and cousin Glendower,
    Will you sit down?
    And uncle Worcester – a plague upon it!   5
    I have forgot the map.
Glendower
                No, here it is.
    Sit, cousin Percy; sit, good cousin Hotspur,
    For by that name as oft as Lancaster
    Doth speak of you, his cheek looks pale, and with
    A rising sigh he wisheth you in heaven.   10
Hotspur
    And you in hell, as oft as he hears
    Owen Glendower spoke of.
Glendower
    I cannot blame him: at my nativity
    The front of heaven was full of fiery shapes,
    Of burning cressets; and at my birth   15
    The frame and huge foundation of the earth
    Shaked like a coward.
Hotspur
    Why, so it would have done at the same season if your
    mother's cat had but kitten'd, though yourself had
    never been born.   20

Glendower

I say the earth did shake when I was born.

Hotspur

And I say the earth was not of my mind,
If you suppose as fearing you it shook.

Glendower

The heavens were all on fire, the earth did tremble.

Hotspur

25   O, then the earth shook to see the heavens on fire,
And not in fear of your nativity.
Diseased nature oftentimes breaks forth
In strange eruptions; oft the teeming earth
Is with a kind of colic pinch'd and vex'd
30   By the imprisoning of unruly wind
Within her womb; which, for enlargement striving,
Shakes the old beldam earth, and topples down
Steeples and moss-grown towers. At your birth,
Our grandam earth, having this distemp'rature,
In passion shook.

Glendower

35   Cousin, of many men
I do not bear these crossings. Give me leave
To tell you once again that at my birth
The front of heaven was full of fiery shapes,
The goats ran from the mountains, and the herds
40   Were strangely clamorous to the frighted fields.
These signs have mark'd me extraordinary;
And all the courses of my life do show
I am not in the roll of common men.
Where is he living, clipp'd in with the sea
45   That chides the banks of England, Scotland, Wales,
Which calls me pupil or hath read to me?
And bring him out that is but woman's son
Can trace me in the tedious ways of art
And hold me pace in deep experiments.

Hotspur

50   I think there's no man speaks better Welsh. I'll to dinner.

Mortimer
Peace, cousin Percy; you will make him mad.
Glendower
I can call spirits from the vasty deep.
Hotspur
Why, so can I, or so can any man;
But will they come when you do call for them?
Glendower
Why, I can teach you, cousin, to command   55
The devil.
Hotspur
And I can teach thee, coz, to shame the devil
By telling truth: tell truth, and shame the devil.
If thou have power to raise him, bring him hither,
And I'll be sworn I have power to shame him hence.   60
O, while you live, tell truth, and shame the devil!
Mortimer
Come, come, no more of this unprofitable chat.
Glendower
Three times hath Henry
Bolingbroke made head
Against my power; thrice from the banks of Wye   65
And sandy-bottom'd Severn have I sent him
Bootless home and weather-beaten back.
Hotspur
Home without boots, and in foul weather too!
How scapes he agues, in the devil's name?
Glendower
Come, here is the map; shall we divide our right   70
According to our threefold order ta'en?
Mortimer
The Archdeacon hath divided it
Into three limits very equally:
England, from Trent and Severn hitherto,
By south and east is to my part assign'd;   75
All westward, Wales beyond the Severn shore,
And all the fertile land within that bound,

To Owen Glendower; and, dear coz, to you
The remnant northward lying off from Trent.
80 And our indentures tripartite are drawn;
Which being sealed interchangeably,
A business that this night may execute,
To-morrow, cousin Percy, you and I
And my good Lord of Worcester will set forth
85 To meet your father and the Scottish power,
As is appointed us, at Shrewsbury.
My father Glendower is not ready yet,
Nor shall we need his help these fourteen days.
[To GLENDOWER*]* Within that space you may have
drawn together
90 Your tenants, friends, and neighbouring gentlemen.
Glendower
A shorter time shall send me to you, lords;
And in my conduct shall your ladies come,
From whom you now must steal and take no leave;
For there will be a world of water shed
95 Upon the parting of your wives and you.
Hotspur
Methinks my moiety, north from Burton here,
In quantity equals not one of yours.
See how this river comes me cranking in,
And cuts me from the best of all my land
100 A huge half-moon, a monstrous cantle out.
I'll have the current in this place damm'd up,
And here the smug and silver Trent shall run
In a new channel, fair and evenly;
It shall not wind with such a deep indent
105 To rob me of so rich a bottom here.
Glendower
Not wind! It shall, it must; you see it doth.
Mortimer
Yea, but
Mark how he bears his course and runs me up
With like advantage on the other side,

Glending the opposed continent as much   110
  As on the other side it takes from you.

Worcester

Yea, but a little charge will trench him here,
  And on this north side win this cape of land,
  And then he runs straight and even.

Hotspur

I'll have it so; a little charge will do it.   115

Glendower

I'll not have it alt'red.

Hotspur

               Will not you?

Glendower

No, nor you shall not.

Hotspur

                Who shall say me nay?

Glendower

Why, that will I.

Hotspur

Let me not understand you, then; speak it in Welsh.

Glendower

I can speak English, lord, as well as you,   120
  For I was train'd up in the English court;
  Where, being but young, I framed to the harp
  Many an English ditty lovely well,
  And gave the tongue a helpful ornament –
  A virtue that was never seen in you.   125

Hotspur

Marry,
  And I am glad of it with all my heart!
  I had rather be a kitten and cry mew
  Than one of these same metre ballad-mongers;
  I had rather hear a brazen canstick turn'd,
  Or a dry wheel grate on the axle-tree;   130
  And that would set my teeth nothing on edge,
  Nothing so much as mincing poetry.
  'Tis like the forc'd gait of a shuffling nag.

    Glendower
      Come, you shall have Trent turn'd.
    Hotspur
135   I do not care; I'll give thrice so much land
      To any well-deserving friend;
      But in the way of bargain, mark ye me,
      I'll cavil on the ninth part of a hair.
      Are the indentures drawn? Shall we be gone?
    Glendower
140   The moon shines fair; you may away by night;
      I'll haste the writer, and withal
      Break with your wives of your departure hence.
      I am afraid my daughter will run mad,
      So much she doteth on her Mortimer.

[Exit.]

    Mortimer
145   Fie, cousin Percy! how you cross my father!
    Hotspur
      I cannot choose. Sometime he angers me
      With telling me of the moldwarp and the ant,
      Of the dreamer Merlin and his prophecies,
      And of a dragon and a finless fish,
150   A clip-wing'd griffin and a moulten raven,
      A couching lion and a ramping cat,
      And such a deal of skimble-skamble stuff
      As puts me from my faith. I tell you what:
      He held me last night at least nine hours
155   In reckoning up the several devils' names
      That were his lackeys. I cried 'hum' and 'well, go to'
      But mark'd him not a word. O, he is as tedious
      As a tired horse, a railing wife;
      Worse than a smoky house; I had rather live
160   With cheese and garlic in a windmill, far,
      Than feed on cates and have him talk to me
      In any summer house in Christendom.

Mortimer

    In faith, he is a worthy gentleman,
    Exceedingly well read, and profited
    In strange concealments; valiant as a lion,   165
    And wondrous affable; and as bountiful
    As mines of India. Shall I tell you, cousin?
    He holds your temper in a high respect,
    And curbs himself even of his natural scope
    When you come 'cross his humour; faith, he does.   170
    I warrant you that man is not alive
    Might so have tempted him as you have done
    Without the taste of danger and reproof;
    But do not use it oft, let me entreat you.

Worcester

    In faith, my lord, you are too wilfulblame;   175
    And since your coming hither have done enough
    To put him quite besides his patience.
    You must needs learn, lord, to amend this fault;
    Though sometimes it show greatness, courage, blood –
    And that's the dearest grace it renders you –   180
    Yet oftentimes it doth present harsh rage,
    Defect of manners, want of government,
    Pride, haughtiness, opinion, and disdain;
    The least of which, haunting a nobleman,
    Loseth men's hearts, and leaves behind a stain   185
    Upon the beauty of all parts besides,
    Beguiling them of commendation.

Hotspur

    Well, I am school'd: good manners be your speed!
    Here come our wives, and let us take our leave.

    [Re-enter GLENDOWER, *with* LADY MORTIMER *and*
                       LADY PERCY.]*

Mortimer

    This is the deadly spite that angers me: 190
    My wife can speak no English, I no Welsh.

Glendower
My daughter weeps: she'll not part with you;
She'll be a soldier too, she'll to the wars.
Mortimer
Good father, tell her that she and my aunt Percy
195 Shall follow in your conduct speedily.

[GLENDOWER *speaks to her in Welsh, and she answers
him in the same.*]

Glendower
She is desperate here; a peevish, self-will'd harlotry,
one that no persuasion can do good upon. *[The Lady
speaks in Welsh.]*
Mortimer
I understand thy looks: that pretty Welsh
Which thou pourest down from these swelling heavens
200 I am too perfect in; and, but for shame,
In such a parley should I answer thee.

[The Lady speaks again in Welsh.]

I understand thy kisses, and thou mine,
And that's a feeling disputation;
But I will never be a truant, love,
205 Till I have learnt thy language; for thy tongue
Makes Welsh as sweet as ditties highly penn'd,
Sung by a fair queen in a summer's bow'r,
With ravishing division, to her lute.
Glendower
Nay, if you melt, then will she run mad. *[The Lady
speaks again in Welsh.]*
Mortimer
210 O, I am ignorance itself in this!
Glendower
She bids you on the wanton rushes lay you down,
And rest your gentle head upon her lap,
And she will sing the song that pleaseth you,
And on your eyelids crown the god of sleep,

Charming your blood with pleasing heaviness,   215
Making such difference 'twixt wake and sleep
As is the difference betwixt day and night
The hour before the heavenly-harness'd team
Begins his golden progress in the east.

Mortimer

With all my heart I'll sit and hear her sing;   220
By that time will our book, I think, be drawn.

Glendower

Do so; And those musicians that shall play to you Hang
in the air a thousand leagues from hence, And straight
they shall be here; sit, and attend.

Hotspur

Come, Kate, thou art perfect in lying down. Come, 225
quick, quick, that I may lay my head in thy lap.

Lady Percy

Go, ye giddy goose. *[The music plays.]*

Hotspur

Now I perceive the devil understands Welsh;
And 'tis no marvel he is so humorous.
By'r lady, he is a good musician.   230

Lady Percy

Then should you be nothing but musical, for you are
altogether govern'd by humours. Lie still, ye thief, and
hear the lady sing in Welsh.

Hotspur

I had rather hear Lady, my brach, howl in Irish.

Lady Percy

Wouldst thou have thy head broken?   235

Hotspur

No.

Lady Percy

Then be still.

Hotspur

Neither, 'tis a woman's fault.

Lady Percy

Now God help thee!

Hotspur

240   To the Welsh lady's bed.

Lady Percy

What's that?

Hotspur

Peace! she sings.

[Here, the Lady sings a Welsh song.]

Hotspur

Come, Kate, I'll have your song too.

Lady Percy

Not mine, in good sooth.

Hotspur

245   Not yours, in good sooth! Heart! you swear like a
comfit-maker's wife. 'Not you, in good sooth' and 'As
true as I live' and 'As God shall mend me' and 'As sure
    a day'.

And givest such sarcenet surety for thy oaths
As if thou never walk'st further than Finsbury.

250   Swear me, Kate, like a lady as thou art,
A good mouth-filling oath; and leave 'in sooth'
And such protest of pepper-gingerbread
To velvet-guards and Sunday-citizens.
Come, sing.

Lady Percy

255   I will not sing.

Hotspur

'Tis the next way to turn tailor, or be redbreast teacher.
An the indentures be drawn, I'll away within these two
hours; and so come in when ye will. *[Exit]*

Glendower

Come, come, Lord Mortimer; you are as slow

260   As hot Lord Percy is on fire to go.
By this our book is drawn; we'll but seal,
And then to horse immediately.

Mortimer

With all my heart. *[Exeunt.]*

SCENE II

London. The palace.

[Enter the KING, *the* PRINCE OF WALES, *and Lords.]*

King

    Lords, give us leave; the Prince of Wales and I
    Must have some private conference; but be near at
        hand,
    For we shall presently have need of you.

[Exeunt Lords.]

    I know not whether God will have it so,
    For some displeasing service I have done,   5
    That, in his secret doom, out of my blood
    He'll breed revengement and a scourge for me;
    But thou dost in thy passages of life
    Make me believe that thou art only mark'd
    For the hot vengeance and the rod of heaven   10
    To punish my mistreadings. Tell me else,
    Could such inordinate and low desires,
    Such poor, such bare, such lewd, such mean
        attempts,
    Such barren pleasures, rude society,
    As thou art match'd withal and grafted to,   15
    Accompany the greatness of thy blood
    And hold their level with thy princely heart?

Prince

    So please your Majesty, I would I could
    Quit all offences with as clear excuse,
    As well as I am doubtless I can purge   20
    Myself of many I am charg'd withal;
    Yet such extenuation let me beg,
    As, in reproof of many tales devis'd,
    Which oft the ear of greatness needs must hear,
    By smiling pick-thanks and base news-mongers,   25
    I may, for some things true, wherein my youth

Hath faulty wand'red and irregular,
Find pardon on my true submission.

King

God pardon thee! Yet let me wonder, Harry,
30   At thy affections, which do hold a wing
Quite from the flight of all thy ancestors.
Thy place in council thou hast rudely lost,
Which by thy younger brother is supplied,
And art almost an alien to the hearts
35   Of all the court and princes of my blood.
The hope and expectation of thy time
Is ruin'd, and the soul of every man
Prophetically do forethink thy fall.
Had I so lavish of my presence been,
40   So common-hackney'd in the eyes of men,
So stale and cheap to vulgar company,
Opinion, that did help me to the crown,
Had still kept loyal to possession
And left me in reputeless banishment
45   A fellow of no mark nor likelihood.
By being seldom seen, I could not stir
But, like a comet, I was wond'red at;
That men would tell their children 'This is he';
Others would say 'Where, which is Bolingbroke?'
50   And then I stole all courtesy from heaven,
And dress'd myself in such humility
That I did pluck allegiance from men's hearts,
Loud shouts and salutations from their mouths,
Even in the presence of the crowned King.
55   Thus did I keep my person fresh and new,
My presence, like a robe pontifical,
Ne'er seen but wond'red at, and so my state,
Seldom but sumptuous, show'd like a feast
And won by rareness such solemnity.
60   The skipping King, he ambled up and down
With shallow jesters and rash bavin wits,
Soon kindled and soon burnt; carded his state,

Mingled his royalty with cap'ring fools;
Had his great name profaned with their scorns,
And gave his countenance, against his name,   65
To laugh at gibing boys and stand the push
Of every beardless vain comparative;
Grew a companion to the common streets,
Enfeoff'd himself to popularity;
That, being daily swallowed by men's eyes,   70
They surfeited with honey and began
To loathe the taste of sweetness, whereof a little
More than a little is by much too much.
So, when he had occasion to be seen,
He was but as the cuckoo is in June,   75
Heard, not regarded, seen, but with such eyes
As, sick and blunted with community,
Afford no extraordinary gaze,
Such as is bent on sun-like majesty
When it shines seldom in admiring eyes;   80
But rather drowz'd and hung their eyelids down,
Slept in his face, and rend'red such aspect
As cloudy men use to their adversaries,
Being with his presence glutted, gorg'd, and full.
And in that very line, Harry, standest thou;   85
For thou hast lost thy princely privilege
With vile participation. Not an eye
But is aweary of thy common sight,
Save mine, which hath desir'd to see thee more;
Which now doth that I would not have it do –   90
Make blind itself with foolish tenderness.
Prince
    I shall hereafter, my thrice-gracious lord,
    Be more myself.
King
                For all the world
    As thou art to this hour was Richard then
    When I from France set foot at Ravenspurgh;   95
    And even as I was then is Percy now.

Now, by my sceptre and my soul to boot,
He hath more worthy interest to the state
Than thou the shadow of succession;
100   For of no right, nor colour like to right,
He doth fill fields with harness in the realm;
Turns head against the lion's armed jaws;
And, being no more in debt to years than thou,
Leads ancient lords and reverend bishops on
105   To bloody battles and to bruising arms.
What never-dying honour hath he got
Against renowned Douglas! whose high deeds,
Whose hot incursions, and great name in arms,
Holds from all soldiers chief majority
110   And military title capital
Through all the kingdoms that acknowledge Christ.
Thrice hath this Hotspur, Mars in swathling clothes,
This infant warrior, in his enterprises
Discomfited great Douglas; ta'en him once,
115   Enlarged him and made a friend of him,
To fill the mouth of deep defiance up
And shake the peace and safety of our throne.
And what say you to this? Percy, Northumberland,
The Archbishop's Grace of York, Douglas, Mortimer,
120   Capitulate against us and are up.
But wherefore do I tell these news to thee?
Why, Harry, do I tell thee of my foes,
Which art my nearest and dearest enemy?
Thou that art like enough, through vassal fear,
125   Base inclination, and the start of spleen,
To fight against me under Percy's pay,
To dog his heels, and curtsy at his frowns,
To show how much thou art degenerate.

Prince

Do not think so; you shall not find it so;
130   And God forgive them that so much have sway'd
Your Majesty's good thoughts away from me!
I will redeem all this on Percy's head,

And in the closing of some glorious day
Be bold to tell you that I am your son,
When I will wear a garment all of blood, 135
And stain my favours in a bloody mask,
Which, wash'd away, shall scour my shame with it;
And that shall be the day, whene'er it lights,
That this same child of honour and renown,
This gallant Hotspur, this all-praised knight, 140
And your unthought-of Harry chance to meet.
For every honour sitting on his helm,
Would they were multitudes, and on my head
My shames redoubled! For the time will come
That I shall make this northern youth exchange 145
His glorious deeds for my indignities.
Percy is but my factor, good my lord,
To engross up glorious deeds on my behalf;
And I will call him to so strict account
That he shall render every glory up, 150
Yea, even the slightest worship of his time,
Or I will tear the reckoning from his heart.
This, in the name of God, I promise here;
The which if He be pleas'd I shall perform,
I do beseech your Majesty may salve 155
The long-grown wounds of my intemperature.
If not, the end of life cancels all bands;
And I will die a hundred thousand deaths
Ere break the smallest parcel of this vow.
King
A hundred thousand rebels die in this· 160
Thou shalt have charge and sovereign trust herein.

[Enter SIR WALTER BLUNT.*]*

How now, good Blunt! Thy looks are full of speed.
Blunt
So hath the business that I come to speak of.
Lord Mortimer of Scotland hath sent word
That Douglas and the English rebels met 165

The eleventh of this month at Shrewsbury.
A mighty and a fearful head they are,
If promises be kept on every hand,
As ever off'red foul play in a state.

King

170 The Earl of Westmoreland set forth to-day,
With him my son, Lord John of Lancaster;
For this advertisement is five days old.
On Wednesday next, Harry, you shall set forward;
On Thursday we ourselves will march. Our meeting
175 Is Bridgenorth. And, Harry, you shall march
Through Gloucestershire; by which account,
Our business valued, some twelve days hence
Our general forces at Bridgenorth shall meet.
Our hands are full of business. Let's away.
180 Advantage feeds him fat while men delay.

[Exeunt.]

SCENE III

Eastcheap. The Boar's Head Tavern.

[*Enter* FALSTAFF *and* BARDOLPH.]

Falstaff
Bardolph, am I not fall'n away vilely since this last
action? Do I not bate? Do I not dwindle? Why, my
skin hangs about me like an old lady's loose gown; I
am withered like an old applejohn. Well, I'll repent,
and that suddenly, while I am in some liking; I shall   5
be out of heart shortly, and then I shall have no
strength to repent. An I have not forgotten what the
inside of a church is made of, I am a peppercorn, a
brewer's horse. The inside of a church! Company,
villainous company, hath been the spoil of me.   10

Bardolph
Sir John, you are so fretful you cannot live long.

Falstaff
Why, there is it; come, sing me a bawdy song, make
me merry. I was as virtuously given as a gentleman
need to be; virtuous enough: swore little, dic'd not
above seven times a week, went to a bawdy-house not   15
above once in a quarter – of an hour, paid money that
I borrowed – three or four times, lived well, and in
good compass; and now I live out of all order, out of
all compass.

Bardolph
Why, you are so fat, Sir John, that you must needs be   20
out of all compass – out of all reasonable compass, Sir
John.

Falstaff
Do thou amend thy face, and I'll amend my life. Thou
art our admiral, thou bearest the lantern in the poop,
but 'tis in the nose of thee; thou art the Knight of the 25
Burning Lamp.

Bardolph

Why, Sir John, my face does you no harm.

Falstaff

No, I'll be sworn; I make as good use of it as many a
man doth of a death's head or a memento mori: I
30 never see thy face but I think upon hell-fire, and Dives
that lived in purple; for there he is in his robes, burning,
burning. If thou wert any way given to virtue, I would
swear by thy face: my oath should be 'By this fire,
that's God's angel'. But thou art altogether given over,
35 and wert indeed, but for the light in thy face, the son
of utter darkness. When thou ran'st up Gadshill in the
night to catch my horse, if I did not think thou hadst
been an ignis fatuus or a ball of wildfire, there's no
purchase in money. O, thou art a perpetual triumph,
40 an everlasting bonfire light! Thou hast saved me a
thousand marks in links and torches, walking with
thee in the night betwixt tavern and tavern; but the
sack that thou hast drunk me would have bought me
lights as good cheap at the dearest chandler's in Europe.
45 I have maintained that salamander of yours with fire
any time this two and thirty years; God reward me for
it!

Bardolph

'Sblood, I would my face were in your belly!

Falstaff

God-a-mercy! so should I be sure to be heart-burnt.

[Enter HOSTESS.]

50 How now, Dame Partlet the hen! Have you inquir'd
yet who pick'd my pocket?

Hostess

Why, Sir John, what do you think, Sir John? Do you
think I keep thieves in my house? I have search'd, I
have inquired, so has my husband, man by man, boy
55 by boy, servant by servant. The tithe of a hair was
never lost in my house before.

Falstaff

Ye lie, hostess: Bardolph was shav'd and lost many a hair, and I'll be sworn my pocket was pick'd. Go to, you are a woman, go.

Hostess

Who, I? No, I defy thee. God's light, I was never call'd   60
so in mine own house before.

Falstaff

Go to, I know you well enough.

Hostess

No, Sir John, you do not know me, Sir John. I know you, Sir John: you owe me money, Sir John; and now you pick a quarrel to beguile me of it. I bought you a   65
dozen of shirts to your back.

Falstaff

Dowlas, filthy dowlas! I have given them away to bakers' wives; they have made bolters of them.

Hostess

Now, as I am a true woman, holland of eight shillings an ell. You owe money here besides, Sir John, for your   70
diet and by-drinkings, and money lent you, four and twenty pound.

Falstaff

He had his part of it; let him pay.

Hostess

He? Alas, he is poor; he hath nothing.

Falstaff

How! poor? Look upon his face: what call you rich?   75
Let them coin his nose, let them coin his cheeks. I'll not pay a denier. What, will you make a younker of me? Shall I not take mine ease in mine inn but I shall have my pocket pick'd? I have lost a seal-ring of my grandfather's worth forty mark.   80

Hostess

O Jesu, I have heard the Prince tell him, I know not how oft, that that ring was copper!

Falstaff

How! the Prince is a Jack, a sneakcup. 'Sblood, an he
were here, I would cudgel him like a dog if he would
85 say so.'

*[Enter the PRINCE marching, with PETO; and FALSTAFF
meets him, playing upon his truncheon like a fife.]*

Falstaff

How now, lad! Is the wind in that door, i' faith? Must
we all march?

Bardolph

Yea, two and two, Newgate fashion.

Hostess

My lord, I pray you hear me.

Prince

90 What say'st thou, Mistress Quickly? How doth thy
husband? I love him well; he is an honest man.

Hostess

Good my lord, hear me.

Falstaff

Prithee, let her alone, and list to me.

Prince

What say'st thou, Jack?

Falstaff

95 The other night I fell asleep here behind the arras and
had my pocket pick'd; this house is turn'd bawdy-
house; they pick pockets.

Prince

What didst thou lose, Jack?

Falstaff

Wilt thou believe me, Hal? Three or four bonds of forty
100 pound a-piece and a seal-ring of my grandfather's.

Prince

A trifle, some eight-penny matter.

Hostess

So I told him, my lord; and I said I heard your Grace
say so; and, my lord, he speaks most vilely of you, like

a foulmouth'd man as he is, and said he would cudgel
you.   105

Prince

What! he did not?

Hostess

There's neither faith, truth, nor womanhood, in me
else.

Falstaff

There's no more faith in thee than in a stewed prune;
nor no more truth in thee than in a drawn fox; and 110
for womanhood, Maid Marian may be the deputy's
wife of the ward to thee. Go, you thing, go.

Hostess

Say, what thing? what thing?

Falstaff

What thing! Why, a thing to thank God on.

Hostess

I am no thing to thank God on, I would thou shouldst 115
know it; I am an honest man's wife; and setting thy
knighthood aside, thou art a knave to call me so.

Falstaff

Setting thy womanhood aside, thou art a beast to say
otherwise.

Hostess

Say, what beast, thou knave, thou?   120

Falstaff

What beast! Why, an otter.

Prince

An otter, Sir John! Why an otter?

Falstaff

Why, she's neither fish nor flesh: a man knows not
where to have her.

Hostess

Thou art an unjust man in saying so: thou or any man 125
knows where to have me, thou knave, thou!

Prince

Thou say'st true, hostess; and he slanders thee most
grossly.

Hostess

130 So he doth you, my lord; and said this other day you ought him a thousand pound.

Prince

Sirrah, do I owe you a thousand pound?

Falstaff

A thousand pound, Hal! A million. Thy love is worth a million: thou owest me thy love.

Hostess

135 Nay, my lord, he call'd you Jack, and said he would cudgel you.

Falstaff

Did I, Bardolph?

Bardolph

Indeed, Sir John, you said so.

Falstaff

Yea, if he said my ring was copper.

Prince

140 I say 'tis copper. Darest thou be as good as thy word now?

Falstaff

Why, Hal, thou knowest, as thou art but man, I dare; but as thou art prince, I fear thee as I fear the roaring of the lion's whelp.

Prince

And why not as the lion?

Falstaff

145 The King himself is to be feared as the lion. Dost thou think I'll fear thee as I fear thy father? Nay, an I do, I pray God my girdle break.

Prince

O, if it should, how would thy guts fall about thy knees! But, sirrah, there's no room for faith, truth, nor
150 honesty, in this bosom of thine – it is all fill'd up with guts and midriff. Charge an honest woman with picking thy pocket! Why, thou whoreson, impudent, emboss'd rascal, if there were anything in thy pocket

but tavern-reckonings, memorandums of bawdy-
houses, and one poor penny-worth of sugar-candy to 155
make thee long-winded – if thy pocket were enrich'd
with any other injuries but these, I am a villain. And
yet you will stand to it, you will not pocket-up wrong.
Art thou not ashamed?

Falstaff

Dost thou hear, Hal? Thou knowest in the state of 160
innocency Adam fell; and what should poor Jack
Falstaff do in the days of villainy? Thou seest I have
more flesh than another man, and therefore more
frailty. You confess, then, you pick'd my pocket?

Prince

It appears so by the story. 165

Falstaff

Hostess, I forgive thee. Go make ready breakfast, love
thy husband, look to thy servants, cherish thy guests.
Thou shalt find me tractable to any honest reason.
Thou seest I am pacified still. Nay, prithee, be gone.
[Exit HOSTESS*]* Now, Hal, to the news at court: for the 170
robbery, lad, how is that answered?

Prince

O, my sweet beef, I must still be good angel to thee:
the money is paid back again.

Falstaff

O, I do not like that paying back; 'tis a double labour.

Prince

I am good friends with my father, and may do 175
anything.

Falstaff

Rob me the exchequer the first thing thou doest, and
do it with unwash'd hands too.

Bardolph

Do, my lord.

Prince

I have procured thee, Jack, a charge of foot. 180

Falstaff

I would it had been of horse. Where shall I find one
that can steal well? O for a fine thief, of the age of
two and twenty or thereabouts! I am heinously unpro-
vided. Well, God be thanked for these rebels – they
185   offened none but the virtuous; I laud them, I praise
them.

Prince

Bardolph!

Bardolph

My lord?

Prince

Go bear this letter to Lord John of Lancaster,
To my brother John; this to my Lord of
190   Westmoreland. *[Exit* BARDOLPH.*]*
Go, Peto, to horse, to horse; for thou and I
Have thirty miles to ride yet ere dinnertime.

[Exit PETO.*]*

Jack, meet me to-morrow in the Temple Hall
At two o'clock in the afternoon;
195   There shalt thou know thy charge, and there receive
Money and order for their furniture.
The land is burning; Percy stands on high;
And either we or they must lower lie.   *[Exit.]*

Falstaff

Rare words! brave world! Hostess, my breakfast,
come
200   O, I could wish this tavern were my drum!

[Exit.]

ACT FOUR
SCENE I

The rebel camp near Shrewsbury.

[Enter HOTSPUR, WORCESTER, *and* DOUGLAS.*]*

Hotspur
　　Well said, my noble Scot. If speaking truth
　　In this fine age were not thought flattery,
　　Such attribution should the Douglas have
　　As not a soldier of this season's stamp
　　Should go so general current through the world.　　　5
　　By God, I cannot flatter; I do defy
　　The tongues of soothers; but a braver place
　　In my heart's love hath no man than yourself.
　　Nay, task me to my word; approve me, lord.
Douglas
　　Thou art the king of honour:　　　　　　　　　　10
　　No man so potent breathes upon the ground
　　But I will beard him.
Hotspur
　　　　　　　　Do so, and 'tis well.

[Enter a MESSENGER *with letters.]*

　　What letters hast thou there? – I can but thank you.
Messenger
　　These letters come from your father.
Hotspur
　　Letters from him! Why comes he not himself?　　　15
Messenger
　　He cannot come, my lord, he is grievous sick.
Hotspur
　　Zounds! how has he the leisure to be sick
　　In such a justling time? Who leads his power?
　　Under whose government come they along?

89

Messenger

20   His letters bears his mind, not I, my lord.

Worcester

I prithee tell me, doth he keep his bed?

Messenger

He did, my lord, four days ere I set forth;
And at the time of my departure thence
He was much fear'd by his physicians.

Worcester

25   I would the state of time had first been whole
Ere he by sickness had been visited:
His health was never better worth than now.

Hotspur

Sick now! droop now! This sickness doth infect
The very life-blood of our enterprise;

30   'Tis catching hither, even to our camp.
He writes me here that inward sickness –
And that his friends by deputation could not
So soon be drawn; nor did he think it meet
To lay so dangerous and dear a trust

35   On any soul remov'd, but on his own.
Yet doth he give us bold advertisement
That with our small conjunction we should on,
To see how fortune is dispos'd to us;
For, as he writes, there is no quailing now,

40   Because the King is certainly possess'd
Of all our purposes. What say you to it?

Worcester

Your father's sickness is a maim to us.

Hotspur

A perilous gash, a very limb lopp'd off.
And yet, in faith, it is not. His present want

45   Seems more than we shall find it. Were it good
To set the exact wealth of all our states
All at one cast? To set so rich a main
On the nice hazard of one doubtful hour?
It were not good; for therein should we read

The very bottom and the soul of hope,   50
The very list, the very utmost bound
Of all our fortunes.

Douglas
              Faith, and so we should;
Where now remains a sweet reversion.
We may boldly spend upon the hope of what
Is to come in.   55
A comfort of retirement lives in this.

Hotspur
A rendezvous, a home to fly unto,
If that the devil and mischance look big
Upon the maidenhead of our affairs.

Worcester
But yet I would your father had been here.   60
The quality and hair of our attempt
Brooks no division. It will be thought
By some, that know not why he is away,
That wisdom, loyalty, and mere dislike
Of our proceedings, kept the earl from hence;   65
And think how such an apprehension
May turn the tide of fearful faction
And breed a kind of question in our cause;
For well you know we of the off ring side
Must keep aloof from strict arbitrement,   70
And stop all sight-holes, every loop from whence
The eye of reason may pry in upon us.
This absence of your father's draws a curtain
That shows the ignorant a kind of fear
Before not dreamt of.

Hotspur
              You strain too far.   75
I rather of his absence make this use:
It lends a lustre and more great opinion,
A larger dare to our great enterprise,
Than if the earl were here; for men must think,
If we, without his help, can make a head   80

To push against a kingdom, with his help
We shall o'erturn it topsy-turvy down.
Yet all goes well, yet all our joints are whole.

Douglas

As heart can think; there is not such a word
85 Spoke of in Scotland as this term of fear.

[Enter SIR RICHARD VERNON.]

Hotspur

My cousin Vernon! welcome, by my soul.

Vernon

Pray God my news be worth a welcome, lord.
The Earl of Westmoreland, seven thousand strong,
Is marching hitherwards; with him Prince John.

Hotspur

No harm; what more?

Vernon

90   And further, I have learn'd
The King himself in person is set forth,
Or hitherwards intended speedily,
With strong and mighty preparation.

Hotspur

He shall be welcome too. Where is his son,
95 The nimble-footed madcap Prince of Wales,
And his comrades that daff'd the world aside
And bid it pass?

Vernon

                    All furnish'd, all in arms;
All plum'd like estridges, that with the wind
Bated like eagles having lately bath'd;
100 Glittering in golden coats, like images;
As full of spirit as the month of May
And gorgeous as the sun at midsummer;
Wanton as youthful goats, wild as young bulls.
I saw young Harry with his beaver on,
105 His cushes on his thighs, gallantly arm'd,
Rise from the ground like feathered Mercury,

deed were never soldiers, but discarded unjust serving-
men, younger sons to younger brothers, revolted
tapsters, and ostlers trade-fall'n; the cankers of a calm
world and a long peace; ten times more dishonourable
ragged than an old-fac'd ancient. And such have I, to
fill up the rooms of them as have bought out their
services, that you would think that I had a hundred
and fifty tattered Prodigals lately come from swine-
keeping, from eating draff and husks. A mad fellow met
me on the way, and told me I had unloaded all the
gibbets and press'd the dead bodies. No eye hath seen
such scarecrows. I'll not march through Coventry with
them, that's flat. Nay, and the villains march wide
betwixt the legs, as if they had gyves on; for indeed I

40   had the most of them out of prison. There's not a shirt
and a half in all my company; and the half shirt is two
napkins tack'd together and thrown over the shoulders
like a herald's coat without sleeves; and the shirt, to
say the truth, stol'n from my host at Saint Albans, or

45   the red-nose innkeeper of Daventry. But that's all one;
they'll find linen enough on every hedge.

[Enter the PRINCE OF WALES *and* WESTMORELAND.]

Prince
How now, blown Jack! how now, quilt!
Falstaff
What, Hal! how now, mad wag! What a devil dost thou
in Warwickshire? My good Lord of Westmoreland, I
50   cry you mercy; I thought your honour had already
been at Shrewsbury.
Westmoreland
Faith, Sir John, 'tis more than time that I were there,
and you too; but my powers are there already. The King,
I can tell you, looks for us all; we must away all night.
Falstaff
Tut, never fear me; I am as vigilant as a cat to steal
cream.

And vaulted with such ease into his seat
As if an angel dropp'd down from the clouds
To turn and wind a fiery Pegasus,
And witch the world with noble horsemanship.   110
Hotspur
No more, no more; worse than the sun in March,
This praise doth nourish agues. Let them come.
They come like sacrifices in their trim,
And to the fire-ey'd maid of smoky war
All hot and bleeding will we offer them.   115
The mailed Mars shall on his altar sit
Up to the ears in blood. I am on fire
To hear this rich reprisal is so nigh
And yet not ours. Come, let me taste my horse,
Who is to bear me like a thunderbolt   120
Against the bosom of the Prince of Wales.
Harry to Harry shall, hot horse to horse,
Meet, and ne'er part till one drop down a corse.
O that Glendower were come!
Vernon
                          There is more news.
I learn'd in Worcester, as I rode along,   125
He cannot draw his power this fourteen days.
Douglas
That's the worst tidings that I hear of yet.
Worcester
Ay, by my faith, that bears a frosty sound.
Hotspur
What may the King's whole battle reach unto?
Vernon
To thirty thousand.
Hotspur
                 Forty let it be: 130
My father and Glendower being both away,
The powers of us may serve so great a day.
Come, let us take a muster speedily.
Doomsday is near; die all, die merrily.

Douglas
135 Talk not of dying; I am out of fear
Of death or death's hand for this one half year.

[Exeunt.]

SCENE II

A public road near Coven...

[Enter FALSTAFF and BARDOLPH...]

Falstaff
Bardolph, get thee before to Coventry; fill...
of sack. Our soldiers shall march throug...
Sutton Co'fil' to-night.
Bardolph
Will you give me money, Captain?
Falstaff
Lay out, lay out.
Bardolph
This bottle makes an angel.
Falstaff
An if it do, take it for thy labour; and if it make twent...
take them all; I'll answer the coinage. Bid my lieutenan...
Peto meet me at town's end.
Bardolph
I will, Captain; farewell. [Exit.]
Falstaff
If I be not ashamed of my soldiers, I am a sous'd gurnet...
I have misused the King's press damnably. I have got...
in exchange of a hundred and fifty soldiers, thre...
hundred and odd pounds. I press me none but goo...
householders, yeomen's sons; inquire me out contracte...
bachelors, such as had been ask'd twice on the bann...
such a commodity of warm slaves as had as lief h...
the devil as a drum; such as fear the report of a cali...
worse than a struck fowl or a hurt wild-duck. I pr...
me none but such toasts-and-butter, with hearts in...
bellies no bigger than pins' heads, and they have b...
out their services; and now my whole charge...
of ancients, corporals, lieutenants, gentlemen of...
nies – slaves as ragged as Lazarus in the paint...
where the Glutton's dogs licked his sores; an...

And vaulted with such ease into his seat
As if an angel dropp'd down from the clouds
To turn and wind a fiery Pegasus,
And witch the world with noble horsemanship.   110

Hotspur

No more, no more; worse than the sun in March,
This praise doth nourish agues. Let them come.
They come like sacrifices in their trim,
And to the fire-ey'd maid of smoky war
All hot and bleeding will we offer them.   115
The mailed Mars shall on his altar sit
Up to the ears in blood. I am on fire
To hear this rich reprisal is so nigh
And yet not ours. Come, let me taste my horse,
Who is to bear me like a thunderbolt   120
Against the bosom of the Prince of Wales.
Harry to Harry shall, hot horse to horse,
Meet, and ne'er part till one drop down a corse.
O that Glendower were come!

Vernon

                              There is more news.
I learn'd in Worcester, as I rode along,   125
He cannot draw his power this fourteen days.

Douglas

That's the worst tidings that I hear of yet.

Worcester

Ay, by my faith, that bears a frosty sound.

Hotspur

What may the King's whole battle reach unto?

Vernon

To thirty thousand.

Hotspur

                    Forty let it be: 130
My father and Glendower being both away,
The powers of us may serve so great a day.
Come, let us take a muster speedily.
Doomsday is near; die all, die merrily.

Douglas
135 Talk not of dying; I am out of fear
Of death or death's hand for this one half year.

[*Exeunt.*]

SCENE II

A public road near Coventry.

[Enter FALSTAFF *and* BARDOLPH.*]*

Falstaff
Bardolph, get thee before to Coventry; fill me a bottle
of sack. Our soldiers shall march through; we'll to
Sutton Co'fil' to-night.

Bardolph
Will you give me money, Captain?

Falstaff
Lay out, lay out.   5

Bardolph
This bottle makes an angel.

Falstaff
An if it do, take it for thy labour; and if it make twenty,
take them all; I'll answer the coinage. Bid my lieutenant
Peto meet me at town's end.

Bardolph
I will, Captain; farewell. *[Exit.]*   10

Falstaff
If I be not ashamed of my soldiers, I am a sous'd gurnet.
I have misused the King's press damnably. I have got,
in exchange of a hundred and fifty soldiers, three
hundred and odd pounds. I press me none but good
householders, yeomen's sons; inquire me out contracted   15
bachelors, such as had been ask'd twice on the banns;
such a commodity of warm slaves as had as lief hear
the devil as a drum; such as fear the report of a caliver
worse than a struck fowl or a hurt wild-duck. I press'd
me none but such toasts-and-butter, with hearts in their   20
bellies no bigger than pins' heads, and they have bought
out their services; and now my whole charge consists
of ancients, corporals, lieutenants, gentlemen of companies – slaves as ragged as Lazarus in the painted cloth,
where the Glutton's dogs licked his sores; and such as   25

indeed were never soldiers, but discarded unjust serving-men, younger sons to younger brothers, revolted tapsters, and ostlers trade-fall'n; the cankers of a calm world and a long peace; ten times more dishonourable
30 ragged than an old-fac'd ancient. And such have I, to fill up the rooms of them as have bought out their services, that you would think that I had a hundred and fifty tattered Prodigals lately come from swine-keeping, from eating draff and husks. A mad fellow met
35 me on the way, and told me I had unloaded all the gibbets and press'd the dead bodies. No eye hath seen such scarecrows. I'll not march through Coventry with them, that's flat. Nay, and the villains march wide betwixt the legs, as if they had gyves on; for indeed I
40 had the most of them out of prison. There's not a shirt and a half in all my company; and the half shirt is two napkins tack'd together and thrown over the shoulders like a herald's coat without sleeves; and the shirt, to say the truth, stol'n from my host at Saint Albans, or
45 the red-nose innkeeper of Daventry. But that's all one; they'll find linen enough on every hedge.

[Enter the PRINCE OF WALES *and* WESTMORELAND.*]*

Prince

How now, blown Jack! how now, quilt!

Falstaff

What, Hal! how now, mad wag! What a devil dost thou in Warwickshire? My good Lord of Westmoreland, I
50 cry you mercy; I thought your honour had already been at Shrewsbury.

Westmoreland

Faith, Sir John, 'tis more than time that I were there, and you too; but my powers are there already. The King, I can tell you, looks for us all; we must away all night.

Falstaff

55 Tut, never fear me; I am as vigilant as a cat to steal cream.

Prince

I think, to steal cream indeed; for thy theft hath already
made thee butter. But tell me, Jack, whose fellows are
these that come after?

Falstaff

Mine, Hal, mine. 60

Prince

I did never see such pitiful rascals.

Falstaff

Tut, tut; good enough to toss; food for powder, food
for powder; they'll fill a pit as well as better: tush, man,
mortal men, mortal men.

Westmoreland

Ay, but, Sir John, methinks they are exceeding poor 65
and bare – too beggarly.

Falstaff

Faith, for their poverty. I know not where they had
that; and for their bareness, I am sure they never learn'd
that of me.

Prince

No, I'll be sworn; unless you call three fingers in the 70
ribs bare. But, sirrah, make haste; Percy is already in
the field. *[Exit.]*

Falstaff

What, is the King encamp'd?

Westmoreland

He is, Sir John: I fear we shall stay too long. *[Exit.]*

Falstaff

Well, 75
To the latter end of a fray and the beginning of a
feast
Fits a dull fighter and a keen guest.

[Exit.]

SCENE III

The rebel camp near Shrewsbury.

[*Enter* HOTSPUR, WORCESTER, DOUGLAS, *and*
VERNON.]

Hotspur
We'll fight with him to-night.

Worcester

It may not be.

Douglas
You give him, then, advantage.

Vernon

Not a whit.

Hotspur
Why say you so? looks he not for supply?

Vernon
So do we.

Hotspur
His is certain, ours is doubtful.

Worcester
5   Good cousin, be advis'd, stir not to-night.

Vernon
Do not, my lord.

Douglas

You do not counsel well;
You speak it out of fear and cold heart.

Vernon
Do me no slander, Douglas; by my life,
And I dare well maintain it with my life,
10   If well-respected honour bid me on,
I hold as little counsel with weak fear
As you, my lord, or any Scot that this day lives;
Let it be seen to-morrow in the battle
Which of us fears.

Douglas

Yea, or to-night.

Vernon

Content.

Hotspur

    To-night, say I.   15

Vernon

    Come, come, it may not be. I wonder much,
    Being men of such great leading as you are,
    That you foresee not what impediments
    Drag back our expedition: certain horse
    Of my cousin Vernon's are not yet come up;   20
    Your uncle Worcester's horse came but today;
    And now their pride and mettle is asleep,
    Their courage with hard labour tame and dull,
    That not a horse is half the half of himself.

Hotspur

    So are the horses of the enemy   25
    In general, journey-bated and brought low;
    The better part of ours are full of rest.

Worcester

    The number of the King exceedeth ours.
    For God's sake, cousin, stay till all come in.

        [The trumpet sounds a parley.]

        [Enter SIR WALTER BLUNT.]

Blunt

    I come with gracious offers from the King,   30
    If you vouchsafe me hearing and respect.

Hotspur

    Welcome, Sir Walter Blunt; and would to God
    You were of our determination!
    Some of us love you well; and even those some
    Envy your great deservings and good name,   35
    Because you are not of our quality,
    But stand against us like an enemy.

Blunt

    And God defend but still I should stand so,

So long as out of limit and true rule
40 You stand against anointed majesty!
But, to my charge. The King hath sent to know
The nature of your griefs; and whereupon
You conjure from the breast of civil peace
Such bold hostility, teaching his duteous land
45 Audacious cruelty. If that the King
Have any way your good deserts forgot,
Which he confesseth to be manifold,
He bids you name your griefs, and with all speed
You shall have your desires with interest,
50 And pardon absolute for yourself and these
Herein misled by your suggestion.

Hotspur

The King is kind; and well we know the King
Knows at what time to promise, when to pay.
My father and my uncle and myself
55 Did give him that same royalty he wears;
And when he was not six and twenty strong,
Sick in the world's regard, wretched and low,
A poor unminded outlaw sneaking home,
My father gave him welcome to the shore;
60 And when he heard him swear and vow to God
He came but to be Duke of Lancaster,
To sue his livery and beg his peace,
With tears of innocency and terms of zeal,
My father, in kind heart and pity mov'd,
65 Swore him assistance, and perform'd it too.
Now when the lords and barons of the realm
Perceiv'd Northumberland did lean to him,
The more and less came in with cap and knee;
Met him in boroughs, cities, villages;
70 Attended him on bridges, stood in lanes,
Laid gifts before him, proffer'd him their oaths,
Gave him their heirs as pages, followed him
Even at the heels in golden multitudes.
He presently – as greatness knows itself –

Steps me a little higher than his vow   75
Made to my father, while his blood was poor,
Upon the naked shore at Ravenspurgh;
And now, forsooth, takes on him to reform
Some certain edicts, and some strait decrees
That lie too heavy on the commonwealth;   80
Cries out upon abuses, seems to weep
Over his country's wrongs; and by this face,
This seeming brow of justice, did he win
The hearts of all that he did angle for;
Proceeded further: cut me off the heads   85
Of all the favourites that the absent King
In deputation left behind him here,
When he was personal in the Irish war.

Blunt

Tut, I came not to hear this.

Hotspur

                    Then to the point.
In short time after, he depos'd the King;   90
Soon after that depriv'd him of his life;
And in the neck of that, task'd the whole state;
To make that worse, suff'red his kinsman March –
Who is, if every owner were well plac'd,
Indeed his king – to be engag'd in Wales,   95
There without ransom to lie forfeited;
Disgrac'd me in my happy victories;
Sought to entrap me by intelligence;
Rated mine uncle from the council-board;
In rage dismiss'd my father from the court;   100
Broke oath on oath, committed wrong on wrong;
And in conclusion drove us to seek out
This head of safety, and withal to pry
Into his title, the which we find
Too indirect for long continuance.   105

Blunt

Shall I return this answer to the King?

Hotspur
    Not so, Sir Walter; we'll withdraw awhile.
    Go to the King; and let there be impawn'd
    Some surety for a safe return again,
110   And in the morning early shall mine uncle
    Bring him our purposes. And so, farewell.
Blunt
    I would you would accept of grace and love.
Hotspur
    And may be so we shall.
Blunt
                Pray God you do.

[Exeunt.]

SCENE IV

York. The Archbishop's palace.

[Enter the ARCHBISHOP OF YORK, *and* SIR MICHAEL.*]*

Archbishop
    Hie, good Sir Michael; bear this sealed brief
    With winged haste to the Lord Marshall;
    This to my cousin Scroop; and all the rest
    To whom they are directed. If you knew
    How much they do import, you would make haste.   5
Sir Michael
    My good lord,
    I guess their tenour.
Archbishop
                  Like enough you do.
    To-morrow, good Sir Michael, is a day
    Wherein the fortune of ten thousand men
    Must bide the touch; for, sir, at Shrewsbury,   10
    As I am truly given to understand,
    The King with mighty and quick-raised power
    Meets with Lord Harry; and I fear, Sir Michael,
    What with the sickness of Northumberland,
    Whose power was in the first proportion,   15
    And what with Owen Glendower's absence thence,
    Who with them was a rated sinew too
    And comes not in, o'errul'd by prophecies,
    I fear the power of Percy is too weak
    To wage an instant trial with the King.   20
Sir Michael
    Why, my good lord, you need not fear;
    There is Douglas and Lord Mortimer.
Archbishop
    No, Mortimer is not there.
Sir Michael
    But there is Mordake, Vernon, Lord Harry Percy,
    And there is my Lord of Worcester, and a head   25

Of gallant warriors, noble gentlemen.

Archbishop

And so there is; but yet the King hath drawn
The special head of all the land together:
The Prince of Wales, Lord John of Lancaster,
30 The noble Westmoreland, and warlike Blunt;
And many moe corrivals and dear men
Of estimation and command in arms.

Sir Michael

Doubt not, my lord, they shall be well oppos'd.

Archbishop

I hope no less, yet needful 'tis to fear;
35 And, to prevent the worst, Sir Michael, speed;
For if Lord Percy thrive not, ere the King
Dismiss his power, he means to visit us –
For he hath heard of our confederacy –
And 'tis but wisdom to make strong against him;
40 Therefore make haste. I must go write again
To other friends; and so farewell, Sir Michael.

[Exeunt severally.]

ACT FIVE
SCENE I

The King's camp near Shrewsbury.

[*Enter the* KING, *the* PRINCE OF WALES, PRINCE JOHN
OF LANCASTER, SIR WALTER BLUNT, *and* SIR JOHN
FALSTAFF.]

King
How bloodily the sun begins to peer
Above yon busky hill! The day looks pale
At his distemp'rature.
Prince
               The southern wind
Doth play the trumpet to his purposes,
And by his hollow whistling in the leaves   5
Foretells a tempest and a blust'ring day.
King
Then with the losers let it sympathize,
For nothing can seem foul to those that win.

[*The trumpet sounds.*]

[*Enter* WORCESTER *and* VERNON.]

How now, my Lord of Worcester! 'Tis not well
That you and I should meet upon such terms   10
As now we meet. You have deceiv'd our trust,
And made us doff our easy robes of peace
To crush our old limbs in ungentle steel;
This is not well, my lord, this is not well.
What say you to it? Will you again unknit   15
This churlish knot of all-abhorred war,
And move in that obedient orb again
Where you did give a fair and natural light,
And be no more an exhal'd meteor,

20 A prodigy of fear, and a portent
  Of broached mischief to the unborn times?

Worcester

  Hear me, my liege:
  For mine own part, I could be well content
  To entertain the lag-end of my life
25 With quiet hours; for I protest
  I have not sought the day of this dislike.

King

  You have not sought it! How comes it then?

Falstaff

  Rebellion lay in his way, and he found it.

Prince

  Peace, chewet, peace!

Worcester

30 It pleas'd your Majesty to turn your looks
  Of favour from myself and all our house;
  And yet I must remember you, my lord,
  We were the first and dearest of your friends.
  For you my staff of office did I break
35 In Richard's time, and posted day and night
  To meet you on the way and kiss your hand,
  When yet you were in place and in account
  Nothing so strong and fortunate as I.
  It was myself, my brother, and his son,
40 That brought you home, and boldly did outdare
  The dangers of the time. You swore to us –
  And you did swear that oath at Doncaster –
  That you did nothing purpose 'gainst the state,
  Nor claim no further than your new-fall'n right,
45 The seat of Gaunt, dukedom of Lancaster;
  To this we swore our aid. But in short space
  It rain'd down fortune show'ring on your head;
  And such a flood of greatness fell on you,
  What with our help, what with the absent King,
50 What with the injuries of a wanton time,
  The seeming sufferances that you had borne,

And the contrarious winds that held the King
So long in his unlucky Irish wars
That all in England did repute him dead;
And from this swarm of fair advantages   55
You took occasion to be quickly woo'd
To gripe the general sway into your hand;
Forgot your oath to us at Doncaster;
And being fed by us you us'd us so
As that ungentle gull, the cuckoo's bird,   60
Useth the sparrow – did oppress our nest,
Grew by our feeding to so great a bulk
That even our love durst not come near your sight
For fear of swallowing; but with nimble wing
We were enforc'd, for safety sake, to fly   65
Out of your sight, and raise this present head;
Whereby we stand opposed by such means
As you yourself have forg'd against yourself,
By unkind usage, dangerous countenance,
And violation of all faith and troth   70
Sworn to us in your younger enterprise.

King

These things, indeed, you have articulate,
Proclaim'd at market-crosses, read in churches,
To face the garment of rebellion
With some fine colour that may please the eye   75
Of fickle changelings and poor discontents,
Which gape and rub the elbow at the news
Of hurlyburly innovation;
And never yet did insurrection want
Such water-colours to impaint his cause,   80
Nor moody beggars, starving for a time
Of pellmell havoc and confusion.

Prince

In both your armies there is many a soul
Shall pay full dearly for this encounter,
If once they join in trial. Tell your nephew   85
The Prince of Wales doth join with all the world

In praise of Henry Percy. By my hopes,
This present enterprise set off his head,
I do not think a braver gentleman,
90 More active-valiant or more valiant-young,
More daring or more bold, is now alive
To grace this latter age with noble deeds.
For my part, I may speak it to my shame,
I have a truant been to chivalry;
95 And so I hear he doth account me too.
Yet this before my father's majesty –
I am content that he shall take the odds
Of his great name and estimation,
And will, to save the blood on either side,
100 Try fortune with him in a single fight.
King
And, Prince of Wales, so dare we venture thee,
Albeit considerations infinite
Do make against it. No, good Worcester, no,
We love our people well; even those we love
105 That are misled upon your cousin's part;
And will they take the offer of our grace,
Both he and they and you, yea, every man
Shall be my friend again, and I'll be his.
So tell your cousin, and bring me word
110 What he will do. But if he will not yield,
Rebuke and dread correction wait on us,
And they shall do their office. So, be gone;
We will not now be troubled with reply.
We offer fair; take it advisedly.

[Exeunt WORCESTER *and* VERNON.*]*

Prince
115 It will not be accepted, on my life:
The Douglas and the Hotspur both together
Are confident against the world in arms.
King
Hence, therefore, every leader to his charge;

For, on their answer, will we set on them;
And God befriend us, as our cause is just!   120

[Exeunt all but the PRINCE *and* FALSTAFF.*]*

Falstaff

Hal, if thou see me down in the battle, and bestride
me, so; 'tis a point of friendship.

Prince

Nothing but a colossus can do thee that friendship.
Say thy prayers, and farewell.

Falstaff

I would 'twere bed-time, Hal, and all well.   125

Prince

Why, thou owest God a death. *[Exit.]*

Falstaff

'Tis not due yet; I would be loath to pay him before
his day. What need I be so forward with him that calls
not on me? Well, 'tis no matter; honour pricks me on.
Yea, but how if honour prick me off when I come on? 130
How then? Can honour set to a leg? No. Or an arm?
No. Or take away the grief of a wound? No. Honour
hath no skill in surgery, then? No. What is honour?
A word. What is in that word? Honour. What is that
honour? Air. A trim reckoning! Who hath it? He that 135
died o' Wednesday. Doth he feel it? No. Doth he hear
it? No. 'Tis insensible, then? Yea, to the dead. But will
it not live with the living? No. Why? Detraction will
not suffer it. Therefore I'll none of it. Honour is a mere
scutcheon. And so ends my catechism.   140

[Exit.]

SCENE II

The rebel camp.

[Enter WORCESTER *and* VERNON.*]*

Worcester

    O, no, my nephew must not know, Sir Richard,
    The liberal and kind offer of the King.

Vernon

    'Twere best he did.

Worcester

                Then are we all undone.
    It is not possible, it cannot be,
5   The King should keep his word in loving us;
    He will suspect us still, and find a time
    To punish this offence in other faults;
    Supposition all our lives shall be stuck full of eyes,
    For treason is but trusted like the fox,
10   Who, never so tame, so cherish'd, and lock'd up,
    Will have a wild trick of his ancestors.
    Look how we can, or sad or merrily,
    Interpretation will misquote our looks,
    And we shall feed like oxen at a stall,
15   The better cherish'd still the nearer death.
    My nephew's trespass may be well forgot;
    It hath the excuse of youth and heat of blood,
    And an adopted name of privilege –
    A hare-brain'd Hotspur, govern'd by a spleen.
20   All his offences live upon my head
    And on his father's: we did train him on;
    And, his corruption being ta'en from us,
    We, as the spring of all, shall pay for all.
    Therefore, good cousin, let not Harry know,
25   In any case, the offer of the King.

Vernon

    Deliver what you will, I'll say 'tis so.
    Here comes your cousin.

[Enter HOTSPUR *and* DOUGLAS.*]*

Hotspur

      My uncle is return'd:
 Deliver up my Lord of Westmoreland.
 Uncle, what news?

Worcester

 The King will bid you battle presently.   30

Douglas

 Defy him by the Lord of Westmoreland.

Hotspur

 Lord Douglas, go you and tell him so.

Douglas

 Marry, and shall, and very willingly.

[Exit.]

Worcester

 There is no seeming mercy in the King.

Hotspur

 Did you beg any? God forbid!   35

Worcester

 I told him gently of our grievances,
 Of his oath-breaking; which he mended thus,
 By now forswearing that he is forsworn.
 He calls us rebels, traitors, and will scourge
 With haughty arms this hateful name in us. 40

[Re-enter DOUGLAS.*]*

Douglas

 Arm, gentlemen, to arms! for I have thrown
 A brave defiance in King Henry's teeth –
 And Westmoreland, that was engag'd, did bear it –
 Which cannot choose but bring him quickly on.

Worcester

 The Prince of Wales stepp'd forth before the King, 45
 And, nephew, challeng'd you to single fight.

Hotspur

 O, would the quarrel lay upon our heads;

And that no man might draw short breath to-day
But I and Harry Monmouth! Tell me, tell me,
50   How show'd his tasking? Seem'd it in contempt?

Vernon

No, by my soul, I never in my life
Did hear a challenge urg'd more modestly,
Unless a brother should a brother dare
To gentle exercise and proof of arms.
55   He gave you all the duties of a man;
Trimm'd up your praises with a princely tongue;
Spoke your deservings like a chronicle;
Making you ever better than his praise,
By still dispraising praise valued with you;
60   And, which became him like a prince indeed,
He made a blushing cital of himself,
And chid his truant youth with such a grace
As if he mast'red there a double spirit,
Of teaching and of learning instantly.
65   There did he pause; but let me tell the world –
If he outlive the envy of this day,
England did never owe so sweet a hope,
So much misconstrued in his wantonness.

Hotspur

Cousin, I think thou art enamoured
70   On his follies. Never did I hear
Of any prince so wild a liberty.
But be he as he will, yet once ere night
I will embrace him with a soldier's arm,
That he shall shrink under my courtesy.
75   Arm, arm with speed! and, fellows, soldiers, friends,
Better consider what you have to do
Than I, that have not well the gift of tongue,
Can lift your blood up with persuasion.

[Enter a Messenger.]

Messenger

My lord, here are letters for you.

Hotspur

    I cannot read them now.   80
    O gentlemen, the time of life is short!
    To spend that shortness basely were too long,
    If life did ride upon a dial's point,
    Still ending at the arrival of an hour.
    And if we live, we live to tread on kings;   85
    If die, brave death, when princes die with us!
    Now, for our consciences, the arms are fair,
    When the intent of bearing them is just.

              [Enter another Messenger.]

Messenger

    My lord, prepare; the King comes on apace.

Hotspur

    I thank him that he cuts me from my tale,   90
    For I profess not talking; only this –
    Let each man do his best. And here draw I
    A sword, whose temper I intend to stain
    With the best blood that I can meet withal
    In the adventure of this perilous day.   95
    Now, Esperance! Percy! and set on.
    Sound all the lofty instruments of war,
    And by that music let us all embrace;
    For, heaven to earth, some of us never shall
    A second time do such a courtesy.   100

      [They embrace. The trumpets sound. Exeunt.]

SCENE III

A plain between the camps.

[The KING passes across with his power. Alarum to the battle. Then enter DOUGLAS and SIR WALTER BLUNT.]

Blunt

What is thy name, that in battle thus Thou crossest me? What honour dost thou seek Upon my head?

Douglas

Know, then, my name is Douglas; And I do haunt thee in the battle thus Because some tell me that thou art
5   a king.

Blunt

They tell thee true.

Douglas

The Lord of Stafford dear to-day hath bought Thy likeness; for instead of thee, King Harry, This sword hath ended him. So shall it thee,
10   Unless thou yield thee as my prisoner.

Blunt

I was not born a yielder, thou proud Scot; And thou shalt find a king that will revenge Lord Stafford's death.

[They fight. DOUGLAS kills BLUNT.]

[Enter HOTSPUR.]

Hotspur

O Douglas, hadst thou fought at Holmedon thus,
15   I never had triumph'd upon a Scot.

Douglas

All's done, all's won; here breathless lies the King.

Hotspur

Where?

Douglas

Here.

Hotspur

This, Douglas? No: I know this face full well;
A gallant knight he was, his name was Blunt;   20
Semblably furnish'd like the King himself.

Douglas

A fool go with thy soul whither it goes!
A borrowed title hast thou bought too dear;
Why didst thou tell me that thou wert a king?

Hotspur

The King hath many marching in his coats.   25

Douglas

Now, by my sword, I will kill all his coats;
I'll murder all his wardrobe, piece by piece,
Until I meet the King.

Hotspur

                    Up, and away!
Our soldiers stand full fairly for the day.

[Exeunt.]

[Alarum. Enter FALSTAFF, solus.]

Falstaff

Though I could scape shot-free at London, I fear the   30
shot here: here's no scoring but upon the pate. Soft!
who are you? Sir Walter Blunt. There's honour for you!
Here's no vanity! I am as hot as molten lead, and as
heavy too. God keep lead out of me! I need no more
weight than mine own bowels. I have led my ragamuf-   35
fins where they are pepper'd; there's not three of my
hundred and fifty left alive, and they are for the town's
end, to beg during life. But who comes here?

[Enter the PRINCE OF WALES.]

Prince

What, stand'st thou idle here? Lend me thy sword.
Many a nobleman lies stark and stiff   40
Under the hoofs of vaunting enemies,

115

Whose deaths are yet unreveng'd. I prithee lend me
   thy sword.

Falstaff

O Hal, I prithee give me leave to breathe awhile. Turk
Gregory never did such deeds in arms as I have done
45   this day. I have paid Percy, I have made him sure.

Prince

He is, indeed, and living to kill thee. I prithee lend me
   thy sword.

Falstaff

Nay, before God, Hal, if Percy be alive, thou get'st not
my sword; but take my pistol, if thou wilt.

Prince

50   Give it me. What, is it in the case?

Falstaff

Ay, Hal; 'tis hot, 'tis hot; there's that will sack a city.
[The PRINCE *draws it out, and finds it to be a bottle of
sack.]*

Prince

What, is it a time to jest and dally now?

[He throws the bottle at him. Exit.]

Falstaff

Well, if Percy be alive, I'll pierce him. If he do come
in my way, so; if he do not, if I come in his willingly,
55   let him make a carbonado of me. I like not such grin-
ning honour as Sir Walter hath. Give me life, which
if I can save, so; if not, honour comes unlook'd for,
and there's an end.

[Exit.]

SCENE IV

Another part of the field.

[Alarums. Excursions. Enter the KING, *the* PRINCE
OF WALES, PRINCE JOHN OF LANCASTER, *and*
WESTMORELAND.]*

King
> I prithee,
> Harry, withdraw thyself; thou bleedest too much;
> Lord John of Lancaster, go you with him.

Prince John
> Not I, my lord, unless I did bleed too.

Prince
> I beseech your Majesty, make up,   5
> Lest your retirement do amaze your friends.

King
> I will do so.
> My Lord of Westmoreland, lead him to his tent.

Westmoreland
> Come, my lord, I'll lead you to your tent.

Prince
> Lead me, my lord? I do not need your help;   10
> And God forbid a shallow scratch should drive
> The Prince of Wales from such a field as this,
> Where stain'd nobility lies trodden on,
> And rebels' arms triumph in massacres!

Prince John
> We breathe too long. Come, cousin Westmoreland,   15
> Our duty this way lies; for God's sake, come.

[Exeunt PRINCE JOHN *and* WESTMORELAND.]*

Prince
> By God, thou hast deceiv'd me, Lancaster!
> I did not think thee lord of such a spirit;
> Before, I lov'd thee as a brother, John,
> But now I do respect thee as my soul.   20

117

King
I saw him hold Lord Percy at the point
With lustier maintenance than I did look for
Of such an ungrown warrior.

Prince
                              O, this boy
Lends mettle to us all! *[Exit.]*

[Enter DOUGLAS.]

Douglas
25   Another king! They grow like Hydra's heads.
I am the Douglas, fatal to all those
That wear those colours on them. What art thou,
That counterfeit'st the person of a king?

King
The King himself, who, Douglas, grieves at heart
30   So many of his shadows thou hast met,
And not the very King. I have two boys
Seek Percy and thyself about the field;
But, seeing thou fall'st on me so luckily,
I will assay thee; so, defend thyself.

Douglas
35   I fear thou art another counterfeit;
And yet, in faith, thou bearest thee like a king;
But mine I am sure thou art, who'er thou be,
And thus I win thee.

[They fight, the KING being in danger.]

[Re-enter the PRINCE.]

Prince
Hold up thy head, vile Scot, or thou art like
40   Never to hold it up again. The spirits
Of valiant Shirley, Stafford, Blunt, are in my arms;
It is the Prince of Wales that threatens thee,
Who never promiseth but he means to pay.

[They fight; DOUGLAS flies.]

Cheerly, my lord: how fares your Grace?
Sir Nicholas Gawsey hath for succour sent, 45
And so hath Clifton. I'll to Clifton straight.

King

Stay, and breathe awhile.
Thou hast redeem'd thy lost opinion;
And show'd thou mak'st some tender of my life,
In this fair rescue thou hast brought to me. 50

Prince

O God, they did me too much injury
That ever said I heark'ned for your death!
If it were so, I might have let alone
The insulting hand of Douglas over you,
Which would have been as speedy in your end 55
As all the poisonous potions in the world,
And sav'd the treacherous labour of your son.

King

Make up to Clifton, I'll to Sir Nicholas Gawsey.
                    [Exit.]

                [Enter HOTSPUR.*]*

Hotspur

If I mistake not, thou art Harry Monmouth.

Prince

Thou speak'st as if I would deny my name. 60

Hotspur

My name is Harry Percy.

Prince

                    Why, then I see
A very valiant rebel of the name.
I am the Prince of Wales; and think not, Percy,
To share with me in glory any more.
Two stars keep not their motion in one sphere, 65
Nor can one England brook a double reign
Of Harry Percy and the Prince of Wales.

Hotspur

Nor shall it, Harry, for the hour is come

To end the one of us; and would to God
70 Thy name in arms were now as great as mine!
Prince
I'll make it greater ere I part from thee,
And all the budding honours on thy crest
I'll crop to make a garland for my head.
Hotspur
I can no longer brook thy vanities.

[They fight.]

[Enter FALSTAFF.*]*

Falstaff
75 Well said, Hal! to it, Hal! Nay, you shall find no boy's
play here, I can tell you.

[Re-enter DOUGLAS; *he fights with* FALSTAFF, *who
falls down as if he were dead;* DOUGLAS *withdraws.*
HOTSPUR *is wounded, and falls.]*

Hotspur
O, Harry, thou hast robb'd me of my youth!
I better brook the loss of brittle life
Than those proud titles thou hast won of me:
They wound my thoughts worse than thy sword my
80   flesh;
But thoughts, the slaves of life, and life, time's fool,
And time, that takes survey of all the world,
Must have a stop. O, I could prophesy,
But that the earthy and cold hand of death
85 Lies on my tongue. No, Percy, thou art dust
And food for – *[Dies.]*
Prince
For worms, brave Percy. Fare thee well, great heart!
Ill-weav'd ambition, how much art thou shrunk!
When that this body did contain a spirit,
90 A kingdom for it was too small a bound;
But now two paces of the vilest earth

Is room enough. This earth that bears thee dead
Bears not alive so stout a gentleman.
If thou wert sensible of courtesy,
I should not make so dear a show of zeal;   95
But let my favours hide thy mangled face,
And, even in thy behalf, I'll thank myself
For doing these fair rites of tenderness.
Adieu, and take thy praise with thee to heaven!
Thy ignominy sleep with thee in the grave,   100
But not rememb'red in thy epitaph!

[He spieth FALSTAFF *on the ground.]*

What, old acquaintance! Could not all this flesh
Keep in a little life? Poor Jack, farewell!
I could have better spar'd a better man.
O, I should have a heavy miss of thee,   105
If I were much in love with vanity!
Death hath not struck so fat a deer to-day,
Though many dearer, in this bloody fray.
Embowell'd will I see thee by and by;
Till then in blood by noble Percy lie. *[Exit.]*   110
Falstaff
[Rising up] Embowell'd! If thou embowel me to-day, I'll
give you leave to powder me and eat me too to-morrow.
'Sblood, 'twas time to counterfeit, or that hot termagant
Scot had paid me scot and lot too. Counterfeit? I lie,
I am no counterfeit: to die is to be a counterfeit; for 115
he is but the counterfeit of a man who hath not the
life of a man; but to counterfeit dying, when a man
thereby liveth, is to be no counterfeit, but the true and
perfect image of life indeed. The better part of valour
is discretion; in the which better part I have saved my 120
life. Zounds, I am afraid of this gunpowder Percy,
though he be dead; how if he should counterfeit too,
and rise? By my faith, I am afraid he would prove the
better counterfeit. Therefore I'll make him sure; yea,
and I'll swear I kill'd him. Why may not he rise as well 125

as I? Nothing confutes me but eyes, and nobody sees
me. Therefore, sirrah [stabbing him], with a new wound
in your thigh, come you along with me.

[He takes up HOTSPUR on his back.]

[Re-enter the PRINCE OF WALES and PRINCE JOHN OF
LANCASTER.]

Prince
Come, brother John, full bravely hast thou flesh'd
130   Thy maiden sword.
Prince John
But, soft! whom have we here?
Did you not tell me this fat man was dead?
Prince
I did; I saw him dead,
Breathless and bleeding on the ground. Art thou
    alive?
135   Or is it fantasy that plays upon our eyesight?
I prithee speak; we will not trust our eyes
Without our ears: thou art not what thou seem'st.
Falstaff
No, that's certain: I am not a double man; but if I be
not Jack Falstaff, then am I a Jack. There is Percy
140   [throwing the body down]; if your father will do me any
honour, so; if not, let him kill the next Percy himself.
I look to be either earl or duke, I can assure you.
Prince
Why, Percy I kill'd myself, and saw thee dead.
Falstaff
Didst thou? Lord, Lord, how this world is given to
145   lying! I grant you I was down and out of breath, and
so was he; but we rose both at an instant, and fought
a long hour by Shrewsbury clock. If I may be believ'd,
so; if not, let them that should reward valour bear the
sin upon their own heads. I'll take it upon my death,
150   I gave him this wound in the thigh; if the man were

alive, and would deny it, zounds, I would make him
eat a piece of my sword.

Prince John

This is the strangest tale that ever I heard.

Prince

This is the strangest fellow, brother John.
Come, bring your luggage nobly on your back.   155
For my part, if a lie may do thee grace,
I'll gild it with the happiest terms I have.

[A retreat is sounded.]

The trumpet sounds retreat; the day is ours.
Come, brother, let us to the highest of the field,
To see what friends are living, who are dead.   160

[Exeunt the PRINCE *and* PRINCE JOHN OF LANCASTER.*]*

Falstaff

I'll follow, as they say, for reward. He that rewards me,
God reward him! If I do grow great, I'll grow less; for
I'll purge, and leave sack, and live cleanly, as a
nobleman should do.

[Exit.]

SCENE V

Another part of the field.

[The Trumpets sound. Enter the KING, *the* PRINCE OF
WALES, PRINCE JOHN OF LANCASTER, WESTMORELAND,
with WORCESTER *and* VERNON *prisoners.]*

King
    Thus ever did rebellion find rebuke.
    Ill-spirited Worcester! did not we send grace,
    Pardon and terms of love to all of you?
    And wouldst thou turn our offers contrary?
5   Misuse the tenour of thy kinsman's trust?
    Three knights upon our party slain to-day,
    A noble earl, and many a creature else,
    Had been alive this hour,
    If like a Christian thou hadst truly borne
10   Betwixt our armies true intelligence.
Worcester
    What I have done my safety urg'd me to;
    And I embrace this fortune patiently,
    Since not to be avoided it falls on me.
King
    Bear Worcester to the death, and Vernon too;
15   Other offenders we will pause upon.

[Exeunt WORCESTER *and* VERNON *guarded.]*

    How goes the field?
Prince
    The noble Scot, Lord Douglas, when he saw
    The fortune of the day quite turn'd from him,
    The noble Percy slain, and all his men
20   Upon the foot of fear, fled with the rest;
    And falling from a hill, he was so bruis'd
    That the pursuers took him. At my tent
    The Douglas is; and I beseech your Grace
    I may dispose of him.

King

                    With all my heart.

Prince

   Then, brother John of Lancaster, to you   25
   This honourable bounty shall belong:
   Go to the Douglas, and deliver him
   Up to his pleasure, ransomless and free;
   His valours shown upon our crests to-day
   Have taught us how to cherish such high deeds   30
   Even in the bosom of our adversaries.

Prince John

   I thank your Grace for this high courtesy,
   Which I shall give away immediately.

King

   Then this remains – that we divide our power.
   You, son John, and my cousin Westmoreland,   35
   Towards York shall bend you with your dearest
      speed
   To meet Northumberland and the prelate Scroop,
   Who, as we hear, are busily in arms.
   Myself, and you, son Harry, will towards Wales
   To fight with Glendower and the Earl of March.   40
   Rebellion in this land shall lose his sway,
   Meeting the check of such another day;
   And since this business so fair is done,
   Let us not leave till all our own be won.

               [Exeunt.]

INTRODUCTION TO PART 2

by Donald MacKenzie

Sequels are always risky and the sequel to a play as packed and brilliant as *1 Henry IV* not least. It would be a plausible guess that *2 Henry IV* has always been the less enjoyed and esteemed of the two. And one can readily argue for that response. The political action is only the mopping up of a rebellion decisively broken by the end of Part One; plus the (too?) long-drawn-out deathbed of Henry IV and succession of Hal. The Eastcheap scenes lack the brio of those in Part One and their satiric dance with high politics. Falstaff himself, diseased, aged (as distinct from old), something of a predator, has lost his comic verve and fertility. The recruiting scene, like his taking of Colville, can seem a mere ripple from the previous play. Above all do we need or want – indeed how seriously can we take? – a Hal who returns to Eastcheap and has to reconcile himself all over again to his father? Has Shakespeare not been defeated – as a playwright drama-tising history is apt to be – by his material: too much, in this case, for five acts and not enough for ten? (cf Jenkins in Armstrong, 1972).

The case is strong; and yet – at the very least – *2 Henry IV* scores its own distinctive successes. Repetition can prove creatively varied. The slackening of the action allows the play space to probe and brood. This can be focussed in a single figure: the sleepless, memory-haunted king of Act 3 Scene 1; the frustrated heir-apparent Hal of Act 2 Scene 2. Or it can expand diversely as in the great central triptych of *temps perdu* [2.4, 3.1, 3.2]. In Act 3 Scene 1 the reversals and betrayals of politics pass into a sombre vision of unresting cosmic change. This is flanked by two Falstaff scenes, steeped in memory and intimations of mortality. The first – the one meeting of Hal and Falstaff in this play before the final rejection – is (purposefully) sleazy as none of the Eastcheap scenes in *Part One* had been. But its sleaziness can muster a Hogarthian vigour or be transfixed by a sudden bleak pathos. Counterpointing all of these are the scenes with Shallow which blend the mellow, the muddled and a haunting prose lyricism in ways that have no parallel till Chekov (cf Nuttall, 1989). Memory in them is also *mis*rembering and, as such, one form of the confusion that permeates the play from the Prologue of Rumour to Mistress Quickly's verbal straggle to Hal's confounding of expectation at the climax. Confusion darkens into a vision of the body politic as diseased, of history as insuperably tangled (the latter voiced by the rebel archbishop as a ground of hope just before, in the most acrid of the play's reversals, his rebellion is quenched by the casuistic treachery of Prince John).

The succession of Hal as Henry V makes a strong bid to knit confusion into order. He succeeds his usurping father as legitimate heir. He rejects the disordered surrogate father Falstaff, choosing in his place the Lord Chief Justice who embodies the authority of impersonal law [5.2.72–121]. The sea imagery of violence and instability now, channelled, celebrates monarchic power [cf 5.2.129–32 with 1.1.153f or 3.1.45f].

Yet what cuts deepest in those final scenes may be, first, the rejection of Falstaff with what it tells of the cost – necessary, even justified – of political success; and second the irony and poignancy of the deathbed itself. There is irony in the fulfilment of Henry's prophesied death in Jerusalem; poignancy in that even in this full reconciliation neither father nor son can speak quite the whole truth (Henry 'met' – he did not take – the crown; the devoted and ambitious Hal gives a slightly but significantly misleading account of his own taking of it in turn).

Henry IV Part One is sinewed by the primal tragic motifs of inherited guilt and family conflict. Recycling the alienation and reconciling of father and son Shakespeare (at the cost of some implausibility) gives those motifs not a resolution but a refocussing that can pluck disorientatingly at the edge of the mind: 'My father is gone wild into his grave,/For in his tomb lie my affections;/And with his spirits sadly I survive'. The conflict and transposing of parent and child end *Henry IV Part Two* where *Lear* begins. Its sense of the burden of the past and of the ironic fulfilments that corrode human action key it to *Hamlet,* as its deployment of mood and memory key it to *Antony* and *Cleopatra.* The history plays (far more than the diploma-piece melodrama of *Titus Andronicus* or the inverted Shakespearean comedy of *Romeo and Juliet*) are the matrix and predecessors of Shakespearean tragedy; and the final case to be made for *Henry IV Part Two* is that it offers the fullest gateway to the latter.

LIST OF CHARACTERS FOR PART 2

Rumour — the Presenter

King Henry The Fourth

Henry, Prince Of Wales, afterwards Henry V
Prince John Of Lancaster
Prince Humphrey Of Gloucester
Thomas, Duke Of Clarence
} sons of Henry IV

Earl Of Northumberland
Scroop
Archbishop Of York
Lord Mowbray
Lord Hastings
Lord Bardolph
Sir John Colville
Travers
Morton
} retainers of Northumberland opposites against King Henry IV

Earl Of Warwick
Earl Of Westmoreland
Earl Of Surrey
Earl Of Kent
Gower
Harcourt
Blunt
} of the King's party

Lord Chief Justice — Servant, to Lord Chief Justice

Sir John Falstaff
Edward Poins
Bardolph
Pistol
Peto
} irregular humorists
Page, to Falstaff

Robert Shallow
Silence
} country Justices

Davy — servant to Shallow

131

| Fang | Sheriff's officers |
| Snare | |

Ralph Mouldy	
Simon Shadow	
Thomas Wart	country soldiers
Francis Feeble	
Peter Bullcalf	

| Francis | a drawer |

Lady Northumberland

| Lady Percy | Percy's widow |

| Hostess Quickly | of the Boar's Head, Eastcheap |

Doll Tearsheet

Lords, Attendants, a Porter, a Messenger, Drawers, Beadles, Grooms and Servants.

The Scene: England.

INDUCTION

[WARKWORTH. Before NORTHUMBERLAND 's castle.]

[Enter RUMOUR, painted full of tongues.]

Rumour

Open your ears; for which of you will stop
The vent of hearing when loud Rumour speaks?
I, from the orient to the drooping west,
Making the wind my post-horse, still unfold
The acts commenced on this ball of earth.   5
Upon my tongues continual slanders ride,
The which in every language I pronounce,
Stuffing the ears of men with false reports.
I speak of peace while covert enmity,
Under the smile of safety, wounds the world;   10
And who but Rumour, who but only I,
Make fearful musters and prepar'd defence,
Whiles the big year, swoln with some other grief,
Is thought with child by the stern tyrant war,
And so such matter? Rumour is a pipe   15
Blown by surmises, jealousies, conjectures,
And of so easy and so plain a stop
That the blunt monster with uncounted heads,
The still-discordant wav'ring multitude,
Can play upon it. But what need I thus   20
My well-known body to anatomize
Among my household? Why is Rumour here?
I run before King Harry's victory,
Who, in a bloody field by Shrewsbury,
Hath beaten down young Hotspur and his troops,   25
Quenching the flame of bold rebellion
Even with the rebels' blood. But what mean I
To speak so true at first? My office is
To noise abroad that Harry Monmouth fell
Under the wrath of noble Hotspur's sword,   30

And that the King before the Douglas' rage
Stoop'd his anointed head as low as death.
This have I rumour'd through the peasant towns
   Between that royal field of Shrewsbury
35 And this worm-eaten hold of ragged stone,
Where Hotspur's father, old Northumberland,
Lies crafty-sick. The posts come tiring on,
And not a man of them brings other news
Than they have learnt of me. From Rumour's
   tongues
They bring smooth comforts false, worse than true
   wrongs.

[Exit.]

ACT ONE
SCENE I.

Warkworth. Before Northumberland's castle.

[Enter LORD BARDOLPH.]

Lord Bardolph
Who keeps the gate here, ho?

[The Porter opens the gate.]

Where is the Earl?

Porter
What shall I say you are?

Lord Bardolph
Tell thou the Earl
That the Lord Bardolph doth attend him here.

Porter
His lordship is walk'd forth into the orchard.
Please it your honour knock but at the gate,   5
And he himself will answer.

[Enter NORTHUMBERLAND.]

Lord Bardolph
Here comes the Earl.

[Exit Porter.]

Northumberland
What news, Lord Bardolph?
Every minute now
Should be the father of some stratagem.
The times are wild; contention, like a horse   10
Full of high feeding, madly hath broke loose
And bears down all before him.

Lord Bardolph
Noble Earl,

I bring you certain news from Shrewsbury.
Northumberland
Good, an God will!
Lord Bardolph
15   As good as heart can wish.
The King is almost wounded to the death;
And, in the fortune of my lord your son,
Prince Harry slain outright; and both the Blunts
Kill'd by the hand of Douglas; young Prince John,
20   And Westmoreland, and Stafford, fled the field;
And Harry Monmouth's brawn, the hulk Sir John,
Is prisoner to your son. O, such a day,
So fought, so followed, and so fairly won,
Came not till now to dignify the times,
Since Caesar's fortunes!
Northumberland
25   How is this deriv'd?
Saw you the field? Came you from Shrewsbury?
Lord Bardolph
I spake with one, my lord, that came from thence;
A gentleman well bred and of good name,
That freely rend'red me these news for true.

[Enter TRAVERS.*]*

Northumberland
30   Here comes my servant Travers, whom I sent
On Tuesday last to listen after news.
Lord Bardolph
My lord, I over-rode him on the way;
And he is furnish'd with no certainties
More than he haply may retail from me.
Northumberland
35   Now, Travers, what good tidings comes with you?
Travers
My lord, Sir John Umfrevile turn'd me back
With joyful tidings; and, being better hors'd,
Out-rode me. After him came spurring hard

A gentleman, almost forspent with speed,
That stopp'd by me to breathe his bloodied horse.   40
He ask'd the way to Chester; and of him
I did demand what news from Shrewsbury.
He told me that rebellion had bad luck,
And that young Harry Percy's spur was cold.
With that he gave his able horse the head   45
And, bending forward, struck his armed heels
Against the panting sides of his poor jade
Up to the rowel-head; and starting so,
He seem'd in running to devour the way,
Staying no longer question.

Northumberland

                       Ha! Again: 50
Said he young Harry Percy's spur was cold?
Of Hotspur, Coldspur? that rebellion
Had met ill luck?

Lord Bardolph

                   My lord, I'll tell you what:
If my young lord your son have not the day,
Upon mine honour, for a silken point   55
I'll give my barony. Never talk of it.

Northumberland

Why should that gentleman that rode by Travers
Give then such instances of loss?

Lord Bardolph

                     Who – he?
He was some hilding fellow that had stol'n
The horse he rode on and, upon my life,   60
Spoke at a venture. Look, here comes more news.

[Enter MORTON.]

Northumberland

Yea, this man's brow, like to a title-leaf,
Foretells the nature of a tragic volume.
So looks the strand whereon the imperious flood
Hath left a witness'd usurpation.   65

Say, Morton, didst thou come from Shrewsbury?

Morton

I ran from Shrewsbury, my noble lord;
Where hateful death put on his ugliest mask
To fright our party.

Northumberland

70 How doth my son and brother?
Thou tremblest; and the whiteness in thy cheek
Is apter than thy tongue to tell thy errand.
Even such a man, so faint, so spiritless,
So dull, so dead in look, so woe-begone,
75 Drew Priam's curtain in the dead of night
And would have told him half his Troy was burnt;
But Priam found the fire ere he his tongue,
And I my Percy's death ere thou report'st it.
This thou wouldst say: 'Your son did thus and thus;
80 Your brother thus; so fought the noble Douglas' –
Stopping my greedy ear with their bold deeds;
But in the end, to stop my ear indeed,
Thou hast a sigh to blow away this praise,
Ending with 'Brother, son, and all, are dead'.

Morton

85 Douglas is living, and your brother, yet;
But for my lord your son –

Northumberland

Why, he is dead.
See what a ready tongue suspicion hath!
He that but fears the thing he would not know
Hath by instinct knowledge from others' eyes
90 That what he fear'd is chanced. Yet speak, Morton;
Tell thou an earl his divination lies,
And I will take it as a sweet disgrace
And make thee rich for doing me such wrong.

Morton

You are too great to be by me gainsaid; Your spirit is
95 too true, your fears too certain.

Northumberland
    Yet, for all this, say not that Percy's dead.
    I see a strange confession in thine eye;
    Thou shak'st thy head, and hold'st it fear or sin
    To speak a truth. If he be slain, say so:
    The tongue offends not that reports his death;   100
    And he doth sin that doth belie the dead,
    Not he which says the dead is not alive.
    Yet the first bringer of unwelcome news
    Hath but a losing office, and his tongue
    Sounds ever after as a sullen bell,   105
    Rememb'red tolling a departing friend.
Lord Bardolph
    I cannot think, my lord, your son is dead.
Morton
    I am sorry I should force you to believe
    That which I would to God I had not seen;
    But these mine eyes saw him in bloody state,   110
    Rend'ring faint quittance, wearied and outbreath'd,
    To Harry Monmouth, whose swift wrath beat down
    The never-daunted Percy to the earth,
    From whence with life he never more sprung up.
    In few, his death – whose spirit lent a fire   115
    Even to the dullest peasant in his camp –
    Being bruited once, took fire and heat away
    From the best-temper'd courage in his troops;
    For from his metal was his party steeled;
    Which once in him abated, all the rest   120
    Turn'd on themselves, like dull and heavy lead.
    And as the thing that's heavy in itself
    Upon enforcement flies with greatest speed,
    So did our men, heavy in Hotspur's loss,
    Lend to this weight such lightness with their fear   125
    That arrows fled not swifter toward their aim
    Than did our soldiers, aiming at their safety,
    Fly from the field. Then was that noble Worcester
    Too soon ta'en prisoner; and that furious Scot,

130 The bloody Douglas, whose well-labouring sword
    Had three times slain th' appearance of the King,
    Gan vail his stomach and did grace the shame
    Of those that turn'd their backs, and in his flight,
    Stumbling in fear, was took. The sum of all
135 Is that the King hath won, and hath sent out
    A speedy power to encounter you, my lord,
    Under the conduct of young Lancaster
    And Westmoreland. This is the news at full.

Northumberland

    For this I shall have time enough to mourn.
140 In poison there is physic; and these news,
    Having been well, that would have made me sick,
    Being sick, have in some measure made me well;
    And as the wretch whose ever-weak'ned joints,
    Like strengthless hinges, buckle under life,
145 Impatient of his fit, breaks like a fire
    Out of his keeper's arms, even so my limbs,
    Weak'ned with grief, being now enrag'd with grief,
    Are thrice themselves. Hence, therefore, thou nice
        crutch!
    A scaly gauntlet now with joints of steel
150 Must glove this hand; and hence, thou sickly coif!
    Thou art a guard too wanton for the head
    Which princes, flesh'd with conquest, aim to hit.
    Now bind my brows with iron; and approach
    The ragged'st hour that time and spite dare bring
155 To frown upon th' enrag'd Northumberland!
    Let heaven kiss earth! Now let not Nature's hand
    Keep the wild flood confin'd! Let order die!
    And let this world no longer be a stage
    To feed contention in a ling'ring act;
160 But let one spirit of the first-born Cain
    Reign in all bosoms, that, each heart being set
    On bloody courses, the rude scene may end
    And darkness be the burier of the dead!

Lord Bardolph

This strained passion doth you wrong, my lord.

Morton

Sweet Earl, divorce not wisdom from your honour.   165
The lives of all your loving complices
Lean on your health; the which, if you give o'er
To stormy passion, must perforce decay.
You cast th' event of war, my noble lord,
And summ'd the account of chance before you said   170
'Let us make head'. It was your presurmise
That in the dole of blows your son might drop.
You knew he walk'd o'er perils on an edge,
More likely to fall in than to get o'er;
You were advis'd his flesh was capable   175
Of wounds and scars, and that his forward spirit
Would lift him where most trade of danger rang'd;
Yet did you say 'Go forth'; and none of this,
Though strongly apprehended, could restrain
The stiff-borne action. What hath then befall'n,   180
Or what hath this bold enterprise brought forth
More than that being which was like to be?

Lord Bardolph

We all that are engaged to this loss
Knew that we ventured on such dangerous seas
That if we wrought out life 'twas ten to one;   185
And yet we ventur'd, for the gain propos'd
Chok'd the respect of likely peril fear'd;
And since we are o'erset, venture again.
Come, we will all put forth, body and goods.

Morton

'Tis more than time. And, my most noble lord,   190
I hear for certain, and dare speak the truth:
The gentle Archbishop of York is up
With well-appointed pow'rs. He is a man
Who with a double surety binds his followers.
My lord your son had only but the corpse,   195
But shadows and the shows of men, to fight;

For that same word 'rebellion' did divide
The action of their bodies from their souls;
And they did fight with queasiness, constrain'd,
200   As men drink potions; that their weapons only
Seem'd on our side, but for their spirits and souls
This word 'rebellion' – it had froze them up,
As fish are in a pond. But now the Bishop
Turns insurrection to religion.
205   Suppos'd sincere and holy in his thoughts,
He's follow'd both with body and with mind;
And doth enlarge his rising with the blood
Of fair King Richard, scrap'd from Pomfret stones;
Derives from heaven his quarrel and his cause;
Tells them he doth bestride a bleeding land,
210   Gasping for life under great Bolingbroke;
And more and less do flock to follow him.

Northumberland

I knew of this before; but, to speak truth,
This present grief had wip'd it from my mind.
215   Go in with me; and counsel every man
The aptest way for safety and revenge.
Get posts and letters, and make friends with speed –
Never so few, and never yet more need.

[Exeunt.]

SCENE II

London. A street.

[Enter SIR JOHN FALSTAFF, *with his* PAGE *bearing his
sword and buckler.]*

Falstaff
Sirrah, you giant, what says the doctor to my water?
Page
He said, sir, the water itself was a good healthy water;
but for the party that owed it, he might have moe
diseases than he knew for.
Falstaff
Men of all sorts take a pride to gird at me. The brain   5
of this foolish-compounded clay, man, is not able to
invent anything that intends to laughter, more than I
invent or is invented on me. I am not only witty in
myself, but the cause that wit is in other men. I do here
walk before thee like a sow that hath overwhelm'd all   10
her litter but one. If the Prince put thee into my service
for any other reason than to set me off, why then I
have no judgment. Thou whoreson mandrake, thou art
fitter to be worn in my cap than to wait at my heels. I
was never mann'd with an agate till now; but I will   15
inset you neither in gold nor silver, but in vile apparel,
and send you back again to your master, for a jewel –
the juvenal, the Prince your master, whose chin is not
yet fledge. I will sooner have a beard grow in the palm
of my hand than he shall get one off his cheek; and   20
yet he will not stick to say his face is a face-royal. God
may finish it when he will, 'tis not a hair amiss yet. He
may keep it still at a face-royal, for a barber shall never
earn sixpence out of it; and yet he'll be crowing as if
he had writ man ever since his father was a bachelor.   25
He may keep his own grace, but he's almost out of
mine, I can assure him. What said Master Dommelton
about the satin for my short cloak and my slops?

Page

He said, sir, you should procure him better assurance
30   than Bardolph. He would not take his band and yours;
he liked not the security.

Falstaff

Let him be damn'd, like the Glutton; pray God his
tongue be hotter! A whoreson Achitophel! A rascal-
yea-forsooth knave, to bear a gentleman in hand, and
35   then stand upon security! The whoreson smooth-pates
do now wear nothing but high shoes, and bunches of
keys at their girdles; and if a man is through with them
in honest taking-up, then they must stand upon security. I had as lief they would put ratsbane in my mouth
40   as offer to stop it with security. I look'd 'a should have
sent me two and twenty yards of satin, as I am a true
knight, and he sends me security. Well, he may sleep
in security; for he hath the horn of abundance, and
the lightness of his wife shines through it; and yet
45   cannot he see, though he have his own lanthorn to
light him. Where's Bardolph?

Page

He's gone into Smithfield to buy your worship a horse.

Falstaff

I bought him in Paul's, and he'll buy me a horse in
Smithfield. An I could get me but a wife in the stews,
50   I were mann'd, hors'd, and wiv'd.

[Enter the LORD CHIEF JUSTICE *and Servant.]*

Page

Sir, here comes the nobleman that committed the
Prince for striking him about Bardolph.

Falstaff

Wait close; I will not see him.

Chief Justice

What's he that goes there?

Servant

55   Falstaff, an't please your lordship.

Chief Justice
He that was in question for the robb'ry?

Servant
He, my lord; but he hath since done good service at Shrewsbury, and, as I hear, is now going with some charge to the Lord John of Lancaster.

Chief Justice
What, to York? Call him back again.   60

Servant
Sir John Falstaff!

Falstaff
Boy, tell him I am deaf.

Page
You must speak louder; my master is deaf.

Chief Justice
I am sure he is, to the hearing of anything good. Go, pluck him by the elbow; I must speak with him.   65

Servant
Sir John!

Falstaff
What! a young knave, and begging! Is there not wars? Is there not employment? Doth not the King lack subjects? Do not the rebels need soldiers? Though it be a shame to be on any side but one, it is worse shame   70 to beg than to be on the worst side, were it worse than the name of rebellion can tell how to make it.

Servant
You mistake me, sir.

Falstaff
Why, sir, did I say you were an honest man? Setting my knighthood and my soldiership aside, I had lied   75 in my throat if I had said so.

Servant
I pray you, sir, then set your knighthood and your soldiership aside; and give me leave to tell you you lie in your throat, if you say I am any other than an honest man.   80

145

Falstaff

I give thee leave to tell me so! I lay aside that which grows to me! If thou get'st any leave of me, hang me; if thou tak'st leave, thou wert better be hang'd. You hunt counter. Hence! Avaunt!

Servant

85   Sir, my lord would speak with you.

Chief Justice

Sir John Falstaff, a word with you.

Falstaff

My good lord! God give your lordship good time of day. I am glad to see your lordship abroad. I heard say your lordship was sick; I hope your lordship goes
90   abroad by advice. Your lordship, though not clean past your youth, hath yet some smack of age in you, some relish of the saltness of time; and I most humbly beseech your lordship to have a reverend care of your health.

Chief Justice

95   Sir John, I sent for you before your expedition to Shrewsbury.

Falstaff

An't please your lordship, I hear his Majesty is return'd with some discomfort from Wales.

Chief Justice

I talk not of his Majesty. You would not come when
100   I sent for you.

Falstaff

And I hear, moreover, his Highness is fall'n into this same whoreson apoplexy.

Chief Justice

Well, God mend him! I pray you let me speak with you.

Falstaff

105   This apoplexy, as I take it, is a kind of lethargy, an't please your lordship, a kind of sleeping in the blood, a whoreson tingling.

Chief Justice

What tell you me of it? Be it as it is.

Falstaff

It hath it original from much grief, from study, and perturbation of the brain. I have read the cause of his effects in Galen; it is a kind of deafness.

Chief Justice

I think you are fall'n into the disease, for you hear not what I say to you.

Falstaff

Very well, my lord, very well. Rather an't please you, it is the disease of not listening, the malady of not marking, that I am troubled withal.

Chief Justice

To punish you by the heels would amend the attention of your ears; and I care not if I do become your physician.

Falstaff

I am as poor as Job, my lord, but not so patient. Your lordship may minister the potion of imprisonment to me in respect of poverty; but how I should be your patient to follow your prescriptions, the wise may make some dram of a scruple, or indeed a scruple itself.

Chief Justice

I sent for you, when there were matters against you for your life, to come speak with me.

Falstaff

As I was then advis'd by my learned counsel in the laws of this land-service, I did not come.

Chief Justice

Well, the truth is, Sir John, you live in great infamy.

Falstaff

He that buckles himself in my belt cannot live in less.

Chief Justice

Your means are very slender, and your waste is great.

Falstaff

I would it were otherwise; I would my means were greater and my waist slenderer.

Chief Justice

135 You have misled the youthful Prince.

Falstaff

The young Prince hath misled me. I am the fellow with the great belly, and he my dog.

Chief Justice

Well, I am loath to gall a newheal'd wound. Your day's service at Shrewsbury hath a little gilded over your
140 night's exploit on Gadshill. You may thank th' unquiet time for your quiet o'erposting that action.

Falstaff

My lord –

Chief Justice

But since all is well, keep it so: wake not a sleeping wolf.

Falstaff

145 To wake a wolf is as bad as smell a fox.

Chief Justice

What! you are as a candle, the better part burnt out.

Falstaff

A wassail candle, my lord – all tallow; if I did say of wax, my growth would approve the truth.

Chief Justice

There is not a white hair in your face but should have
150 his effect of gravity.

Falstaff

His effect of gravy, gravy, gravy.

Chief Justice

You follow the young Prince up and down, like his ill angel.

Falstaff

Not so, my lord. Your ill angel is light; but I hope he
155 that looks upon me will take me without weighing. And yet in some respects, I grant, I cannot go – I

cannot tell. Virtue is of so little regard in these coster-
mongers' times that true valour is turn'd berod;
pregnancy is made a tapster, and his quick wit wasted
in giving reckoning; all the other gifts appertinent to 160
man, as the malice of this age shapes them, are not
worth a gooseberry. You that are old consider not the
capacities of us that are young; you do measure the
heat of our livers with the bitterness of your galls; and
we that are in the vaward of our youth, I must confess, 165
are wags too.

Chief Justice

Do you set down your name in the scroll of youth,
that are written down old with all the characters of
age? Have you not a moist eye, a dry hand, a yellow
cheek, a white beard, a decreasing leg, an increasing 170
belly? Is not your voice broken, your wind short, your
chin double, your wit single, and every part about you
blasted with antiquity? And will you yet call yourself
young? Fie, fie, fie, Sir John!

Falstaff

My lord, I was born about three of the clock in the 175
afternoon, with a white head and something a round
belly. For my voice – I have lost it with hallooing and
singing of anthems. To approve my youth further, I
will not. The truth is, I am only old in judgement and
understanding; and he that will caper with me for a 180
thousand marks, let him lend me the money, and have
at him. For the box of the ear that the Prince gave you
– he gave it like a rude prince, and you took it like a
sensible lord. I have check'd him for it; and the young
lion repents – marry, not in ashes and sackcloth, but 185
in new silk and old sack.

Chief Justice

Well, God send the Prince a better companion!

Falstaff

God send the companion a better prince! I cannot rid
my hands of him.

Chief Justice

190 Well, the King hath sever'd you. I hear you are going with Lord John of Lancaster against the Archbishop and the Earl of Northumberland.

Falstaff

Yea; I thank your pretty sweet wit for it. But look you pray, all you that kiss my Lady Peace at home, that our

195 armies join not in a hot day; for, by the Lord, I take but two shirts out with me, and I mean not to sweat extraordinarily. If it be a hot day, and I brandish anything but a bottle, I would I might never spit white again. There is not a dangerous action can peep out his head but I

200 am thrust upon it. Well, I cannot last ever; but it was alway yet the trick of our English nation, if they have a good thing, to make it too common. If ye will needs say I am an old man, you should give me rest. I would to God my name were not so terrible to the enemy as

205 it is. I were better to be eaten to death with a rust than to be scoured to nothing with perpetual motion.

Chief Justice

Well, be honest, be honest; and God bless your expedition!

Falstaff

Will your lordship lend me a thousand pound to

210 furnish me forth?

Chief Justice

Not a penny, not a penny; you are too impatient to bear crosses. Fare you well. Commend me to my cousin Westmoreland.

[Exeunt CHIEF JUSTICE *and Servant.]*

Falstaff

If I do, fillip me with a three-man beetle. A man can

215 no more separate age and covetousness than 'a can part young limbs and lechery; but the gout galls the one, and the pox pinches the other; and so both the degrees prevent my curses. Boy!

Page

    Sir?

Falstaff

    What money is in my purse?   220

Page

    Seven groats and two pence.

Falstaff

    I can get no remedy against this consumption of the
    purse; borrowing only lingers and lingers it out, but
    the disease is incurable. Go bear this letter to my Lord
    of Lancaster; this to the Prince; this to the Earl of 225
    Westmoreland; and this to old Mistress Ursula, whom
    I have weekly sworn to marry since I perceiv'd the first
    white hair of my chin. About it; you know where to
    find me. *[Exit* PAGE*]* A pox of this gout! or, a gout of
    this pox! for the one or the other plays the rogue with 230
    my great toe. 'Tis no matter if I do halt; I have the
    wars for my colour, and my pension shall seem the
    more reasonable. A good wit will make use of anything.
    I will turn diseases to commodity.

                        [Exit.]

SCENE III

York. The Archbishop's palace.

[Enter the ARCHBISHOP, THOMAS MOWBRAY *the Earl
Marshal,* LORD HASTINGS *and* LORD BARDOLPH.]

Archbishop
    Thus have you heard our cause and known our means;
    And, my most noble friends, I pray you all
    Speak plainly your opinions of our hopes –
    And first, Lord Marshal, what say you to it?
5 *Mowbray*
    I well allow the occasion of our arms;
    But gladly would be better satisfied
    How, in our means, we should advance ourselves
    To look with forehead bold and big enough
    Upon the power and puissance of the King.
10 *Hastings*
    Our present musters grow upon the file
    To five and twenty thousand men of choice;
    And our supplies live largely in the hope
    Of great Northumberland, whose bosom burns
    With an incensed fire of injuries.
15 *Lord Bardolph*
    The question then, Lord Hastings, standeth thus:
    Whether our present five and twenty thousand
    May hold up head without Northumberland?
Hastings
    With him, we may.
Lord Bardolph
                Yea, marry, there's the point;
20   But if without him we be thought too feeble,
    My judgement is we should not step too far
    Till we had his assistance by the hand;
    For, in a theme so bloody-fac'd as this,
    Conjecture, expectation, and surmise
    Of aids incertain, should not be admitted.

Archbishop   25
    'Tis very true, Lord Bardolph; for indeed
    It was young Hotspur's case at Shrewsbury.
Lord Bardolph
    It was, my lord; who lin'd himself with hope,
    Eating the air and promise of supply,
    Flatt'ring himself in project of a power   30
    Much smaller than the smallest of his thoughts;
    And so, with great imagination
    Proper to madmen, led his powers to death,
    And, winking, leapt into destruction.
Hastings
    But, by your leave, it never yet did hurt   35
    To lay down likelihoods and forms of hope.
Lord Bardolph
    Yes, if this present quality of war –
    Indeed the instant action, a cause on foot –
    Lives so in hope, as in an early spring
    We see th' appearing buds; which to prove fruit   40
    Hope gives not so much warrant, as despair
    That frosts will bite them. When we mean to build,
    We first survey the plot, then draw the model;
    And when we see the figure of the house,
    Then must we rate the cost of the erection;   45
    Which if we find outweighs ability,
    What do we then but draw anew the model
    In fewer offices, or at least desist
    To build at all? Much more, in this great work –
    Which is almost to pluck a kingdom down   50
    And set another up – should we survey
    The plot of situation and the model,
    Consent upon a sure foundation,
    Question surveyors, know our own estate
    How able such a work to undergo –   55
    To weigh against his opposite; or else
    We fortify in paper and in figures,
    Using the names of men instead of men;

Like one that draws the model of a house
60   Beyond his power to build it; who, half through,
Gives o'er and leaves his part-created cost
A naked subject to the weeping clouds
And waste for churlish winter's tyranny.

Hastings

Grant that our hopes – yet likely of fair birth –
65   Should be still-born, and that we now possess'd
The utmost man of expectation,
I think we are so a body strong enough,
Even as we are, to equal with the King.

Lord Bardolph

What, is the King but five and twenty thousand?

Hastings

70   To us no more; nay, not so much, Lord Bardolph;
For his divisions, as the times do brawl,
Are in three heads: one power against the French,
And one against Glendower; perforce a third
Must take up us. So is the unfirm King
75   In three divided; and his coffers sound
With hollow poverty and emptiness.

Archbishop

That he should draw his several strengths together
And come against us in full puissance
Need not be dreaded.

Hastings

                    If he should do so,
80   He leaves his back unarm'd, the French and Welsh
Baying him at the heels. Never fear that.

Lord Bardolph

Who is it like should lead his forces hither?

Hastings

The Duke of Lancaster and Westmoreland;
Against the Welsh, himself and Harry Monmouth;
But who is substituted against the French
I have no certain notice.

Archbishop   85
                    Let us on,
And publish the occasion of our arms.
The commonwealth is sick of their own choice;
Their over-greedy love hath surfeited.
An habitation giddy and unsure   90
Hath he that buildeth on the vulgar heart.
O thou fond many, with what loud applause
Didst thou beat heaven with blessing Bolingbroke
Before he was what thou wouldst have him be!
And being now trimm'd in thine own desires,   95
Thou, beastly feeder, art so full of him
That thou provok'st thyself to cast him up.
So, so, thou common dog, didst thou disgorge
Thy glutton bosom of the royal Richard;
And now thou wouldst eat thy dead vomit up,   100
And howl'st to find it. What trust is in these times?
They that, when Richard liv'd, would have him die
Are now become enamour'd on his grave.
Thou that threw'st dust upon his goodly head,
When through proud London he came sighing on   105
After th' admired heels of Bolingbroke,
Criest now 'O earth, yield us that king again,
And take thou this!' O thoughts of men accurs'd!
Past and to come seems best; things present, worst.
Mowbray
Shall we go draw our numbers, and set on?
Hastings   110
We are time's subjects, and time bids be gone.

                    [Exeunt.]

ACT TWO
SCENE I

London. A street.

[Enter HOSTESS *with two officers,* FANG *and* SNARE.*]*

Hostess
Master Fang, have you ent'red the action?

Fang
It is ent'red.

Hostess
Where's your yeoman? Is't a lusty yeoman? Will 'a
stand to't?

Fang
5   Sirrah, where's Snare?

Hostess
O Lord, ay! good Master Snare.

Snare
Here, here.

Fang
Snare, we must arrest Sir John Falstaff.

Hostess
Yea, good Master Snare; I have ent'red him and all.

Snare
10   It may chance cost some of us our lives, for he will
stab.

Hostess
Alas the day! take heed of him; he stabb'd me in mine
own house, and that most beastly. In good faith, 'a
cares not what mischief he does, if his weapon be out;
he will foin like any devil; he will spare neither man,
15   woman, nor child.

Fang
If I can close with him, I care not for his thrust.

Hostess

No, nor I neither; I'll be at your elbow.

Fang

An I but fist him once; an 'a come but within my vice!

Hostess

I am undone by his going; I warrant you, he's an 20
infinitive thing upon my score. Good Master Fang,
hold him sure. Good Master Snare, let him not scape.
'A comes continuantly to Piecorner – saving your
manhoods – to buy a saddle; and he is indited to dinner
to the Lubber's Head in Lumbert Street, to Master 25
Smooth's the silkman. I pray you, since my exion is
ent'red, and my case so openly known to the world,
let him be brought in to his answer. A hundred mark
is a long one for a poor lone woman to bear; and I
have borne, and borne, and borne; and have been 30
fubb'd off, and fubb'd off, and fubb'd off, from this
day to that day, that it is a shame to be thought on.
There is no honesty in such dealing; unless a woman
should be made an ass and a beast, to bear every knave's
wrong. 35

[Enter SIR JOHN FALSTAFF, PAGE, *and* BARDOLPH.*]*

Yonder he comes; and that arrant malmsey-nose knave,
Bardolph, with him. Do your offices, do your offices,
Master Fang and Master Snare; do me, do me, do me
your offices.

Falstaff

How now! whose mare's dead? 40
What's the matter?

Fang

Sir John, I arrest you at the suit of Mistress Quickly.

Falstaff

Away, varlets! Draw, Bardolph. Cut me off the villain's
head. Throw the quean in the channel.

Hostess

Throw me in the channel! I'll throw thee in the 45

channel. Wilt thou? wilt thou? thou bastardly rogue!
Murder, murder! Ah, thou honeysuckle villain! wilt
thou kill God's officers and the King's? Ah, thou honey-
seed rogue! thou art a honey-seed; a man-queller and
50 a woman-queller.

Falstaff
Keep them off, Bardolph.

Fang
A rescue! a rescue!

Hostess
Good people, bring a rescue or two. Thou wot, wot
thou! thou wot, wot ta? Do, do, thou rogue! do, thou
55 hemp-seed!

Page
Away, you scullion! you rampallian! you fustilarian!
I'll tickle your catastrophe.

[Enter the LORD CHIEF JUSTICE *and his Men.]*

Chief Justice
What is the matter? Keep the peace here, ho!

Hostess
Good my lord, be good to me. I beseech you, stand to
60 me.

Chief Justice
How now, Sir John! what, are you brawling here?
Doth this become your place, your time, and
    business?
You should have been well on your way to York.
Stand from him, fellow; wherefore hang'st thou
    upon him?

Hostess
65 O my most worshipful lord, an't please your Grace, I
am a poor widow of Eastcheap, and he is arrested at
my suit.

Chief Justice
For what sum?

Hostess

It is more than for some, my lord; it is for all – all I
have. He hath eaten me out of house and home; he   70
hath put all my substance into that fat belly of his.
But I will have some of it out again, or I will ride thee
a nights like the mare.

Falstaff

I think I am as like to ride the mare, if I have any
vantage of ground to get up.   75

Chief Justice

How comes this, Sir John? Fie! What man of good
temper would endure this tempest of exclamation? Are
you not ashamed to enforce a poor widow to so rough
a course to come by her own?

Falstaff

What is the gross sum that I owe thee?   80

Hostess

Marry, if thou wert an honest man, thyself and the
money too. Thou didst swear to me upon a parcel-gilt
goblet, sitting in my Dolphin chamber, at the round
table, by a sea-coal fire, upon Wednesday in Wheeson
week, when the Prince broke thy head for liking his   85
father to a singing-man of Windsor – thou didst swear
to me then, as I was washing thy wound, to marry me
and make me my lady thy wife. Canst thou deny it?
Did not goodwife Keech, the butcher's wife, come in
then and call me gossip Quickly? Coming in to borrow 90
a mess of vinegar, telling us she had a good dish of
prawns, whereby thou didst desire to eat some, whereby
I told thee they were ill for a green wound? And didst
thou not, when she was gone down stairs, desire me
to be no more so familiarity with such poor people,   95
saying that ere long they should call me madam? And
didst thou not kiss me, and bid me fetch thee thirty
shillings? I put thee now to thy book-oath. Deny it, if
thou canst.

Falstaff

100   My lord, this is a poor mad soul, and she says up and
down the town that her eldest son is like you. She
hath been in good case, and, the truth is, poverty hath
distracted her. But for these foolish officers, I beseech
you I may have redress against them.

Chief Justice

105   Sir John, Sir John, I am well acquainted with your
manner of wrenching the true cause the false way. It
is not a confident brow, nor the throng of words that
come with such more than impudent sauciness from
you, can thrust me from a level consideration. You

110   have, as it appears to me, practis'd upon the easy
yielding spirit of this woman, and made her serve your
uses both in purse and in person.

Hostess

Yea, in truth, my lord.

Chief Justice

Pray thee, peace. Pay her the debt you owe her, and

115   unpay the villainy you have done with her; the one
you may do with sterling money, and the other with
current repentance.

Falstaff

My lord, I will not undergo this sneap without reply.
You call honourable boldness impudent sauciness; if

120   a man will make curtsy and say nothing, he is virtuous.
No, my lord, my humble duty rememb'red, I will not
be your suitor. I say to you I do desire deliverance from
these officers, being upon hasty employment in the
King's affairs.

Chief Justice

125   You speak as having power to do wrong; but answer
in th' effect of your reputation, and satisfy the poor
woman.

Falstaff

Come hither hostess.

[Enter GOWER]

Chief Justice

Now, Master Gower, what news?

Gower

The King, my lord, and Harry Prince of Wales   130
Are near at hand. The rest the paper tells.

[Gives a letter.]

Falstaff

As I am a gentleman!

Hostess

Faith, you said so before.

Falstaff

As I am a gentleman! Come, no more words of it.

Hostess

By this heavenly ground I tread on, I must be fain to 135
pawn both my plate and the tapestry of my
dining-chambers.

Falstaff

Glasses, glasses, is the only drinking; and for thy walls,
a pretty slight drollery, or the story of the Prodigal, or
the German hunting, in water-work, is worth a thou- 140
sand of these bed-hangers and these fly-bitten tapestries.
Let it be ten pound, if thou canst. Come, an 'twere
not for thy humours, there's not a better wench in
England. Go, wash thy face, and draw the action.
Come, thou must not be in this humour with me; dost 145
not know me? Come, come, I know thou wast set on
to this.

Hostess

Pray thee, Sir John, let it be but twenty nobles; i' faith,
I am loath to pawn my plate, so God save me, la!

Falstaff

Let it alone; I'll make other shift. You'll be a fool still. 150

Hostess

Well, you shall have it, though I pawn my gown. I
hope you'll come to supper. You'll pay me all together?

Falstaff

Will I live? *[To* BARDOLPH*] Go*, with her, with her; hook on, hook on.

Hostess

155   Will you have Doll Tearsheet meet you at supper?

Falstaff

No more words; let's have her.

      [Exeunt HOSTESS, BARDOLPH*, and Officers.]*

Chief Justice

I have heard better news.

Falstaff

What's the news, my lord?

Chief Justice

Where lay the King to-night?

Gower

160   At Basingstoke, my lord.

Falstaff

I hope, my lord, all's well. What is the news, my lord?

Chief Justice

Come all his forces back?

Gower

No; fifteen hundred foot, five hundred horse,
Are march'd up to my Lord of Lancaster,

165   Against Northumberland and the Archbishop.

Falstaff

Comes the King back from Wales, my noble lord?

Chief Justice

You shall have letters of me presently.
Come, go along with me, good Master Gower.

Falstaff

My lord!

Chief Justice

170   What's the matter?

Falstaff

Master Gower, shall I entreat you with me to dinner?

Gower

I must wait upon my good lord here, I thank you,
good Sir John.

Chief Justice

Sir John, you loiter here too long, being you are to
take soldiers up in counties as you go.   180

Falstaff

Will you sup with me, Master Gower?

Chief Justice

What foolish master taught you these manners, Sir
John?

Falstaff

Master Gower, if they become me not, he was a fool
that taught them me. This is the right fencing grace, 185
my lord: tap for tap, and so part fair.

Chief Justice

Now, the Lord lighten thee!
Thou art a great fool.

[Exeunt.]

SCENE II

London. Another street.

[Enter PRINCE HENRY *and* POINS.*]*

Prince

Before God, I am exceeding weary.

Poins

Is't come to that? I had thought weariness durst not
have attach'd one of so high blood.

Prince

Faith, it does me; though it discolours the complexion
5 of my greatness to acknowledge it. Doth it not show
vilely in me to desire small beer?

Poins

Why, a prince should not be so loosely studied as to
remember so weak a composition.

Prince

Belike then my appetite was not princely got; for, by
10 my troth, I do now remember the poor creature, small
beer. But indeed these humble considerations make
me out of love with my greatness. What a disgrace is
it to me to remember thy name, or to know thy face
to-morrow, or to take note how many pair of silk
15 stockings thou hast – viz., these, and those that were
thy peach-colour'd ones – or to bear the inventory of
thy shirts – as, one for superfluity, and another for
use! But that the tennis-court-keeper knows better than
I; for it is a low ebb of linen with thee when thou
20 keepest not racket there; as thou hast not done a great
while, because the rest of thy low countries have made
a shift to eat up thy holland. And God knows whether
those that bawl out the ruins of thy linen shall inherit
his kingdom; but the midwives say the children are
25 not in the fault; whereupon the world increases, and
kindreds are mightily strengthened.

Poins

How ill it follows, after you have laboured so hard,
you should talk so idly! Tell me, how many good young
princes would do so, their fathers being so sick as yours
at this time is?   30

Prince

Shall I tell thee one thing, Poins?

Poins

Yes, faith; and let it be an excellent good thing.

Prince

It shall serve among wits of no higher breeding than
thine.

Poins

Go to; I stand the push of your one thing that you   35
will tell.

Prince

Marry, I tell thee it is not meet that I should be sad,
now my father is sick; albeit I could tell to thee – as
to one it pleases me, for fault of a better, to call my
friend – I could be sad and sad indeed too.   40

Poins

Very hardly upon such a subject.

Prince

By this hand, thou thinkest me as far in the devil's
book as thou and Falstaff for obduracy and persistency:
let the end try the man. But I tell thee my heart bleeds
inwardly that my father is so sick; and keeping such   45
vile company as thou art hath in reason taken from
me all ostentation of sorrow.

Poins

The reason?

Prince

What wouldst thou think of me if I should weep?

Poins

I would think thee a most princely hypocrite.   50

Prince

It would be every man's thought; and thou art a blessed

fellow to think as every man thinks. Never a man's
thought in the world keeps the road-way better than
thine. Every man would think me an hypocrite indeed.
55 And what accites your most worshipful thought to
think so?

Poins

Why, because you have been so lewd and so much
engraffed to Falstaff.

Prince

And to thee.

Poins

60 By this light, I am well spoke on; I can hear it with
mine own ears. The worst that they can say of me is
that I am a second brother and that I am a proper
fellow of my hands; and those two things, I confess,
I cannot help. By the mass, here comes Bardolph.

[Enter BARDOLPH and Page.]

Prince

65 And the boy that I gave Falstaff. 'A had him from me
Christian; and look if the fat villain have not
transform'd him ape.

Bardolph

God save your Grace!

Prince

And yours, most noble Bardolph!

Poins

70 Come, you virtuous ass, you bashful fool, must you
be blushing? Wherefore blush you now? What a maid-
enly man-at-arms are you become! Is't such a matter
to get a pottle-pot's maidenhead?

Page

'A calls me e'en now, my lord, through a red lattice,
75 and I could discern no part of his face from the window.
At last I spied his eyes; and methought he had made
two holes in the alewife's new petticoat, and so peep'd
through.

Prince

    Has not the boy profited?

Bardolph

    Away, you whoreson upright rabbit, away!   80

Page

    Away, you rascally Althaea's dream, away!

Prince

    Instruct us, boy; what dream, boy?

Page

    Marry, my lord, Althaea dreamt she was delivered of
    a fire-brand; and therefore I call him her dream.

Prince

    A crown's worth of good interpretation.   85
    There 'tis, boy. *[Giving a crown.]*

Poins

    O that this blossom could be kept from cankers! Well,
    there is sixpence to preserve thee.

Bardolph

    An you do not make him be hang'd among you, the
    gallows shall have wrong.   90

Prince

    And how doth thy master, Bardolph?

Bardolph

    Well, my lord. He heard of your Grace's coming to
    town. There's a letter for you.

Poins

    Deliver'd with good respect. And how doth the
    martlemas, your master?   95

Bardolph

    In bodily health, sir.

Poins

    Marry, the immortal part needs a physician; but that
    moves not him. Though that be sick, it dies not.

Prince

    I do allow this wen to be as familiar with me as my
    dog; and he holds his place, for look you how he writes. 100

Poins

[Reads] 'John Falstaff, knight' –
Every man must know that as oft as he has occasion
to name himself, even like those that are kin to the
King; for they never prick their finger but they say
105 'There's some of the King's blood spilt'. 'How comes
that?' says he that takes upon him not to conceive.
The answer is as ready as a borrower's cap: 'I am the
King's poor cousin, sir'.

Prince

Nay, they will be kin to us, or they will fetch it from
110 Japhet. But the letter: *[Reads]* 'Sir John Falstaff, knight,
to the son of the King nearest his father, Harry Prince
of Wales, greeting'.

Poins

Why, this is a certificate.

Prince

Peace! *[Reads]* 'I will imitate the honourable Romans
115 in brevity.' –

Poins

He sure means brevity in breath, short-winded.

Prince

[Reads] 'I commend me to thee, I commend thee, and
I leave thee. Be not too familiar with Poins; for he
misuses thy favours so much that he swears thou art
120 to marry his sister Nell. Repent at idle times as thou
mayst, and so farewell.

> Thine, by yea and no – which is as
> much as to say as thou usest him
> – JACK FALSTAFF with my familiars,
125 JOHN with my brothers and sisters,
> and SIR JOHN with all Europe.'

Poins

My lord, I'll steep this letter in sack and make him eat
it.

Prince

That's to make him eat twenty o his words. But do
130 you use me thus, Ned? Must I marry your sister?

Poins

God send the wench no worse fortune. But I never said so.

Prince

Well, thus we play the fools with the time, and the spirits of the wise sit in the clouds and mock us. Is your master here in London?   135

Bardolph

Yea, my lord.

Prince

Where sups he? Doth the old boar feed in the old frank?

Bardolph

At the old place, my lord, in Eastcheap.

Prince

What company?   140

Page

Ephesians, my lord, of the old church.

Prince

Sup any women with him?

Page

None, my lord, but old Mistress Quickly and Mistress Doll Tearsheet.

Prince

What pagan may that be?   145

Page

A proper gentlewoman, sir, and a kinswoman of my master's.

Prince

Even such kin as the parish heifers are to the town bull. Shall we steal upon them, Ned, at supper?

Poins

I am your shadow, my lord; I'll follow you.   150

Prince

Sirrah, you boy, and Bardolph, no word to your master that I am yet come to town. There's for your silence.

Bardolph

I have no tongue, sir.

Page
    And for mine, sir, I will govern it.
Prince
155   Fare you well; go. *[Exeunt* BARDOLPH *and* PAGE*]* This
    Doll Tearsheet should be some road.
Poins
    I warrant you, as common as the way between Saint
    Albans and London.
Prince
    How might we see Falstaff bestow himself to-night in
160   his true colours, and not ourselves be seen?
Poins
    Put on two leathern jerkins and aprons, and wait upon
    him at his table as drawers.
Prince
    From a god to a bull? A heavy descension! It was Jove's
    case. From a prince to a prentice? A low transforma-
165   tion! That shall be mine; for in everything the purpose
    must weigh with the folly. Follow me, Ned.

[Exeunt.]

SCENE III

Warkworth. Before the castle.

[Enter NORTHUMBERLAND, LADY NORTHUMBERLAND,
and LADY PERCY.*]*

Northumberland
    I pray thee, loving wife, and gentle daughter,
    Give even way unto my rough affairs;
    Put not you on the visage of the times
    And be, like them, to Percy troublesome.
Lady Northumberland
    I have given over, I will speak no more.   5
    Do what you will; your wisdom be your guide.
Northumberland
    Alas, sweet wife, my honour is at pawn;
    And but my going nothing can redeem it.
Lady Percy
    O, yet, for God's sake, go not to these wars!
    The time was, father, that you broke your word,   10
    When you were more endear'd to it than now;
    When your own Percy, when my heart's dear Harry,
    Threw many a northward look to see his father
    Bring up his powers; but he did long in vain.
    Who then persuaded you to stay at home?   15
    There were two honours lost, yours and your son's.
    For yours, the God of heaven brighten it!
    For his, it stuck upon him as the sun
    In the grey vault of heaven; and by his light
    Did all the chivalry of England move   20
    To do brave acts. He was indeed the glass
    Wherein the noble youth did dress themselves.
    He had no legs that practis'd not his gait;
    And speaking thick, which nature made his blemish,
    Became the accents of the valiant;   25
    For those that could speak low and tardily

Would turn their own perfection to abuse
To seem like him: so that in speech, in gait,
In diet, in affections of delight,
30 In military rules, humours of blood,
He was the mark and glass, copy and book,
That fashion'd others. And him – O wondrous him!
O miracle of men! – him did you leave –
Second to none, unseconded by you –
35 To look upon the hideous god of war
In disadvantage, to abide a field
Where nothing but the sound of Hotspur's name
Did seem defensible. So you left him.
Never, O never, do his ghost the wrong
40 To hold your honour more precise and nice
With others than with him! Let them alone.
The Marshal and the Archbishop are strong.
Had my sweet Harry had but half their numbers,
To-day might I, hanging on Hotspur's neck,
Have talk'd of Monmouth's grave.

Northumberland
45   Beshrew your heart,
Fair daughter, you do draw my spirits from me
With new lamenting ancient oversights.
But I must go and meet with danger there,
Or it will seek me in another place,
And find me worse provided.

Lady Northumberland
50   O, fly to Scotland
Till that the nobles and the armed commons
Have of their puissance made a little taste.

Lady Percy
If they get ground and vantage of the King,
Then join you with them, like a rib of steel,
55 To make strength stronger; but, for all our loves,
First let them try themselves. So did your son;
He was so suffred; so came I a widow;
And never shall have length of life enough

To rain upon remembrance with mine eyes,
That it may grow and sprout as high as heaven,   60
For recordation to my noble husband.

Northumberland

Come, come, go in with me. 'Tis with my mind
As with the tide swell'd up unto his height,
That makes a still-stand, running neither way.
Fain would I go to meet the Archbishop,   65
But many thousand reasons hold me back.
I will resolve for Scotland. There am I,
Till time and vantage crave my company.

[Exeunt.]

SCENE IV

London. The Boar's Head Tavern in Eastcheap.

[Enter FRANCIS *and another* DRAWER.]

Francis
> What the devil hast thou brought there – apple-johns?
> Thou knowest Sir John cannot endure an
> apple-john.

2 Drawer
> Mass, thou say'st true. The Prince once set a dish of
> 5   apple-johns before him, and told him there were five
> more Sir Johns; and, putting off his hat, said 'I will
> now take my leave of these six dry, round, old, withered
> knights'. It ang'red him to the heart; but he hath forgot
> that.

Francis
> 10 Why, then, cover and set them down; and see if thou
> canst find out Sneak's noise; Mistress Tearsheet would
> fain hear some music.

[Enter THIRD DRAWER.]

3 Drawer
> Dispatch! The room where they supp'd is too hot;
> they'll come in straight.

Francis
> 15 Sirrah, here will be the Prince and Master Poins anon;
> and they will put on two of our jerkins and aprons;
> and Sir John must not know of it. Bardolph hath
> brought word.

3 Drawer
> By the mass, here will be old utis; it will be an excel-
> 20 lent stratagem.

2 Drawer
> I'll see if I can find out Sneak.

[Exeunt SECOND *and* THIRD DRAWERS.]

[Enter HOSTESS *and* DOLL TEARSHEET.*]*

Hostess

I' faith, sweetheart, methinks now you are in an excellent good temperality. Your pulsidge beats as extraordinarily as heart would desire; and your colour, I warrant you, is as red as any rose, in good truth, la! 25
But, i' faith, you have drunk too much canaries; and that's a marvellous searching wine, and it perfumes the blood ere one can say 'What's this?' How do you now?

Doll

Better than I was – hem.

Hostess

Why, that's well said; a good heart's worth gold. Lo, 30
here comes Sir John.

[Enter FALSTAFF.*]*

Falstaff

[Singing] 'When Arthur first in court' – Empty the jordan. *[Exit* FRANCIS*]* – *[Singing]* 'And was a worthy king' – How now, Mistress Doll!

Hostess

Sick of a calm; yea, good faith. 35

Falstaff

So is all her sect; an they be once in a calm, they are sick.

Doll

A pox damn you, you muddy rascal! Is that all the comfort you give me?

Falstaff

You make fat rascals, Mistress Doll. 40

Doll

I make them! Gluttony and diseases make them: I make them not.

Falstaff

If the cook help to make the gluttony, you help to make the diseases, Doll. We catch of you, Doll, we catch of you; grant that, my poor virtue, grant that. 45

Doll

Yea, joy, our chains and our jewels.

Falstaff

'Your brooches, pearls, and ouches.' For to serve bravely
is to come halting off; you know, to come off the
breach with his pike bent bravely, and to surgery
50 bravely; to venture upon the charg'd chambers bravely
–

Doll

Hang yourself, you muddy conger, hang yourself!

Hostess

By my troth, this is the old fashion; you two never
meet but you fall to some discord. You are both, i'
good truth, as rheumatic as two dry toasts; you cannot
55 one bear with another's confirmities. What the good-
year! one must bear, and that must be you. You are
the weaker vessel, as they say, the emptier vessel.

Doll

Can a weak empty vessel bear such a huge full hogs-
head? There's a whole merchant's venture of Bourdeaux
60 stuff in him; you have not seen a hulk better stuff'd
in the hold. Come, I'll be friends with thee, Jack. Thou
art going to the wars; and whether I shall ever see thee
again or no, there is nobody cares.

[Re-enter FRANCIS.]

Francis

Sir, Ancient Pistol's below and would speak with you.

Doll

65 Hang him, swaggering rascal! Let him not come hither;
it is the foulmouth'dst rogue in England.

Hostess

If he swagger, let him not come here. No, by my faith!
I must live among my neighbours; I'll no swaggerers.
I am in good name and fame with the very best. Shut
70 the door. There comes no swaggerers here; I have not
liv'd all this while to have swaggering now. Shut the
door, I pray you.

Falstaff

Dost thou hear, hostess?

Hostess

Pray ye, pacify yourself, Sir John; there comes no swagg- 75
gerers here.

Falstaff

Dost thou hear? It is mine ancient.

Hostess

Tilly-fally, Sir John, ne'er tell me; and your ancient
swagg'rer comes not in my doors. I was before Master
Tisick, the debuty, t' other day; and, as he said to me
– 'twas no longer ago than Wednesday last i' good 80
faith! – 'Neighbour Quickly,' says he – Master Dumbe,
our minister, was by then – 'Neighbour Quickly,' says
he 'receive those that are civil, for' said he 'you are in
an ill name.' Now 'a said so, I can tell whereupon.
'For' says he 'you are an honest woman and well 85
thought on, therefore take heed what guests you
receive. Receive' says he 'no swaggering companions.'
There comes none here. You would bless you to hear
what he said. No, I'll no swagg'rers.

Falstaff

He's no swagg'rer, hostess; a tame cheater, i' faith; you 90
may stroke him as gently as a puppy greyhound. He'll
not swagger with a Barbary hen, if her feathers turn
back in any show of resistance. Call him up, drawer.

[Exit FRANCIS.]

Hostess

Cheater, call you him? I will bar no honest man my
house, nor no cheater; but I do not love swaggering, 95
by my troth. I am the worse when one says 'swagger'.
Feel, masters, how I shake; look you, I warrant you.

Doll

So you do, hostess.

Hostess

Do I? Yea, in very truth, do I, an 'twere an aspen leaf.
I cannot abide swagg'rers. 100

[Enter PISTOL, BARDOLPH, and PAGE.]

Pistol

God save you, Sir John!

Falstaff

Welcome, Ancient Pistol. Here, Pistol, I charge you
with a cup of sack; do you discharge upon mine hostess.

Pistol

I will discharge upon her, Sir John, with two bullets.

Falstaff

105   She is pistol-proof, sir; you shall not hardly offend her.

Hostess

Come, I'll drink no proofs nor no bullets. I'll drink no
more than will do me good, for no man's pleasure, I.

Pistol

Then to you, Mistress Dorothy; I will charge you.

Doll

Charge me! I scorn you, scurvy companion. What! you
110   poor, base, rascally, cheating, lack-linen mate! Away,
you mouldy rogue, away! I am meat for your master.

Pistol

I know you, Mistress Dorothy.

Doll

Away, you cut-purse rascal! you filthy bung, away! By
this wine, I'll thrust my knife in your mouldy chaps,
115   an you play the saucy cuttle with me. Away, you
bottle-ale rascal! you basket-hilt stale juggler, you!
Since when, I pray you, sir? God's light, with two
points on your shoulder? Much!

Pistol

God let me not live but I will murder your ruff for
120   this.

Falstaff

No more, Pistol; I would not have you go off here.
Discharge yourself of our company, Pistol.

Hostess

No, good Captain Pistol; not here, sweet captain.

Doll

Captain! Thou abominable damn'd cheater, art thou
not ashamed to be called captain? An captains were 125
of my mind, they would truncheon you out, for taking
their names upon you before you have earn'd them.
You a captain! you slave, for what? For tearing a poor
whore's ruff in a bawdy-house? He a captain! hang
him, rouge! He lives upon mouldy stew'd prunes and 130
dried cakes. A captain! God's light, these villains will
make the word as odious as the word 'occupy'; which
was an excellent good word before it was ill sorted.
Therefore captains had need look to't.

Bardolph

Pray thee go down, good ancient. 140

Falstaff

Hark thee hither, Mistress Doll.

Pistol

Not I! I tell thee what, Corporal
Bardolph, I could tear her; I'll be reveng'd of her.

Page

Pray thee go down.

Pistol

I'll see her damn'd first; to Pluto's damn'd lake, by this 145
hand, to th' infernal deep, with Erebus and tortures
vile also. Hold hook and line, say I. Down, down, dogs!
down, faitors! Have we not Hiren here?

Hostess

Good Captain Peesel, be quiet; 'tis very late, i' faith; I
beseek you now, aggravate your choler. 150

Pistol

These be good humours, indeed! Shall packhorses,
And hollow pamper'd jades of Asia,
Which cannot go but thirty mile a day,
Compare with Caesars, and with Cannibals,
And Troiant Greeks? Nay, rather damn them with 155
King Cerberus; and let the welkin roar.
Shall we fall foul for toys?

Hostess

By my troth, Captain, these are very bitter words.

Bardolph

Be gone, good ancient; this will grow to a brawl anon.

Pistol

160   Die men like dogs! Give crowns like pins!

Have we not Hiren here?

Hostess

O' my word, Captain, there's none such here. What the good-year! do you think I would deny her? For God's sake, be quiet.

Pistol

165   Then feed and be fat, my fair Calipolis.

Come, give some sack.

'Si fortune me tormente sperato me contento.'

Fear we broadsides? No, let the fiend give fire.

Give me some sack; and, sweetheart, lie thou there.

    [Laying down his sword.]

Come we to full points here, and are etceteras

170   nothings?

Falstaff

Pistol, I would be quiet.

Pistol

Sweet knight, I kiss thy neaf. What! we have seen the seven stars.

Doll

For God's sake thrust him down stairs; I cannot endure

175   such a fustian rascal.

Pistol

Thrust him down stairs! Know we not

Galloway nags?

Falstaff

Quoit him down, Bardolph, like a shove-groat shilling.

Nay, an 'a do nothing but speak nothing, 'a shall be

180   nothing here.

Bardolph

Come, get you down stairs.

Pistol

    What! shall we have incision? Shall we imbrue?

      [Snatching up his sword.]

    Then death rock me asleep, abridge my doleful days!

    Why, then, let grievous, ghastly, gaping wounds

    Untwine the Sisters Three! Come, Atropos, I say!   185

Hostess

    Here's goodly stuff toward!

Falstaff

    Give me my rapier, boy.

Doll

    I pray thee, Jack, I pray thee, do not draw.

Falstaff

    Get you down stairs.

      [Drawing and driving PISTOL *out.]*

Host

    Here's a goodly tumult! I'll forswear keeping house 190
    afore I'll be in these tirrits and frights. So; murder, I
    warrant now. Alas, alas! put up your naked weapons,
    put up your naked weapons. *[Exeunt* PISTOL *and*
    BARDOLPH.*]*

Doll

    I pray thee, Jack, be quiet; the rascal's gone.

    Ah, you whoreson little valiant villain, you!   195

Hostess

    Are you not hurt i' th' groin?

    Methought 'a made a shrewd thrust at your belly.

      [Re-enter BARDOLPH.*]*

Falstaff

    Have you turn'd him out a doors?

Bardolph

    Yea, sir. The rascal's drunk. You have hurt him, sir, i'
    th' shoulder.   200

Falstaff

    A rascal! to brave me!

Doll

Ah, you sweet little rogue, you! Alas, poor ape, how thou sweat'st! Come, let me wipe thy face. Come on, you whoreson chops. Ah, rogue! i' faith, I love thee.
205 Thou art as valorous as Hector of Troy, worth five of Agamemnon, and ten times better than the Nine Worthies. Ah, villain!

Falstaff

A rascally slave! I will toss the rogue in a blanket.

Doll

Do, an thou dar'st for thy heart. An thou dost, I'll
210 canvass thee between a pair of sheets.

[Enter Musicians.]

Page

The music is come, sir.

Falstaff

Let them play. Play, sirs. Sit on my knee, Doll. A rascal bragging slave! The rogue fled from me like quicksilver.

Doll

215 I' faith, and thou follow'dst him like a church. Thou whoreson little tidy Bartholomew boar-pig, when wilt thou leave fighting a days and foining a nights, and begin to patch up thine old body for heaven?

[Enter, behind, PRINCE HENRY and POINS disguised as drawers.]

Falstaff

Peace, good Doll! Do not speak like a death's-head; do
210 not bid me remember mine end.

Doll

Sirrah, what humour's the Prince of?

Falstaff

A good shallow young fellow. 'A would have made a good pantler; 'a would ha' chipp'd bread well.

Doll

They say Poins has a good wit.

Falstaff

He a good wit! hang him, baboon! His wit's as thick 225
as Tewksbury mustard; there's no more conceit in him
than is in a mallet.

Doll

Why does the Prince love him so, then?

Falstaff

Because their legs are both of a bigness, and 'a plays
at quoits well, and eats conger and fennel, and drinks 230
off candles' ends for flap-dragons, and rides the wild
mare with the boys, and jumps upon join'd-stools, and
swears with a good grace, and wears his boots very
smooth, like unto the sign of the Leg, and breeds no
bate with telling of discreet stories; and such other 235
gambol faculties 'a has, that show a weak mind and
an able body, for the which the Prince admits him.
For the Prince himself is such another; the weight of
a hair will turn the scales between their avoirdupois.

Prince

Would not this nave of a wheel have his ears cut off? 240

Poins

Let's beat him before his whore.

Prince

Look whe'er the wither'd elder hath not his poll claw'd
like a parrot.

Poins

Is it not strange that desire should so many years
outlive performance?   245

Falstaff

Kiss me, Doll.

Prince

Saturn and Venus this year in conjunction! What says
th' almanac to that?

Poins

And look whether the fiery Trigon, his man, be not
lisping to his master's old tables, his note-book, his 250
counsel-keeper.

Falstaff

Thou dost give me flattering busses.

Doll

By my troth, I kiss thee with a most constant heart.

Falstaff

I am old, I am old.

Doll

255 I love thee better than I love e'er a scurvy young boy of them all.

Falstaff

What stuff wilt have a kirtle of? I shall receive money a Thursday. Shalt have a cap to-morrow. A merry song, come. 'A grows late; we'll to bed. Thou't forget me

260 when I am gone.

Doll

By my troth, thou't set me a-weeping, an thou say'st so. Prove that ever I dress myself handsome till thy return. Well, hearken a' th' end.

Falstaff

Some sack, Francis.

Prince, Poins

275 Anon, anon, sir. *[Advancing]*

Falstaff

Ha! a bastard son of the King's? And art thou not Poins his brother?

Prince

Why, thou globe of sinful continents, what a life dost thou lead!

Falstaff

275 A better than thou. I am a gentleman: thou art a drawer.

Prince

Very true, sir, and I come to draw you out by the ears.

Hostess

O, the Lord preserve thy Grace! By my troth, welcome to London. How the Lord bless that sweet face of thine!

280 O Jesus, are you come from Wales?

Falstaff

Thou whoreson mad compound of majesty, by this light flesh and corrupt blood, thou art welcome. *[Leaning his hand upon DOLL.]*

Doll

How, you fat fool! I scorn you.

Poins

My lord, he will drive you out of your revenge and turn all to a merriment, if you take not the heat.   285

Prince

You whoreson candle-mine, you, how vilely did you speak of me even now before this honest, virtuous, civil gentlewoman!

Hostess

God's blessing of your good heart! and so she is, by my troth.   290

Falstaff

Didst thou hear me?

Prince

Yea; and you knew me, as you did when you ran away by Gadshill. You knew I was at your back, and spoke it on purpose to try my patience.

Falstaff

No, no, no; not so; I did not think thou wast within 295 hearing.

Prince

I shall drive you then to confess the wilful abuse, and then I know how to handle you.

Falstaff

No abuse, Hal, o' mine honour; no abuse.

Prince

Not – to dispraise me, and call me pantler, and bread- 300 chipper, and I know not what!

Falstaff

No abuse, Hal.

Poins

No abuse!

Falstaff

No abuse Ned, i' th' world; honest Ned, none. I
305   disprais'd him before the wicked – that the wicked
might not fall in love with thee; in which doing. I
have done the part of a careful friend and a true subject;
and thy father is to give me thanks for it. No abuse,
Hal; none, Ned, none; no, faith, boys, none.

Prince

310   See now, whether pure fear and entire cowardice doth
not make thee wrong this virtuous gentlewoman to
close with us? Is she of the wicked? Is thine hostess here
of the wicked? Or is thy boy of the wicked? Or honest
Bardolph, whose zeal burns in his nose, of the wicked?

Poins

315   Answer, thou dead elm, answer.

Falstaff

The fiend hath prick'd down Bardolph irrecoverable;
and his face is Lucifer's privy-kitchen, where he doth
nothing but roast malt-worms. For the boy – there is
a good angel about him; but the devil outbids him
320   too.

Prince

For the women?

Falstaff

For one of them – she's in hell already, and burns poor
souls. For th' other – I owe her money; and whether
she be damn'd for that, I know not.

Hostess

325   No, I warrant you.

Falstaff

No, I think thou art not; I think thou are quit for that.
Marry, there is another indictment upon thee for
suffering flesh to be eaten in thy house, contrary to
the law; for the which I think thou wilt howl.

Hostess

330   All vict'lers do so. What's a joint of mutton or two in
a whole Lent?

Prince

You, gentlewoman –

Doll

What says your Grace?

Falstaff

His Grace says that which his flesh rebels against.
[Knocking within.]

Hostess

Who knocks so loud at door? Look to th' door there, 335
Francis.

[Enter PETO.*]*

Prince

Peto, how now! What news?

Peto

The King your father is at Westminster;
And there are twenty weak and wearied posts
Come from the north; and as I came along   340
I met and overtook a dozen captains,
Bare-headed, sweating, knocking at the taverns,
And asking every one for Sir John Falstaff.

Prince

By heaven, Points, I feel me much to blame
So idly to profane the precious time,   345
When tempest of commotion, like the south,
Borne with black vapour, doth begin to melt
And drop upon our bare unarmed heads.
Give me my sword and cloak. Falstaff, good night.

[Exeunt PRINCE, POINS, PETO, *and* BARDOLPH.*]*

Falstaff

Now comes in the sweetest morsel of the night, and 350
we must hence, and leave it unpick'd. *[Knocking within]*
More knocking at the door!

[Re-enter BARDOLPH.*]*

How now! What's the matter?

Bardolph

You must away to court, sir, presently;
355   A dozen captains stay at door for you.

Falstaff

[*To the Page*] Pay the musicians, sirrah. – Farewell, hostess; farewell, Doll. You see, my good wenches, how men of merit are sought after; the underserver may sleep, when the man of action is call'd on. Farewell,
360   good wenches. If I be not sent away post, I will see you again ere I go.

Doll

I cannot speak. If my heart be not be ready to burst! Well, sweet Jack, have a care of thyself.

Falstaff

Farewell, farewell.

[Exeunt FALSTAFF *and* BARDOLPH.*]*

Hostess

365   Well, fare thee well. I have known thee these twenty-nine years, come peascodtime; but an honester and truer-hearted man – well, fare thee well.

Bardolph

[*Within*] Mistress Tearsheet!

Hostess

What's the matter?

Bardolph

370   [*Within*] Bid Mistress Tearsheet come to my master.

Hostess

O, run Doll, run, run, good Doll. Come. [*To* BARDOLPH*]* She comes blubber'd. – Yea, will you come, Doll? [*Exeunt.*]

ACT THREE

SCENE I

Westminster. The palace.

[Enter the KING *in his nightgown, with a Page.]*

King
Go call the Earls of Surrey and of Warwick;
But, ere they come, bid them o'er-read these letters
And well consider of them. Make good speed.

[Exit Page.]

How many thousand of my poorest subjects
Are at this hour asleep! O sleep, O gentle sleep,   5
Nature's soft nurse, how have I frighted thee,
That thou no more wilt weigh my eyelids down,
And steep my senses in forgetfulness?
Why rather, sleep, liest thou in smoky cribs,
Upon uneasy pallets stretching thee,   10
And hush'd with buzzing night-flies to thy slumber,
Than in the perfum'd chambers of the great,
Under the canopies of costly state,
And lull'd with sound of sweetest melody?
O thou dull god, why liest thou with the vile   15
In loathsome beds, and leav'st the kingly couch
A watch-case or a common 'larum-bell?
Wilt thou upon the high and giddy mast
Seal up the ship-boy's eyes, and rock his brains
In cradle of the rude imperious surge,   20
And in the visitation of the winds,
Who take the ruffian billows by the top,
Curling their monstrous heads, and hanging them
With deafing clamour in the slippery clouds,
That with the hurly death itself awakes?   25
Canst thou, O partial sleep, give thy repose

To the wet sea-boy in an hour so rude;
And in the calmest and most stillest night,
With all appliances and means to boot,
30 Deny it to a king? Then, happy low, lie down!
Uneasy lies the head that wears a crown.

[Enter WARWICK *and* SURREY.*]*

Warwick
   Many good morrows to your Majesty!
King
   Is it good morrow, lords?
Warwick
   'Tis one o'clock, and past.
King
35 Why then, good morrow to you all, my lords.
   Have you read o'er the letters that I sent you?
Warwick
   We have, my liege.
King
   Then you perceive the body of our kingdom
   How foul it is; what rank diseases grow,
40 And with what danger, near the heart of it.
Warwick
   It is but as a body yet distempered;
   Which to his former strength may be restored
   With good advice and little medicine.
   My Lord Northumberland will soon be cool'd.
King
45 O God! that one might read the book of fate,
   And see the revolution of the times
   Make mountains level, and the continent,
   Weary of solid firmness, melt itself
   Into the sea; and other times to see
50 The beachy girdle of the ocean
   Too wide for Neptune's hips; how chances mock,
   And changes fill the cup of alteration
   With divers liquors! O, if this were seen,

The happiest youth, viewing his progress through,
What perils past, what crosses to ensue,   55
Would shut the book and sit him down and die.
'Tis not ten years gone
Since Richard and Northumberland, great friends,
Did feast together, and in two years after
Were they at wars. It is but eight years since   60
This Percy was the man nearest my soul;
Who like a brother toil'd in my affairs
And laid his love and life under my foot;
Yea, for my sake, even to the eyes of Richard
Gave him defiance. But which of you was by –   65
[To WARWICK] You, cousin Nevil, as I may remember –
When Richard, with his eye brim full of tears,
Then check'd and rated by Northumberland,
Did speak these words, now prov'd a prophecy?
'Northumberland, thou ladder by the which   70
My cousin Bolingbroke ascends my throne' –
Though then, God knows, I had no such intent
But that necessity so bow'd the state
That I and greatness were compell'd to kiss –
'The time shall come' – thus did he follow it –   75
'The time will come that foul sin, gathering head,
Shall break into corruption' so went on,
Foretelling this same time's condition
And the division of our amity.

Warwick
There is a history in all men's lives,   80
Figuring the natures of the times deceas'd;
The which observ'd, a man may prophesy,
With a near aim, of the main chance of things
As yet not come to life, who in their seeds
And weak beginning lie intreasured.   85
Such things become the hatch and brood of time;
And, by the necessary form of this,
King Richard might create a perfect guess
That great Northumberland, then false to him,

90 Would of that seed grow to a greater falseness;
  Which should not find a ground to root upon Unless
  on you.

King

  Are these things then necessities?
  Then let us meet them like necessities;
95 And that same word even now cries out on us.
  They say the Bishop and Northumberland
  Are fifty thousand strong.

Warwick

        It cannot be, my lord.
  Rumour doth double, like the voice and echo,
  The numbers of the feared. Please it your Grace
100 To go to bed. Upon my soul, my lord,
  The powers that you already have sent forth
  Shall bring this prize in very easily.
  To comfort you the more, I have receiv'd
  A certain instance that Glendower is dead.
105 Your Majesty hath been this fortnight ill;
  And these unseasoned hours perforce must add
  Unto your sickness.

King

       I will take your counsel.
  And, were these inward wars once out of hand,
  We would, dear lords, unto the Holy Land.

      [Exeunt.]

SCENE II

Gloucestershire. Before Justice Shallow's house.

[Enter SHALLOW *and* SILENCE, *meeting;* MOULDY, SHADOW, WART, FEEBLE, BULLCALF, *and Servants, behind.]*

Shallow

Come on, come on, come on; give me your hand, sir;
give me your hand, sir. An early stirrer, by the rood!
And how doth my good cousin Silence?

Silence

Good morrow, good cousin Shallow.

Shallow

And how doth my cousin, your bedfellow? and your   5
fairest daughter and mine, my god-daughter Ellen?

Silence

Alas, a black ousel, cousin Shallow!

Shallow

By yea and no, sir. I dare say my cousin William is
become a good scholar; he is at Oxford still, is he not?

Silence

Indeed, sir, to my cost.   10

Shallow

'A must, then, to the Inns o' Court shortly. I was once
of Clement's Inn; where I think they will talk of mad
Shallow yet.

Silence

You were call'd 'lusty Shallow' then, cousin.

Shallow

By the mass, I was call'd anything; and I would have   15
done anything indeed too, and roundly too. There was
I, and little John Doit of Staffordshire, and black George
Barnes, and Francis Pickbone, and Will Squele a Cotsole
man – you had not four such swinge-bucklers in all
the Inns o' Court again. And I may say to you we knew   20
where the bona-robas were, and had the best of them

all at commandment. Then was Jack Falstaff, now Sir
John, a boy, and page to Thomas Mowbray, Duke of
Norfolk.

Silence

25   This Sir John, cousin, that comes hither anon about
soldiers?

Shallow

The same Sir John, the very same. I see him break
Scoggin's head at the court gate, when 'a was a crack
not thus high; and the very same day did I fight with
30   one Sampson Stockfish, a fruiterer, behind Gray's Inn.
Jesu, Jesu, the mad days that I have spent! and to see
how many of my old acquaintance are dead!

Silence

We shall all follow, cousin.

Shallow

Certain, 'tis certain; very sure, very sure. Death, as the
35   Psalmist saith, is certain to all; all shall die. How a
good yoke of bullocks at Stamford fair?

Silence

By my troth, I was not there.

Shallow

Death is certain. Is old double of your town living yet?

Silence

Dead, Sir.

Shallow

40   Jesu, Jesu, dead! 'A drew a good bow; and dead! 'A shot
a fine shoot. John a Gaunt loved him well, and betted
much money on his head. Dead! 'A would have clapp'd
I' th' clout at twelve score, and carried you a forehand
shaft a fourteen and fourteen and a half, that it would
45   have done a man's heart good to see. How a score of
ewes now?

Silence

Thereafter as they be – a score of good ewes may be
worth ten pounds.

Shallow

And is old Double dead?

[Enter BARDOLPH *and One with him.]*

Silence
Here come two of Sir John Falstaff's men, as I think.　50

Shallow
Good morrow, honest gentlemen.

Bardolph
I beseech you, which is Justice Shallow?

Shallow
I am Robert Shallow, Sir, a poor esquire of this county,
and one of the King's justices of the peace. What is
your good pleasure with me?　55

Bardolph
My captain, sir, commends him to you; my captain,
Sir John Falstaff – a tall gentleman, by heaven, and a
most gallant leader.

Shallow
He greets me well, sir; i knew him a good backsword
man. How doth the good knight? May I ask how my　60
lady his wife doth?

Bardolph
Sir, pardon; a solider is better accommodated than with
a wife.

Shallow
It is well said, in faith, sir; and it is well said indeed,
too. 'Better accommodated'! It is good; yea, indeed, is　65
it. Good phrases are surely, and ever were, very
commendable. 'Accommodated'! It comes of accom-
modo. Very good; a good phrase.

Bardolph
Pardon, Sir; I have heard the word. 'Phrase' call you
it? By this day, I know not the phrase; but I will main-　70
tain the word with my sword to be a soldier-like word,
and a word of exceeding good command, by heaven.
Accommodated: that is, when a man is, as they say,
accommodated; or when a man is being – whereby 'a
may be thought to be accommodated; which is an　75
excellent thing.

195

[Enter FALSTAFF.]

Shallow

It is very just. Look, here comes good Sir John. Give
me your good hand, give me your worship's good
hand. By my troth, you like well and bear your years
80   very well. Welcome, good Sir John.

Falstaff

I am glad to see you well, good Master Robert Shallow.
Master Surecard, as I think?

Shallow

No, Sir John; it is my cousin Silence, in commission
with me.

Falstaff

85   Good Master Silence, it well befits you should be of
the peace.

Silence

Your good worship is welcome.

Falstaff

Fie! this is hot weather. Gentlemen, have you provided
me here half a dozen sufficient men?

Shallow

90   Marry, have we, sir. Will you sit?

Falstaff

Let me see them, I beseech you.

Shallow

Where's the roll? Where's the roll? Where's the roll?
Let me see, let me see, let me see. So, so, so, so, so –
so, so – yea, marry, sir. Rafe Mouldy! Let them appear
95   as I call; let them do so, let them do so. Let me see;
where is Mouldy?

Mouldy

Here, an't please you.

Shallow

What think you, Sir John? A good limb'd fellow; young,
strong, and of good friends.

Falstaff

100   Is thy name Mouldy?

Mouldy

Yea, an't please you.

Falstaff

'Tis the more time thou wert us'd.

Shallow

Ha, ha, ha! most excellent, i' faith! Things that are mouldy lack use. Very singular good! In faith, well said, Sir John; very well said.   105

Falstaff

Prick him.

Mouldy

I was prick'd well enough before, an you could have let me alone. My old dame will be undone now for one to do her husbandry and her drudgery. You need not to have prick'd me; there are other men fitter to 110 go out than I.

Falstaff

Go to; peace, Mouldy; you shall go.

Mouldy, it is time you were spent.

Mouldy

Spent!

Shallow

Peace, fellow, peace; stand aside; know you where you 115 are? For th' other, Sir John – let me see. Simon Shadow!

Falstaff

Yea, marry, let me have him to sit under. He's like to be a cold soldier.

Shallow

Where's Shadow?

Shadow

Here, sir.   120

Falstaff

Shadow, whose son art thou?

Shadow

My mother's son, sir.

Falstaff

Thy mother's son! Like enough; and thy father's

197

shadow. So the son of the female is the shadow of the
125   male. It is often so indeed; but much of the father's
substance!

Shallow

Do you like him, Sir John?

Falstaff

Shadow will serve for summer. Prick him; for we have
a number of shadows fill up the muster-book.

Shallow

130   Thomas Wart!

Falstaff

Where's he?

Wart

Here, sir.

Falstaff

Is thy name Wart?

Wart

Yea, sir.

Falstaff

135   Thou art a very ragged wart.

Shallow

Shall I prick him, Sir John?

Falstaff

It were superfluous; for his apparel is built upon his
back, and the whole frame stands upon pins. Prick him
no more.

Shallow

140   Ha, ha, ha! You can do it, sir; you can do it. I commend
you well. Francis Feeble!

Feeble

Here, Sir.

Falstaff

What trade art thou, Feeble?

Feeble

A woman's tailor, sir.

Shallow

145   Shall I prick him, sir?

Falstaff

You may; but if he had been a man's tailor, he'd ha'
prick'd you. Wilt thou make as many holes in an
enemy's battle as thou hast done in a woman's
petticoat?

Feeble

I will do my good will, sir; you can have no more. 150

Falstaff

Well said, good woman's tailor! well said, courageous
Feeble! Thou wilt be as valiant as the wrathful dove
or most magnanimous mouse. Prick the woman's tailor
– well, Master Shallow, deep, Master Shallow.

Feeble

I would Wart might have gone, sir. 155

Falstaff

I would thou wert a man's tailor, that thou mightst
mend him and make him fit to go. I cannot put him
to a private soldier, that is the leader of so many
thousands. Let that suffice, most forcible Feeble.

Feeble

It shall suffice, sir. 160

Falstaff

I am bound to thee, reverend Feeble.
Who is next?

Shallow

Peter Bullcalf o' th' green!

Falstaff

Yea, marry, let's see Bullcalf.

Bullcalf

Here, sir. 165

Falstaff

Fore God, a likely fellow! Come, prick me Bullcalf till
he roar again.

Bullcalf

O Lord! good my lord captain –

Falstaff

What, dost thou roar before thou art prick'd?

Bullcalf

170   O Lord, sir! I am a diseased man.

Falstaff

What disease hast thou?

Bullcalf

A whoreson cold, sir, a cough, sir, which I caught with ringing in the King's affairs upon his coronation day, sir.

Falstaff

175   Come, thou shalt go to the wars in a gown. We will have away thy cold; and I will take such order that thy friends shall ring for thee. Is here all?

Shallow

Here is two more call'd than your number. You must have but four here, sir; and so, I pray you, go in with

180   me to dinner.

Falstaff

Come, I will go drink with you, but I cannot tarry dinner. I am glad to see you, by my troth, Master Shallow.

Shallow

O, Sir John, do you remember since we lay all night

185   in the windmill in Saint George's Field?

Falstaff

No more of that, Master Shallow, no more of that.

Shallow

Ha, 'twas a merry night. And is Jane Nightwork alive?

Falstaff

She lives, Master Shallow.

Shallow

She never could away with me.

Falstaff

190   Never, never; she would always say she could not abide Master Shallow.

Shallow

By the mass, I could anger her to th' heart. She was then a bona-roba. Doth she hold her own well?

Falstaff

Old, old, Master Shallow.

Shallow

Nay, she must be old; she cannot choose but be old; 195
certain she's old; and had Robin Nightwork, by old
Nightwork, before I came to Clement's Inn.

Silence

That's fifty-five year ago.

Shallow

Ha, cousin Silence, that thou hadst seen that that this
knight and I have seen! Ha, Sir John, said I well? 200

Falstaff

We have heard the chimes at midnight, Master Shallow.

Shallow

That we have, that we have, that we have; in faith, Sir
John, we have. Our watchword was 'Hem, boys!' Come,
let's to dinner; come, let's to dinner. Jesus, the days
that we have seen! Come, come. 205

[Exeunt FALSTAFF *and the Justices.]*

Bullcalf

Good Master Corporate Bardolph, stand my friend; and
here's four Harry ten shillings in French crowns for
you. In very truth, sir, I had as lief be hang'd, sir, as
go. And yet, for mine own part, sir, I do not care; but
rather because I am unwilling and, for mine own part, 210
have a desire to stay with my friends; else, sir, I did
not care for mine own part so much.

Bardolph

Go to; stand aside.

Mouldy

And, good Master Corporal Captain, for my old dame's
sake, stand my friend. She has nobody to do anything 215
about her when I am gone; and she is old, and cannot
help herself. You shall have forty, sir.

Bardolph

Go to; stand aside.

Feeble

220 By my troth, I care not; a man can die but once; we owe God a death. I'll ne'er bear a base mind. An't be my destiny, so; an't be not, so. No man's too good to serve's Prince; and, let it go which way it will, he that dies this year is quit for the next.

Bardolph

Well said; th'art a good fellow.

Feeble

225 Faith, I'll bear no base mind.

[Re-enter FALSTAFF *and the Justices.]*

Falstaff

Come, sir, which men shall I have?

Shallow

Four of which you please.

Bardolph

Sir, a word with you. I have three pound to free Mouldy and Bullcalf.

Falstaff

230 Go to; well.

Shallow

Come, Sir John, which four will you have?

Falstaff

Do you choose for me.

Shallow

Marry, then – Mouldy, Bullcalf, Feeble, and Shadow.

Falstaff

Mouldy and Bullcalf: for you, Mouldy, stay at home
235 till you are past service; and for your part, Bullcalf, grow till you come unto it. I will none of you.

Shallow

Sir John, Sir John, do not yourself wrong. They are your likeliest men, and I would have you serv'd with the best.

Falstaff

240 Will you tell me, Master Shallow, how to choose a

man? Care I for the limb, the thews, the stature, bulk,
and big assemblance of a man! Give me the spirit,
Master Shallow. Here's Wart; you see what a ragged
appearance it is. 'A shall charge you and discharge you
with the motion of a pewterer's hammer, come off and 245
on swifter than he that gibbets on the brewer's bucket.
And this same half-fac'd fellow, Shadow – give me this
man. He presents no mark to the enemy; the foeman
may with as great aim level at the edge of a penknife.
And, for a retreat – how swiftly will this Feeble, the 250
woman's tailor, run off! O, give me the spare men, and
spare me the great ones. Put me a caliver into Wart's
hand, Bardolph.

Bardolph

Hold, Wart. Traverse – thus, thus, thus.

Falstaff

Come, manage me your caliver. So – very well. Go to; 255
very good; exceeding good. O, give me always a little,
lean, old, chopt, bald shot. Well said, i' faith, Wart;
th'art a good scab. Hold, there's a tester for thee.

Shallow

He is not his craft's master, he doth not do it right. I
remember at Mile-end Green, when I lay at Clement's 260
Inn – I was then Sir Dagonet in Arthur's show – there
was a little quiver fellow, and 'a would manage you
his piece thus; and 'a would about and about, and
come you in and come you in. 'Rah, tah, tah!' would
'a say; 'Bounce!' would 'a say; and away again would 265
'a go, and again would 'a come. I shall ne'er see such
a fellow.

Falstaff

These fellows will do well. Master Shallow, God keep
you! Master Silence, I will not use many words with
you: Fare you well! Gentlemen both, I thank you. I 270
must a dozen mile to-night. Bardolph, give the soldiers
coats.

Shallow

Sir John, the Lord bless you; God prosper your affairs;
God send us peace! At your return, visit our house; let
275 our old acquaintance be renewed. Peradventure I will
with ye to the court.

Falstaff

Fore God, would you would.

Shallow

Go to; I have spoke at a word. God keep you.

Falstaff

Fare you well, gentle gentlemen. *[Exeunt JUSTICES]* On,
280 Bardolph; lead the men away. *[Exeunt all but FALSTAFF]*
As I return, I will fetch off these justices. I do see the
bottom of Justice Shallow. Lord, Lord, how subject we
old men are to this vice of lying! This same starv'd
justice hath done nothing but prate to me of the wild-
285 ness of his youth and the feats he hath done about
Turnbull Street; and every third word a lie, duer paid
to the hearer that the Turk's tribute. I do remember
him at Clement's Inn, like a man made after supper
of a cheese-paring. When 'a was naked, he was for all
290 the world like a fork'd radish, with a head fantastically
carved upon it with a knife. 'A was so forlorn that his
dimensions to any thick sight were invisible. 'A was
the very genius of famine; yet lecherous as a monkey,
and the whores call'd him mandrake. 'A came ever in
295 the rearward of the fashion, and sung those tunes to
the overscutch'd huswifes that he heard the carmen
whistle, and sware they were his fancies or his good-
nights. And now is this Vice's dagger become a squire,
and talks as familiarly of John a Gaunt as if he had
300 been sworn brother to him; and I'll be sworn 'a ne'er
saw him but once in the Tiltyard; and then he burst
his head for crowding among the marshal's men. I saw
it, and told John a Gaunt he beat his own name; for
you might have thrust him and all his apparel into an
305 eel-skin; the case of a treble hautboy was a mansion

for him, a court – and now has he land and beeves.
Well, I'll be acquainted with him if I return; and't shall
go hard but I'll make him a philosopher's two stones
to me. If the young dace be a bait for the old pike, I
see no reason in the law of nature but I may snap at 310
him. Let time shape, and there an end.

[Exit.]

ACT FOUR

SCENE I

Yorkshire. Within the Forest of Gaultree.

[Enter the ARCHBISHOP OF YORK, MOWBRAY,
HASTINGS, *and Others.]*

Archbishop
    What is this forest call'd?
Hastings
    'Tis Gaultree Forest, an't shall please your Grace.
Archbishop
    Here stand, my lords, and send discoverers forth
    To know the numbers of our enemies.
Hastings
    We have sent forth already.
Archbishop
5   'Tis well done.
    My friends and brethren in these great affairs,
    I must acquaint you that I have receiv'd
    New-dated letters from Northumberland;
    Their cold intent, tenour, and substance, thus:
10   Here doth he wish his person, with such powers
    As might hold sortance with his quality,
    The which he could not levy; whereupon
    He is retir'd, to ripe his growing fortunes,
    To Scotland; and concludes in hearty prayers
15   That your attempts may overlive the hazard
    And fearful meeting of their opposite.
Mowbray
    Thus do the hopes we have in him touch ground
    And dash themselves to pieces.

[Enter a Messenger.]

Hastings
                              Now, what news?
Messenger
    West of this forest, scarcely off a mile,
    In goodly form comes on the enemy;   20
    And, by the ground they hide, I judge their number
    Upon or near the rate of thirty thousand.
Mowbray
    The just proportion that we gave them out.
    Let us sway on and face them in the field.

                    [Enter WESTMORELAND.*]*

Archbishop
    What well-appointed leader fronts us here?   25
Mowbray
    I think it is my Lord of Westmoreland.
Westmoreland
    Health and fair greeting from our general,
    The Prince, Lord John and Duke of Lancaster.
Archbishop
    Say on, my Lord of Westmoreland, in peace,
    What doth concern your coming.
Westmoreland
                              Then, my lord,   30
    Unto your Grace do I in chief address
    The substance of my speech. If that rebellion
    Came like itself, in base and abject routs,
    Led on by bloody youth, guarded with rags,
    And countenanc'd by boys and beggary –   35
    I say, if damn'd commotion so appear'd
    In his true, native, and most proper shape,
    You, reverend father, and these noble lords,
    Had not been here to dress the ugly form
    Of base and bloody insurrection   40
    With your fair honours. You, Lord Archbishop,
    Whose see is by a civil peace maintain'd,
    Whose beard the silver hand of peace hath touch'd,

Whose learning and good letters peace hath tutor'd,
45   Whose white investments figure innocence,
The dove, and very blessed spirit of peace –
Wherefore do you so ill translate yourself
Out of the speech of peace, that bears such grace,
Into the harsh and boist'rous tongue of war;
50   Turning your books to graves, your ink to blood,
Your pens to lances, and your tongue divine
To a loud trumpet and a point of war?

Archbishop

Wherefore do I this? So the question stands.
Briefly to this end: we are all diseas'd
55   And with our surfeiting and wanton hours
Have brought ourselves into a burning fever,
And we must bleed for it; of which disease
Our late King, Richard, being infected, died.
But, my most noble Lord of Westmoreland,
60   I take not on me here as a physician;
Nor do I as an enemy to peace
Troop in the throngs of military men;
But rather show awhile like fearful war
To diet rank minds sick of happiness,
65   And purge th' obstructions which begin to stop
Our very veins of life. Hear me more plainly.
I have in equal balance justly weigh'd
What wrongs our arms may do, what wrongs we suffer,
And find our griefs heavier than our offences.
70   We see which way the stream of time doth run
And are enforc'd from our most quiet there
By the rough torrent of occasion;
And have the summary of all our griefs,
When time shall serve, to show in articles;
75   Which long ere this we offer'd to the King,
And might by no suit gain our audience:
When we are wrong'd, and would unfold our griefs,
We are denied access unto his person,

Even by those men that most have done us wrong.
The dangers of the days but newly gone,   80
Whose memory is written on the earth
With yet appearing blood, and the examples
Of every minute's instance, present now,
Hath put us in these ill-beseeming arms;
Not to break peace, or any branch of it,   85
But to establish here a peace indeed,
Concurring both in name and quality.

Westmoreland

When ever yet was your appeal denied;
Wherein have you been galled by the King;
What peer hath been suborn'd to grate on you   90
That you should seal this lawless bloody book
Of forg'd rebellion with a seal divine,
And consecrate commotion's bitter edge?

Archbishop

My brother general, the commonwealth,
To brother born an household cruelty,   95
I make my quarrel in particular.

Westmoreland

There is no need of any such redress;
Or if there were, it not belongs to you.

Mowbray

Why not to him in part, and to us all
That feel the bruises of the days before,   100
And suffer the condition of these times
To lay a heavy and unequal hand
Upon our honours?

Westmoreland

        O my good Lord Mowbary,
Construe the times to their necessities,
And you shall say, indeed, it is the time,   105
And not the King, that doth you injuries.
Yet, for your part, it not appears to me,
Either from the King or in the present time,
That you should have an inch of any ground

110   To build a grief on. Were you not restor'd
        To all the Duke of Norfolk's signiories,
        Your noble and right well-rememb'red father's?

Mowbray

        What thing, in honour, had my father lost
        That need to be reviv'd and breath'd in me?
115   The King that lov'd him, as the state stood then,
        Was force perforce compell'd to banish him,
        And then that Henry Bolingbroke and he,
        Being mounted and both roused in their seats,
        Their neighing coursers daring of the spur,
120   Their armed staves in charge, their beavers down,
        Their eyes of fire sparkling through sights of steel,
        And the loud trumpet blowing them together –
        Then, then, when there was nothing could have
           stay'd
        My father from the breast of Bolingbroke,
125   O, when the King did throw his warder down –
        His own life hung upon the staff he threw –
        Then threw he down himself, and all their lives
        That by indictment and by dint of sword
        Have since miscarried under Bolingbroke.

Westmoreland

130   You speak, Lord Mowbray, now you know not what.
        The Earl of Hereford was reputed then
        In England the most valiant gentleman.
        Who knows on whom fortune would then have
           smil'd?
        But if your father had been victor there,
135   He ne'er had borne it out of Coventry;
        For all the country, in a general voice,
        Crie hate upon him; and all their prayers and love
        Were set on Hereford, whom they doted on,
        And bless'd and grac'd indeed more than the King.
140   But this is mere digression from my purpose.
        Here come I from our princely general
        To know your griefs; to tell you from his Grace
        That he will give you audience; and wherein

It shall appear that your demands are just,
You shall enjoy them, everything set off   145
That might so much as think you enemies.
Mowbray
But he hath forc'd us to compel this offer;
And it proceeds from policy, not love.
Westmoreland
Mowbray, you overween to take it so.
This offer comes from mercy, not from fear;   150
For, lo! within a ken our army lies –
Upon mine honour, all too confident
To give admittance to a thought of fear.
Our battle is more full of names than yours,
Our men more perfect in the use of arms,   155
Our armour all as strong, our cause the best;
Then reason will our hearts should be as good.
Say you not, then, our offer is compell'd.
Mowbray
Well, by my will we shall admit no parley.
Westmoreland
That argues but the shame of your offence: 160
A rotten case abides no handling.
Hastings
Hath the Prince John a full commission,
In very ample virtue of his father,
To hear and absolutely to determine
Of what conditions we shall stand upon?   165
Westmoreland
That is intended in the general's name.
I muse you make so slight a question.
Archbishop
Then take, my Lord of Westmoreland, this schedule,
For this contains our general grievances.
Each several article herein redress'd,   170
All members of our cause, both here and hence,
That are insinewed to this action,
Acquitted by a true substantial form,
And present execution of our wills

175   To us and to our purposes confin'd –
     We come within our awful banks again,
     And knit our powers to the arm of peace.
Westmoreland
     This will I show the general. Please you, lords,
     In sight of both our battles we may meet;
180   And either end in peace – which God so frame! –
     Or to the place of diff'rence call the swords
     Which must decide it.
Archbishop

                    My lord, we will do so.

        [Exit WESTMORELAND.*]*

Mowbray
     There is a thing within my bosom tells me
     That no conditions of our peace can stand.
Hastings
185   Fear you not that: if we can make our peace
     Upon such large terms and so absolute
     As our conditions shall consist upon,
     Our peace shall stand as firm as rocky mountains.
Mowbray
     Yea, but our valuation shall be such
190   That every slight and false-derived cause,
     Yea, every idle, nice, and wanton reason,
     Shall to the King taste of this action;
     That, were our royal faiths martyrs in love,
     We shall be winnow'd with so rough a wind
195   That even our corn shall seem as light as chaff,
     And good from bad find no partition.
Archbishop
     No, no, my lord. Note this: the King is weary
     Of dainty and such picking grievances;
     For he hath found to end one doubt by death
200   Revives two greater in the heirs of life;
     And therefore will he wipe his tables clean,
     And keep no tell-tale to his memory
     That may repeat and history his loss

To new remembrance. For full well he knows
He cannot so precisely weed this land   205
As his misdoubts present occasion:
His foes are so enrooted with his friends
That, plucking to unfix an enemy,
He doth unfasten so and shake a friend.
So that this land, like an offensive wife   210
That hath enrag'd him on to offer strokes,
As he is striking, holds his infant up,
And hangs resolv'd correction in the arm
That was uprear'd to execution.

Hastings

Besides, the King hath wasted all his rods   215
On late offenders, that he now doth lack
The very instruments of chastisement;
So that his power, like to a fangless lion,
May offer, but not hold.

Archbishop

                'Tis very true;
And therefore be assur'd, my good Lord Marshal,   220
If we do now make our atonement well,
Our peace will, like a broken limb united,
Grow stronger for the breaking.

Mowbray

                Be it so.
Here is return'd my Lord of Westmoreland.

[Re-enter WESTMORELAND.]

Westmoreland

The Prince is here at hand. Pleaseth your lordship   225
To meet his Grace just distance 'tween our armies?

Mowbray

Your Grace of York, in God's name then, set
    forward.

Archbishop

Before, and greet his Grace. My lord, we come.

[Exeunt.]

SCENE II

Another part of the forest.

[Enter, from one side, MOWBRAY, *attended; afterwards,*
the ARCHBISHOP, HASTINGS, *and Others: from*
the other side, PRINCE JOHN OF LANCASTER,
WESTMORELAND, *Officers and Others.]*

Prince John
You are well encount'red here, my cousin Mowbray.
Good day to you, gentle Lord Archbishop;
And so to you, Lord Hastings, and to all.
My Lord of York, it better show'd with you
5   When that your flock, assembled by the bell,
Encircled you to hear with reverence
Your exposition on the holy text
Than now to see you here an iron man,
Cheering a rout of rebels with your drum,
10   Turning the word to sword, and life to death.
That man that sits within a monarch's heart
And ripens in the sunshine of his favour,
Would he abuse the countenance of the king,
Alack, what mischiefs might be set abroach
15   In shadow of such greatness! With you, Lord Bishop,
It is even so. Who hath not heard it spoken
How deep you were within the books of God?
To us the speaker in His parliament,
To us th' imagin'd voice of God himself,
20   The very opener and intellingencer
Between the grace, the sanctities of heaven,
And our dull workings. O, who shall believe
But you misuse the reverence of your place,
Employ the countenance and grace of heav'n
25   As a false favourite doth his prince's name,
In deeds dishonourable? You have ta'en up,
Under the counterfeited zeal of God,
The subjects of His substitute, my father,

And both against the peace of heaven and him
Have here up-swarm'd them.

Archbishop

Good my Lord of Lancaster, 30
I am not here against your father's peace;
But, as I told my Lord of Westmoreland,
The time misord'red doth, in common sense,
Crowd us and crush us to this monstrous form
To hold our safety up. I sent your Grace 35
The parcels and particulars of our grief,
The which hath been with scorn shov'd from the
    court,
Whereon this hydra son of war is born;
Whose dangerous eyes may well be charm'd asleep
With grant of our most just and right desires; 40
And true obedience, of this madness cur'd,
Stoop tamely to the foot of majesty.

Mowbray

If not, we ready are to try our fortunes
To the last man.

Hastings

And though we here fall down,
We have supplies to second our attempt. 45
If they miscarry, theirs shall second them;
And so success of mischief shall be born,
And heir from heir shall hold this quarrel up
Whiles England shall have generation.

Prince John

You are too shallow, Hastings, much too shallow, 50
To sound the bottom of the after-times.

Westmoreland

Pleaseth your Grace to answer them directly
How far forth you do like their articles.

Prince John

I like them all and do allow them well;
And swear here, by the honour of my blood, 55
My father's purposes have been mistook;

And some about him have too lavishly
Wrested his meaning and authority.
My lord, these griefs shall be with speed redress'd;
60   Upon my soul, they shall. If this may please you,
Discharge your powers unto their several counties,
As we will ours; and here, between the armies,
Let's drink together friendly and embrace,
That all their eyes may bear those tokens home
65   Of our restored love and amity.
Archbishop
I take your princely word for these redresses.
Prince John
I give it you, and will maintain my word;
And thereupon I drink unto your Grace.
Hastings
Go, Captain, and deliver to the army
70   This news of peace. Let them have pay, and part.
I know it will well please them. Hie thee, Captain.

[Exit Officer.]

Archbishop
To you, my noble Lord of Westmoreland.
Westmoreland
I pledge your Grace; and if you knew what pains
I have bestow'd to breed this present peace,
75   You would drink freely; but my love to ye
Shall show itself more openly hereafter.
Archbishop
I do not doubt you.
Westmoreland
                          I am glad of it.
Health to my lord and gentle cousin, Mowbray.
Mowbray
You wish me health in very happy season,
80   For I am on the sudden something ill.
Archbishop
Against ill chances men are ever merry;
But heaviness foreruns the good event.

Westmoreland
Therefore be merry, coz; since sudden sorrow
Serves to say thus; 'Some good thing comes
to-morrow'.
Archbishop
Believe me, I am passing light in spirit.   85
Mowbray
So much the worse, if your own rule be true.
[Shouts within.]
Prince John
The word of peace is rend'red.
Hark, how they shout!
Mowbray
This had been cheerful after victory.
Archbishop
A peace is of the nature of a conquest;   90
For then both parties nobly are subdu'd,
And neither party loser.
Prince John
Go, my lord,
And let our army be discharged too.

[Exit WESTMORELAND.]

And, good my lord, so please you let our trains
March by us, that we may peruse the men   95
We should have cop'd withal.
Archbishop
Go, good Lord Hastings,
And, ere they be dismiss'd, let them march by.

[Exit HASTINGS.]

Prince John
I trust, lords, we shall lie tonight together.

[Re-enter WESTMORELAND.]

Now, cousin, wherefore stands our army still?

Westmoreland

100 The leaders, having charge from you to stand,
Will not go off until they hear you speak.

Prince John

They know their duties.

[Re-enter HASTINGS.]

Hastings

My lord, our army is dispers'd already.
Like youthful steers unyok'd, they take their courses
105 East, west, north, south; or like a school broke up,
Each hurries toward his home and sporting-place.

Westmoreland

Good tidings, my Lord Hastings; for the which
I do arrest thee, traitor, of high treason;
And you, Lord Archbishop, and you, Lord Mowbray,
110 Of capital treason I attach you both.

Mowbray

Is this proceeding just and honourable?

Westmoreland

Is your assembly so?

Archbishop

Will you thus break your faith?

Prince John

I pawn'd thee none:
I promis'd you redress of these same grievances
115 Whereof you did complain; which, by mine honour,
I will perform with a most Christian care.
But for you, rebels – look to taste the due
Meet for rebellion and such acts as yours.
Most shallowly did you these arms commence,
120 Fondly brought here, and foolishly sent hence.
Strike up our drums, pursue the scatt'red stray.
God, and not we, hath safely fought to-day.
Some guard these traitors to the block of death,
Treason's true bed and yielder-up of breath.

[Exeunt.]

SCENE III

Another part of the forest.

[Alarum; excursions. Enter FALSTAFF *and* COLVILLE, *meeting.]*

Falstaff
What's your name, sir? Of what condition are you, and of what place, I pray?

Colville
I am a knight sir; and my name is Colville of the Dale.

Falstaff
Well then, Colville is your name, a knight is your degree, and your place the Dale. Colville shall be still   5
your name, a traitor your degree, and the dungeon your place – a place deep enough; so shall you be still Colville of the Dale.

Colville
Are not you Sir John Falstaff?

Falstaff
As good a man as he, sir, whoe'er I am. Do ye yield,   10
sir, or shall I sweat for you? If I do sweat, they are the drops of thy lovers, and they weep for thy death; therefore rouse up fear and trembling, and do observance to my mercy.

Colville
I think you are Sir John Falstaff, and in that thought   15
yield me.

Falstaff
I have a whole school of tongues in this belly of mine; and not a tongue of them all speaks any other word but my name. An I had but a belly of any indifferency, I were simply the most active fellow in Europe. My   20
womb, my womb, my womb undoes me. Here comes our general.

[Enter PRINCE JOHN OF LANCASTER, WESTMORELAND, BLUNT, *and Others.]*

Prince John

The heat is past; follow no further now.
Call in the powers, good cousin Westmoreland.

[Exit WESTMORELAND.*]*

25 Now, Falstaff, where have you been all this while?
When everything is ended, then you come.
These tardy tricks of yours will, on my life,
One time or other break some gallows' back.

Falstaff

I would be sorry, my lord, but it should be thus: I
30 never knew yet but rebuke and check was the reward
of valour. Do you think me a swallow, an arrow, or a
bullet? Have I, in my poor and old motion, the expedition of thought? I have speeded hither with the very
extremest inch of possibility; I have found'red nine
35 score and odd posts; and here, travel tainted as I am,
have in my pure and immaculate valour, taken Sir John
Colville of the Dale, a most furious knight and valorous
enemy. But what of that? He saw me, and yielded; that
I may justly say with the hook-nos'd fellow of Rome
40 – I came, saw, and overcame.

Prince John

It was more of his courtesy than your deserving.

Falstaff

I know not. Here he is, and here I yield him; and I
beseech your Grace, let it be book'd with the rest of
this day's deeds; or, by the Lord, I will have it in a
45 particular ballad else, with mine own picture on the
top on't, Colville kissing my foot; to the which course
if I be enforc'd, if you do not all show like gilt
twopences to me, and I, in the clear sky of fame,
o'ershine you as much as the full moon doth the
50 cinders of the element, which show like pins' heads
to her, believe not the word of the noble. Therefore
let me have right, and let desert mount.

Prince John
Thine's too heavy to mount.
Falstaff
Let it shine, then.
Prince John
Thine's too thick to shine. 55
Falstaff
Let it do something, my good lord, that may do me
good, and call it what you will.
Prince John
Is thy name Colville?
Colville
It is, my lord.
Prince John
A famous rebel art thou, Colville. 60
Falstaff
And a famous true subject took him.
Colville
I am, my lord, but as my betters are That led me hither.
Had they been rul'd by me, You should have won them
dearer than you have.
Falstaff
I know not how they sold themselves; but thou, like 65
a kind fellow, gavest thyself away gratis; and I thank
thee for thee.

[Re-enter WESTMORELAND.]

Prince John
Now, have you left pursuit?
Westmoreland
Retreat is made, and execution stay'd.
Prince John
Send Colville, with his confederates, 70
To York, to present execution.
Blunt, lead him hence; and see you guard him sure.
    [Exeunt BLUNT and others.]
And now dispatch we toward the court, my lords.

I hear the King my father is sore sick.
75 Our news shall go before us to his Majesty,
Which, cousin, you shall bear to comfort him;
And we with sober speed will follow you.

Falstaff

My lord, I beseech you, give me leave to go through
Gloucestershire; and, when you come to court, stand
80 my good lord, pray, in your good report.

Prince John

Fare you well, Falstaff. I, in my condition,
Shall better speak of you than you deserve.

[Exeunt all but FALSTAFF.]

Falstaff

I would you had but the wit; 'twere better than your
dukedom. Good faith, this same young sober-blooded
85 boy doth not love me; nor a man cannot make him
laugh – but that's no marvel; he drinks no wine. There's
never none of these demure boys come to any proof;
for thin drink doth so over-cool their blood, and
making many fish-meals, that they fall into a kind of
90 male green-sickness; and then, when they marry, they
get wenches. They are generally fools and cowards –
which some of us should be too, but for inflammation.
A good sherris-sack hath a twofold operation in it. It
ascends me into the brain; dries me there all the foolish
95 and dull and crudy vapours which environ it; makes
it apprehensive, quick, forgetive, full of nimble, fiery,
and delectable shapes; which delivered o'er to the voice,
the tongue, which is the birth, becomes excellent wit.
The second property of your excellent sherris is the
100 warming of the blood; which before, cold and settled,
left the liver white and pale, which is the badge of
pusillanimity and cowardice; but the sherris warms it,
and makes it course from the inwards to the parts
extremes. It illumineth the face, which, as a beacon,
105 gives warning to all the rest of this little kingdom,

man, to arm; and then the vital commoners and inland
petty spirits muster me all to their captain, the heart,
who, great and puff'd up with this retinue, doth any
deed of courage – and this valour comes of sherris. So
that skill in the weapon is nothing without sack, for 110
that sets it a-work; and learning, a mere hoard of gold
kept by a devil till sack commences it and sets it in
act and use. Hereof comes it that Prince Harry is valiant;
for the cold blood he did naturally inherit of his father,
he hath, like lean, sterile, and bare land, manured, 115
husbanded, and till'd, with excellent endeavour of
drinking good and good store of fertile sherris, that he
is become very hot and valiant. If I had a thousand
sons, the first humane principle I would teach them
should be to forswear thin potations, and to addict 120
themselves to sack.

[Enter BARDOLPH.]

How now, Bardolph!
Bardolph
  The army is discharged all and gone.
Falstaff
  Let them go. I'll through Gloucestershire, and there
  will I visit Master Robert Shallow, Esquire. I have him 125
  already temp'ring between my finger and my thumb,
  and shortly will I seal with him. Come away.

[Exeunt.]

SCENE IV

Westminster. The Jerusalem Chamber.

[*Enter the* KING, PRINCE THOMAS OF CLARENCE,
PRINCE HUMPHREY OF GLOUCESTER, WARWICK, *and
Others.*]

King

Now, lords, if God doth give successful end
To this debate that bleedeth at our doors,
We will our youth lead on to higher fields,
And draw no swords but what are sanctified.
5   Our navy is address'd, our power collected,
Our substitutes in absence well invested,
And everything lies level to our wish.
Only we want a little personal strength;
And pause us till these rebels, now afoot,
10   Come underneath the yoke of government.

Warwick

Both which we doubt not but your Majesty
Shall soon enjoy.

King

               Humphrey, my son of Gloucester,
Where is the Prince your brother?

Gloucester

I think he's gone to hunt, my lord, at Windsor.

King

And how accompanied?

Gloucester

15   I do not know, my lord.

King

Is not his brother, Thomas of Clarence, with him?

Gloucester

No, my good lord, he is in presence here.

Clarence

What would my lord and father?

King
    Nothing but well to thee, Thomas of Clarence.
    How chance thou art not with the Prince thy
      brother?   20
    He loves thee, and thou dost neglect him, Thomas.
    Thou hast a better place in his affection
    Than all thy brothers; cherish it, my boy,
    And noble offices thou mayst effect
    Of mediation, after I am dead,   25
    Between his greatness and thy other brethren.
    Therefore omit him not; blunt not his love,
    Nor lose the good advantage of his grace
    By seeming cold or careless of his will;
    For he is gracious if he be observ'd.   30
    He hath a tear for pity and a hand
    Open as day for melting charity;
    Yet notwithstanding, being incens'd, he is flint;
    As humorous as winter, and as sudden
    As flaws congealed in the spring of day.   35
    His temper, therefore, must be well observ'd.
    Chide him for faults, and do it reverently,
    When you perceive his blood inclin'd to mirth;
    But, being moody, give him line and scope
    Till that his passions, like a whale on ground,   40
    Confound themselves with working. Learn this,
      Thomas,
    And thou shalt prove a shelter to thy friends,
    A hoop of gold to bind thy brothers in,
    That the united vessel of their blood,
    Mingled with venom of suggestion –   45
    As, force perforce, the age will pour it in –
    Shall never leak, though it do work as strong
    As aconitum or rash gunpowder.
Clarence
    I shall observe him with all care and love.
King
    Why art thou not at Windsor with him, Thomas?   50

Clarence

He is not there to-day; he dines in London.

King

And how accompanied? Canst thou tell that?

Clarence

With Poins, and other his continual followers.

King

Most subject is the fattest soil to weeds;
55 And he, the noble image of my youth,
Is overspread with them; therefore my grief
Stretches itself beyond the hour of death.
The blood weeps from my heart when I do shape,
In forms imaginary, th' unguided days
60 And rotten times that you shall look upon
When I am sleeping with my ancestors.
For when his headstrong riot hath no curb,
When rage and hot blood are his counsellors,
When means and lavish manners meet together,
65 O, with what wings shall his affections fly
Towards fronting peril and oppos'd decay!

Warwick

My gracious lord, you look beyond him quite.
The Prince but studies his companions
Like a strange tongue, wherein, to gain the language,
70 'Tis needful that the most immodest word
Be look'd upon and learnt; which once attain'd,
Your Highness knows, comes to no further use
But to be known and hated. So, like gross terms,
The Prince will, in the perfectness of time,
75 Cast off his followers; and their memory
Shall as a pattern or a measure live
By which his Grace must mete the lives of other,
Turning past evils to advantages.

King

'Tis seldom when the bee doth leave her comb
In the dead carrion.

[Enter WESTMORELAND.]

Who's here? Westmoreland?   80

Westmoreland

Health to my sovereign, and new happiness
Added to that that I am to deliver!
Prince John, your son, doth kiss your Grace's hand.
Mowbray, the Bishop Scroop, Hastings, and all,
Are brought to the correction of your law.   85
There is not now a rebel's sword unsheath'd,
But Peace puts forth her olive everywhere.
The manner how this action hath been borne
Here at more leisure may your Highness read,
With every course in his particular.   90

King

O Westmoreland, thou art a summer bird,
Which ever in the haunch of winter sings
The lifting up of day.

[Enter HARCOURT.]

Look here's more news.

Harcourt

From enemies heaven keep your Majesty;
And, when they stand against you, may they fall   95
As those that I am come to tell you of!
The Earl Northumberland and the Lord Bardolph,
With a great power of English and of Scots,
Are by the shrieve of Yorkshire overthrown.
The manner and true order of the fight   100
This packet, please it you, contains at large.

King

And wherefore should these good news make me
    sick?
Will Fortune never come with both hands full,
But write her fair words still in foulest letters?
She either gives a stomach and no food –   105
Such are the poor, in health – or else a feast,
And takes away the stomach – such are the rich
That have abundance and enjoy it not.

I should rejoice now at this happy news;
110   And now my sight fails, and my brain is giddy.
O me! come near me now I am much ill.

Gloucester

Comfort, your Majesty!

Clarence

                O my royal father!

Westmoreland

My sovereign lord, cheer up yourself, look up.

Warwick

Be patient, Princes; you do know these fits
115   Are with his Highness very ordinary.
Stand from him, give him air; he'll straight be well.

Clarence

No, no; he cannot long hold out these pangs.
Th' incessant care and labour of his mind
Hath wrought the mure that should confine it in
120   So thin that life looks through, and will break out.

Gloucester

The people fear me; for they do observe
Unfather'd heirs and loathly births of nature.
The seasons change their manners, as the year
Had found some months asleep, and leapt them
    over.

Clarence

125   The river hath thrice flow'd, no ebb between;
And the old folk, Time's doting chronicles,
Say it did so a little time before
That our great grandsire, Edward, sick'd and died.

Warwick

Speak lower, Princes, for the King recovers.

Gloucester

130   This apoplexy will certain be his end.

King

I pray you take me up, and bear me hence
Into some other chamber. Softly, pray.

SCENE V

Westminster. Another chamber.

[The KING *lying on a bed;* CLARENCE, GLOUCESTER,
WARWICK, *and Others in attendance.]*

King
    Let there be no noise made, my gentle friends;
    Unless some dull and favourable hand
    Will whisper music to my weary spirit.
Warwick
    Call for the music in the other room.
King
    Set me the crown upon my pillow here.   5
Clarence
    His eye is hollow, and he changes much.
Warwick
    Less noise, less noise!

          [Enter PRINCE HENRY.*]*

Prince
    Who saw the Duke of Clarence?
Clarence
    I am here, brother, full of heaviness.
Prince
    How now! Rain within doors, and none abroad!   10
    How doth the King?
Gloucester
    Exceeding ill.
Prince
    Heard he the good news yet? Tell it him.
Gloucester
    He alt'red much upon the hearing it.
Prince
    If he be sick with joy, he'll recover without physic.   15
Warwick
    Not so much noise, my lords. Sweet Prince, speak low;

The King your father is dispos'd to sleep.
Clarence
Let us withdraw into the other room.
Warwick
Will't please your Grace to go along with us?
Prince
20 No; I will sit and watch here by the King.

[Exeunt all but the PRINCE.*]*

Why doth the crown lie there upon his pillow,
Being so troublesome a bedfellow?
O polish'd perturbation! golden care!
That keep'st the ports of slumber open wide
25 To many a watchful night! Sleep with it now!
Yet not so sound and half so deeply sweet
As he whose brow with homely biggen bound
Snores out the watch of night. O majesty!
When thou dost pinch thy bearer, thou dost sit
30 Like a rich armour worn in heat of day
That scald'st with safety. By his gates of breath
There lies a downy feather which stirs not.
Did he suspire, that light and weightless down
Perforce must move. My gracious lord! my father!
35 This sleep is sound indeed; this is a sleep
That from this golden rigol hath divorc'd
So many English kings. Thy due from me
Is tears and heavy sorrows of the blood
Which nature, love, and filial tenderness,
40 Shall, O dear father, pay thee plenteously.
My due from thee is this imperial crown,
Which, as immediate from thy place and blood,
Derives itself to me. *[Putting on the crown]* Lo where
it sits –
Which God shall guard; and put the world's whole
strength
45 Into one giant arm, it shall not force
This lineal honour from me. This from thee
Will I to mine leave as 'tis left to me. *[Exit.]*

King
　Warwick! Gloucester! Clarence!

　　[Re-enter WARWICK, GLOUCESTER, CLARENCE.*]*

Clarence
　Doth the King call?
Warwick
　What would your Majesty? How fares your Grace?　　50
King
　Why did you leave me here alone, my lords?
Clarence
　We left the Prince my brother here, my liege,
　Who undertook to sit and watch by you.
King
　The Prince of Wales! Where is he? Let me see him.
　He is not here.　　55
Warwick
　This door is open; he is gone this way.
Gloucester
　He came not through the chamber where we stay'd.
King
　Where is the crown? Who took it from my pillow?
Warwick
　When we withdrew, my liege, we left it here.
King
　The Prince hath ta'en it hence. Go, seek him out.　　60
　Is he so hasty that he doth suppose
　My sleep my death?
　Find him, my Lord of Warwick; chide him hither.
　　[Exit WARWICK.*]*
　This part of his conjoins with my disease
　And helps to end me. See, sons, what things you
　　are!　　65
　How quickly nature falls into revolt
　When gold becomes her object!
　For this the foolish over-careful fathers
　Have broke their sleep with thoughts,
　Their brains with care, their bones with industry;　　70

For this they have engrossed and pil'd up
The cank'red heaps of strange-achieved gold;
For this they have been thoughtful to invest
Their sons with arts and martial exercises;
75 When, like the bee, tolling from every flower
The virtuous sweets,
Our thighs with wax, our mouths with honey
pack'd,
We bring it to the hive, and, like the bees,
Are murd'red for our pains. This bitter taste
80 Yields his engrossments to the ending father.

[Re-enter WARWICK.*]*

Now where is he that will not stay so long
Till his friend sickness hath determin'd me?
Warwick
My lord, I found the Prince in the next room,
Washing with kindly tears his gentle cheeks,
85 With such a deep demeanour in great sorrow,
That tyranny, which never quaff'd but blood,
Would, by beholding him, have wash'd his knife
With gentle eye-drops. He is coming hither.
King
But wherefore did he take away the crown?

[Re-enter PRINCE HENRY.*]*

90 Lo where he comes. Come hither to me, Harry.
Depart the chamber, leave us here alone.

[Exeunt all but the KING *and the* PRINCE.*]*

Prince
I never thought to hear you speak again.
King
Thy wish was father, Harry, to that thought.
I stay too long by thee, I weary thee.
95 Dost thou so hunger for mine empty chair
That thou wilt needs invest thee with my honours

Before thy hour be ripe? O foolish youth!
Thou seek'st the greatness that will overwhelm thee.
Stay but a little, for my cloud of dignity
Is held from falling with so weak a wind   100
That it will quickly drop; my day is dim.
Thou hast stol'n that which, after some few hours,
Were thine without offence; and at my death
Thou hast seal'd up my expectation.
Thy life did manifest thou lov'dst me not,   105
And thou wilt have me die assur'd of it.
Thou hid'st a thousand daggers in thy thoughts,
Which thou hast whetted on thy stony heart,
To stab at half an hour of my life.
What, canst thou not forbear me half an hour?   110
Then get thee gone, and dig my grave thyself;
And bid the merry bells ring to thine ear
That thou art crowned, not that I am dead.
Let all the tears that should bedew my hearse
Be drops of balm to sanctify thy head;   115
Only compound me with forgotten dust;
Give that which gave thee life unto the worms.
Pluck down my officers, break my decrees;
For now a time is come to mock at form –
Harry the Fifth is crown'd. Up, vanity: 120
Down, royal state. All you sage counsellors, hence.
And to the English court assemble now,
From every region, apes of idleness.
Now, neighbour confines, purge you of your scum.
Have you a ruffian that will swear, drink, dance,   125
Revel the night, rob, murder, and commit
The oldest sins the newest kind of ways?
Be happy, he will trouble you no more.
England shall double gild his treble guilt;
England shall give him office, honour, might;   130
For the fifth Harry from curb'd license plucks
The muzzle of restraint, and the wild dog
Shall flesh his tooth on every innocent.

O my poor kingdom, sick with civil blows!
135   When that my care could not withhold thy riots,
What wilt thou do when riot is thy care?
O, thou wilt be a wilderness again,
Peopled with wolves, thy old inhabitants!

Prince

O, pardon me, my liege! But for my tears,
140   The moist impediments unto my speech,
I had forestall'd this dear and deep rebuke
Ere you with grief had spoke and I had heard
The course of it so far. There is your crown,
And He that wears the crown immortally
145   Long guard it yours! *[Kneeling]* If I affect it more
Than as your honour and as your renown,
Let me no more from this obedience rise,
Which my most inward true and duteous spirit
Teacheth this prostrate and exterior bending!
150   God witness with me, when I here came in
And found no course of breath within your Majesty,
How cold it struck my heart! If I do feign,
O, let me in my present wildness die,
And never live to show th' incredulous world
155   The noble change that I have purposed!
Coming to look on you, thinking you dead –
And dead almost, my liege, to think you were –
I spake unto this crown as having sense,
And thus upbraided it: 'The care on thee depending
160   Hath fed upon the body of my father;
Therefore thou best of gold art worst of gold.
Other, less fine in carat, is more precious,
Preserving life in med'cine potable;
But thou, most fine, most honour'd, most renown'd,
165   Hast eat thy bearer up'. Thus, my most royal liege,
Accusing it, I put it on my head,
To try with it – as with an enemy
That had before my face murd'red my father –
The quarrel of a true inheritor.

But if it did infect my blood with joy,   170
Or swell my thoughts to any strain of pride;
If any rebel or vain spirit of mine
Did with the least affection of a welcome
Give entertainment to the might of it,
Let God for ever keep it from my head,   175
And make me as the poorest vassal is,
That doth with awe and terror kneel to it!

King
O my son,
God put it in thy mind to take it hence,
That thou mightst win the more thy father's love,   180
Pleading so wisely in excuse of it!
Come hither, Harry; sit thou by my bed,
And hear, I think, the very latest counsel
That ever I shall breathe. God knows, my son,
By what by-paths and indirect crook'd ways   185
I met this crown; and I myself know well
How troublesome it sat upon my head:
To thee it shall descend with better quiet,
Better opinion, better confirmation;
For all the soil of the achievement goes   190
With me into the earth. It seem'd in me
But as an honour snatch'd with boist'rous hand;
And I had many living to upbraid
My gain of it by their assistances;
Which daily grew to quarrel and to bloodshed,   195
Wounding supposed peace. All these bold fears
Thou seest with peril I have answered;
For all my reign hath been but as a scene
Acting that argument. And now my death
Changes the mood; for what in me was purchas'd   200
Falls upon thee in a more fairer sort;
So thou the garland wear'st successively.
Yet, though thou stand'st more sure than I could
    do,
Thou art not firm enough, since griefs are green;

And all my friends, which thou must make thy
205   friends,
Have but their stings and teeth newly ta'en out;
By whose fell working I was first advanc'd,
And by whose power I well might lodge a fear
To be again displac'd; which to avoid,
210 I cut them off; and had a purpose now
To lead out many to the Holy Land,
Lest rest and lying still might make them look
Too near unto my state. Therefore, my Harry,
Be it thy course to busy giddy minds
215 With foreign quarrels, that action, hence borne out,
May waste the memory of the former days.
More would I, but my lungs are wasted so
That strength of speech is utterly denied me.
How I came by the crown, O God, forgive;
220 And grant it may with thee in true peace live!

Prince

My gracious liege,
You won it, wore it, kept it, gave it me;
Then plain and right must my possession be;
Which I with more than with a common pain
225 'Gainst all the world will rightfully maintain.

[*Enter* PRINCE JOHN OF LANCASTER, WARWICK, *Lords,
and Others.*]

King

Look, look, here comes my John of Lancaster.

Prince John

Health, peace, and happiness, to my royal father!

King

Thou bring'st me happiness and peace, son John;
But health, alack, with youthful wings is flown
230 From this bare wither'd trunk. Upon thy sight
My worldly business makes a period.
Where is my Lord of Warwick?

Prince

                              My Lord of Warwick!

King

   Doth any name particular belong
   Unto the lodging where I first did swoon?

Warwick

   'Tis call'd Jerusalem, my noble lord.   235

King

   Laud be to God! Even there my life must end.
   It hath been prophesied to me many years,
   I should not die but in Jerusalem;
   Which vainly I suppos'd the Holy Land.
   But bear me to that chamber; there I'll lie;   240
   In that Jerusalem shall Harry die.

[Exeunt.]

ACT FIVE
SCENE I

Gloucestershire. Shallow's house.

[*Enter* SHALLOW, FALSTAFF, BARDOLPH, *and Page.*]

Shallow
By cock and pie, sir, you shall not away to-night. What, Davy, I say!

Falstaff
You must excuse me, Master Robert Shallow.

Shallow
5 I will not excuse you; you shall not be excus'd; excuses shall not be admitted; there is no excuse shall serve; you shall not be excus'd. Why, Davy!

[*Enter* DAVY.]

Davy
Here, sir.

Shallow
Davy, Davy, Davy, Davy; let me see, Davy; let me see, Davy; let me see – yea, marry, William cook, bid him
10 come hither. Sir John, you shall not be excus'd.

Davy
Marry, sir, thus: those precepts cannot be served; and, again, sir – shall we sow the headland with wheat?

Shallow
With red wheat, Davy. But for William cook – are there no young pigeons?

Davy
15 Yes, sir. Here is now the smith's note for shoeing and plough-irons.

Shallow
Let it be cast, and paid. Sir John, you shall not be excused.

Davy

    Now, sir, a new link to the bucket must needs be had;
    and, sir, do yo mean to stop any of William's wages   20
    about the sack he lost the other day at Hinckley fair?

Shallow

    'A shall answer it. Some pigeons, Davy, a couple of
    short-legg'd hens, a joint of mutton, and any pretty
    little tiny kickshaws, tell William cook.

Davy

    Doth the man of war stay all night, sir?   25

Shallow

    Yea, Davy; I will use him well. A friend i' th' court is
    better than a penny in purse. Use his men well, Davy;
    for they are arrant knaves and will backbite.

Davy

    No worse than they are backbitten, sir; for they have
    marvellous foul linen.   30

Shallow

    Well conceited, Davy – about thy business, Davy.

Davy

    I beseech you, sir, to countenance William Visor of
    Woncot against Clement Perkes o' th' hill.

Shallow

    There is many complaints, Davy, against that Visor.
    That Visor is an arrant knave, on my knowledge.   35

Davy

    I grant your worship that he is a knave, sir; but yet
    God forbid, sir, but a knave should have some coun-
    tenance at his friend's request. An honest man, sir, is
    able to speak for himself, when a knave is not. I have
    serv'd your worship truly, sir, this eight years; an I   40
    cannot once or twice in a quarter bear out a knave
    against an honest man, I have but a very little credit
    with your worship. The knave is mine honest friend,
    sir; therefore, I beseech you, let him be countenanc'd.

Shallow

    Go to; I say he shall have no wrong. Look about, Davy.   45

[Exit DAVY*]* Where are you, Sir John? Come, come, come, off with your boots. Give me your hand, Master Bardolph.

Bardolph

I am glad to see your worship.

Shallow

50   I thank thee with all my heart, kind Master Bardolph. *[To the* PAGE*]* And welcome, my tall fellow. Come, Sir John.

Falstaff

I'll follow you, good Master Robert Shallow. *[Exit* SHALLOW*]* Bardolph, look to our horses. *[Exeunt*
55   BARDOLPH *and* PAGE*]* If I were sawed into quantities, I should make four dozen of such bearded hermits' staves as Master Shallow. It is a wonderful thing to see the semblable coherence of his men's spirits and his. They, by observing of him, do bear themselves like foolish
60   justices: he, by conversing with them, is turned into a justice-like serving-man. Their spirits are so married in conjunction with the participation of society that they flock together in consent, like so many wild geese. If I had a suit to Master Shallow, I would humour his
65   men with the imputation of being near their master; if to his men, I would curry with Master Shallow that no man could better command his servants. It is certain that either wise bearing or ignorant carriage is caught, as men take diseases, one of another; therefore let men
70   take heed of their company. I will devise matter enough out of this Shallow to keep Prince Harry in continual laughter the wearing out of six fashions, which is four terms, or two actions; and 'a shall laugh without inter-vallums. O, it is much that a lie with a slight oath,
75   and a jest with a sad brow, will do with a fellow that never had the ache in his shoulders! O, you shall see him laugh still his face be like a wet cloak ill laid up!

Shallow

[Within] Sir John!

Falstaff
I come, Master Shallow; I come, Master Shallow.

[Exit.]

SCENE II

Westminster. The palace.

[Enter, severally, WARWICK *and the* LORD CHIEF
JUSTICE.*]*

Warwick
　　How now, my Lord Chief Justice; whither away?
Chief Justice
　　How doth the King?
Warwick
　　Exceeding well; his cares are now all ended.
Chief Justice
　　I hope, not dead.
Warwick
　　　　　　　　He's walk'd the way of nature;
5　　And to our purposes he lives no more.
Chief Justice
　　I would his Majesty had call'd me with him.
　　The service that I truly did his life
　　Hath left me open to all injuries.
Warwick
　　Indeed I think the young King loves you not.
Chief Justice
10　　I know he doth not, and do arm myself
　　To welcome the condition of the time,
　　Which cannot look more hideously upon me
　　Than I have drawn it in my fantasy.

[Enter LANCASTER, CLARENCE, GLOUCESTER,
WESTMORELAND, *and Others.]*

Warwick
　　Here come the heavy issue of dead Harry.
15　　O that the living Harry had the temper
　　Of he, the worst of these three gentlemen!
　　How many nobles then should hold their places
　　That must strike sail to spirits of vile sort!

Chief Justice

O God, I fear all will be overturn'd.

Prince John

Good morrow, cousin Warwick, good morrow.   20

Gloucester, Clarence

Good morrow, cousin.

Prince John

We meet like men that had forgot to speak.

Warwick

We do remember; but our argument
Is all too heavy to admit much talk.

Prince John

Well, peace be with him that hath made us heavy!   25

Chief Justice

Peace be with us, lest we be heavier!

Gloucester

O, good my lord, you have lost a friend indeed;
And I dare swear you borrow not that face
Of seeming sorrow – it is sure your own.

Prince John

Though no man be assur'd what grace to find,   30
You stand in coldest expectation.
I am the sorrier; would 'twere otherwise.

Clarence

Well, you must now speak Sir John Falstaff fair;
Which swims against your stream of quality.

Chief Justice

Sweet Princes, what I did, I did in honour,   35
Led by th' impartial conduct of my soul;
And never shall you see that I will beg
A ragged and forestall'd remission.
If truth and upright innocency fail me,
I'll to the King my master that is dead,   40
And tell him who hath sent me after him.

Warwick

Here comes the Prince.

[Enter KING HENRY THE FIFTH, *attended.]*

Chief Justice
Good morrow, and God save your Majesty!
King
This new and gorgeous garment, majesty,
45 Sits not so easy on me as you think.
Brothers, you mix your sadness with some fear.
This is the English, not the Turkish court;
Not Amurath an Amurath succeeds,
But Harry Harry. Yet be sad, good brothers,
50 For, by my faith, it very well becomes you.
Sorrow so royally in you appears
That I will deeply put the fashion on,
And wear it in my heart. Why, then, be sad;
But entertain no more of it, good brothers,
55 Than a joint burden laid upon us all.
For me, by heaven, I bid you be assur'd,
I'll be your father and your brother too;
Let me but bear your love, I'll bear your cares.
Yet weep that Harry's dead, and so will I;
60 But Harry lives that shall convert those tears
By number into hours of happiness.
Brothers
We hope no otherwise from your Majesty.
King
You all look strangely on me; and you most.
You are, I think, assur'd I love you not.
Chief Justice
65 I am assur'd, if I be measur'd rightly,
Your Majesty hath no just cause to hate me.
King
No?
How might a prince of my great hopes forget
So great indignities you laid upon me?
70 What, rate, rebuke, and roughly send to prison,
Th' immediate heir of England! Was this easy?
May this be wash'd in Lethe and forgotten?
Chief Justice
I then did use the person of your father;

The image of his power lay then in me;
And in th' administration of his law,   75
Whiles I was busy for the commonwealth,
Your Highness pleased to forget my place,
The majesty and power of law and justice,
The image of the King whom I presented,
And struck me in my very seat of judgment;   80
Whereon, as an offender to your father,
I gave bold way to my authority
And did commit you. If the deed were ill,
Be you contented, wearing now the garland,
To have a son set your decrees at nought,   85
To pluck down justice from your awful bench,
To trip the course of law, and blunt the sword
That guards the peace and safety of your person;
Nay, more, to spurn at your most royal image,
And mock your workings in a second body.   90
Question your royal thoughts, make the case yours;
Be now the father, and propose a son;
Hear your own dignity so much profan'd,
See your most dreadful laws so loosely slighted,
Behold yourself so by a son disdain'd;   95
And then imagine me taking your part
And, in your power, soft silencing your son.
After this cold considerance, sentence me;
And, as you are a king, speak in your state
What I have done that misbecame my place,   100
My person, or my liege's sovereignty.

King

You are right, Justice, and you weigh this well;
Therefore still bear the balance and the sword;
And I do wish your honours may increase
Till you do live to see a son of mine   105
Offend you, and obey you, as I did.
So shall I live to speak my father's words:
'Happy am I that have a man so bold
That dares do justice on my proper son;
And not less happy, having such a son   110

245

That would deliver up his greatness so
Into the hands of justice'. You did commit me;
For which I do commit into your hand
Th' unstained sword that you have us'd to bear;
115   With this remembrance – that you use the same
With the like bold, just, and impartial spirit
As you have done 'gainst me. There is my hand.
You shall be as a father to my youth;
My voice shall sound as you do prompt mine ear;
120   And I will stoop and humble my intents
To your well-practis'd wise directions.
And, Princes all, believe me, I beseech you,
My father is gone wild into his grave,
For in his tomb lie my affections;
125   And with his spirits sadly I survive,
To mock the expectation of the world,
To frustrate prophecies, and to raze out
Rotten opinion, who hath writ me down
After my seeming. The tide of blood in me
130   Hath proudly flow'd in vanity till now.
Now doth it turn and ebb back to the sea,
Where it shall mingle with the state of floods,
And flow henceforth in formal majesty.
Now call we our high court of parliament;
135   And let us choose such limbs of noble counsel,
That the great body of our state may go
In equal rank with the best govern'd nation;
That war, or peace, or both at once, may be
As things acquainted and familiar to us;
140   In which you, father, shall have foremost hand.
Our coronation done, we will accite,
As I before rememb'red, all our state;
And – God consigning to my good intents –
No prince nor peer shall have just cause to say,
145   God shorten Harry's happy life one day.

[Exeunt.]

SCENE III

Gloucestershire. Shallow's orchard.

[Enter FALSTAFF, SHALLOW, SILENCE, BARDOLPH, *the Page, and* DAVY.*]*

Shallow
    Nay, you shall see my orchard, where, in an arbour,
    we will eat a last year's pippin of mine own graffing,
    with a dish of caraways, and so forth. Come, cousin
    Silence. And then to bed.

Falstaff
    Fore God, you have here a goodly dwelling and rich.   5

Shallow
    Barren, barren, barren; beggars all, beggars all, Sir John
    – marry, good air. Spread, Davy, spread, Davy; well
    said, Davy.

Falstaff
    This Davy serves you for good uses; he is your serving-
    man and your husband.   10

Shallow
    A good varlet, a good varlet, a very good varlet, Sir
    John. By the mass, I have drunk too much sack at
    supper. A good varlet. Now sit down, now sit down;
    come, cousin.

Silence
    Ah, sirrah! quoth-a – we shall *[Singing.]*   15
    Do nothing but eat and make good cheer,
    And praise God for the merry year;
    When flesh is cheap and females dear,
    And lusty lads roam here and there,
    So merrily,
             And ever among so merrily.   20

Falstaff
    There's a merry heart! Good Master
    Silence, I'll give you a health for that anon.

247

Shallow
Give Master Bardolph some wine, Davy.
Davy
Sweet sir, sit; I'll be with you anon; most sweet sir, sit.
25   Master Page, good Master Page, sit. Proface! What you
want in meat, we'll have in drink. But you must bear;
the heart's all. *[Exit.]*
Shallow
Be merry, Master Bardolph; and, my little soldier there,
be merry.
Silence
[Singing]
30   Be merry, be merry, my wife has all;
For women are shrews, both short and tall;
'Tis merry in hall when beards wag all;
And welcome merry Shrove-tide.
Be merry, be merry.
Falstaff
35   I did not think Master Silence had been a man of this
mettle.
Silence
Who, I? I have been merry twice and once ere now.

[Re-enter DAVY.]

Davy
[To BARDOLPH] There's a dish of leather-coats for you.
Shallow
Davy!
Davy
40   Your worship! I'll be with you straight. *[To BARDOLPH]*
A cup of wine, sir?
Silence
[Singing]
A cup of wine that's brisk and fine,
And drink unto the leman mine;
    And a merry heart lives long-a.

Falstaff

Well said, Master Silence. 45

Silence

An we shall be merry, now comes in the sweet o' th' night.

Falstaff

Health and long life to you, Master Silence!

Silence

[Singing]

Fill the cup, and let it come, I'll pledge you a mile to th' bottom. 50

Shallow

Honest Bardolph, welcome; if thou want'st anything and wilt not call, beshrew thy heart. Welcome, my little tiny thief and welcome indeed too. I'll drink to Master Bardolph, and to all the cabileros about London.

Davy

I hope to see London once ere I die. 55

Bardolph

An I might see you there, Davy!

Shallow

By the mass, you'll crack a quart together – ha! will you not, Master Bardolph?

Bardolph

Yea, sir, in a pottle-pot.

Shallow

By God's liggens, I thank thee. The knave will stick by 60 thee, I can assure thee that. 'A will not out, 'a; 'tis true bred.

Bardolph

And I'll stick by him, sir.

Shallow

Why, there spoke a king. Lack nothing; be merry.

[One knocks at door]

Look who's at door there, ho! Who knocks? 65

[Exit DAVY.]

Falstaff

[*To* SILENCE, *who has drunk a bumper*]

Why, now you have done me right.

Silence

[*Singing*] Do me right,

> And dub me knight.

> > Samingo.

70 Is't not so?

Falstaff

'Tis so.

Silence

Is't so? Why then, say an old man can do somewhat.

[*Re-enter* DAVY.]

Davy

An't please your worship, there's one Pistol come from

75 the court with news.

Falstaff

From the court? Let him come in.

[*Enter* PISTOL.]

How now, Pistol?

Pistol

Sir John, God save you!

Falstaff

What wind blew you hither, Pistol?

Pistol

85 Not the ill wind which blows no man to good. Sweet knight, thou art now one of the greatest men in this realm.

Silence

By'r lady, I think 'a be, but goodman Puff of Barson.

Pistol

Puff!

90 Puff in thy teeth, most recreant coward base!

Sir John, I am thy Pistol and thy friend,

And helter-skelter have I rode to thee;
And tidings do I bring, and lucky joys,
And golden times, and happy news of price.

Falstaff

I pray thee now, deliver them like a man of this world.　95

Pistol

A foutra for the world and worldlings base!
I speak of Africa and golden joys.

Falstaff

O base Assyrian knight, what is thy news?
Let King Cophetua know the truth thereof.

Silence

[*Singing*] And Robin Hood, Scarlet, and John.　　　100

Pistol

Shall dunghill curs confront the Helicons?
And shall good news be baffled?
Then, Pistol, lay thy head in Furies' lap.

Shallow

Honest gentleman, I know not your breeding.

Pistol

Why, then, lament therefore.　　　　　　　105

Shallow

Give me pardon, sir. If, sir, you come with news from
the court, I take it there's but two ways – either to
utter them or conceal them. I am, sir, under the King,
in some authority.

Pistol

Under which king, Bezonian? Speak, or die.　　110

Shallow

Under King Harry.

Pistol

　　　　　　Harry the Fourth – or Fifth?

Shallow

Harry the Fourth.

Pistol

　　　　　A foutra for thine office!
Sir John, thy tender lambkin now is King;

Harry the Fifth's the man. I speak the truth.
115 When Pistol lies, do this; and fig me, like
The bragging Spaniard.

Falstaff
What, is the old king dead?

Pistol
As nail in door. The things I speak are just.

Falstaff
Away, Bardolph! saddle my horse. Master Robert
120 Shallow, choose what office thou wilt in the land, 'tis
thine. Pistol, I will double-charge thee with dignities.

Bardolph
O joyful day!
I would not take a knighthood for my fortune.

Pistol
What, I do bring good news?

Falstaff
125 Carry Master Silence to bed. Master Shallow, my Lord
Shallow, be what thou wilt – I am Fortune's steward.
Get on thy boots; we'll ride all night. O sweet Pistol!
Away, Bardolph! *[Exit* BARDOLPH*]* Come, Pistol, utter
more to me; and withal devise something to do thyself
130 good. Boot, boot, Master Shallow! I know the young
King is sick for me. Let us take any man's horses: the
laws of England are at my commandment. Blessed are
they that have been my friends; and woe to my Lord
Chief Justice!

Pistol
135 Let vultures vile seize on his lungs also!
'Where is the life that late I led?' say they.
Why, here it is. Welcome these pleasant days!

[Exeunt]

SCENE IV

London. A street.

[Enter Beadles, dragging in HOSTESS QUICKLY *and*
DOLL TEARSHEET.*]*

Hostess
No, thou arrant knave; I would to God that I might
die, that I might have thee hang'd. Thou hast drawn
my shoulder out of joint.

I Beadle
The constables have delivered her over to me; and she
shall have whipping-cheer enough, I warrant her. There   5
hath been a man or two lately kill'd about her.

Doll
Nut-hook, nut-hook, you lie. Come on; I'll tell thee
what, thou damn'd tripe-visag'd rascal, an the child I
now go with do miscarry, thou wert better thou hadst
struck thy mother, thou wert better thou hadst struck   10
thy mother, thou paper-fac'd villain.

Hostess
O the Lord, that Sir John were come!
He would make this a bloody day to somebody.
But I pray God the fruit of her womb miscarry!

I Beadle
If it do, you shall have a dozen of cushions again; you   15
have but eleven now. Come, I charge you both go with
me; for the man is dead that you and Pistol beat
amongst you.

Doll
I'll tell you what, you thin man in a censer, I will have
you as soundly swing'd for this – you due-bottle rogue,   20
you filthy famish'd correctioner, if you be not swing'd,
I'll forswear half-kirtles.

I Beadle
Come, come, you she knight-errant, come.

Hostess

O God, that right should thus overcome might! Well,
25   of sufferance comes ease.

Doll

Come, you rogue, come; bring me to a justice.

Hostess

Ay, come, you starv'd bloodhound.

Doll

Goodman death, goodman bones!

Hostess

Thou atomy, thou!

Doll

30   Come, you thin thing! come, you rascal!

I Beadle

Very well.

[Exeunt.]

SCENE V

Westminster. Near the Abbey.

[Enter Grooms, strewing rushes.]

1 Groom
 More rushes, more rushes!
2 Groom
 The trumpets have sounded twice.
3 Groom
 'Twill be two o'clock ere they come from the coronation. Dispatch, dispatch.

[Exeunt.]

[Trumpets sound, and the KING *and his Train pass
over the stage. After them enter* FALSTAFF, SHALLOW,
PISTOL, BARDOLPH, *and Page.]*

Falstaff
 Stand here by me, Master Robert Shallow; I will make   5
 the King do you grace. I will leer upon him, as 'a comes
 by; and do but mark the countenance that he will give
 me.
Pistol
 God bless thy lungs, good knight!
Falstaff
 Come here, Pistol; stand behind me. *[To* SHALLOW*]* O,   10
 if I had had time to have made new liveries, I would
 have bestowed the thousand pound I borrowed of you.
 But 'tis no matter; this poor show doth better; this
 doth infer the zeal I had to see him.
Shallow
 It doth so.   15
Falstaff
 It shows my earnestness of affection –
Shallow
 It doth so.

Falstaff
My devotion –
Shallow
It doth, it doth, it' doth.
Falstaff
20   As it were, to ride day and night; and not to deliberate,
not to remember, not to have patience to shift me –
Shallow
It is best, certain.
Falstaff
But to stand stained with travel, and sweating with
desire to see him; thinking of nothing else, putting all
25   affairs else in oblivion, as if there were nothing else to
be done but to see him.
Pistol
'Tis 'semper idem' for 'obsque hoc nihil est'. 'Tis all in
every part.
Shallow
'Tis so, indeed.
Pistol
My knight, I will inflame thy noble liver And make
30   thee rage.
Thy Doll, and Helen of thy noble thoughts,
Is in base durance and contagious prison;
Hal'd thither
By most mechanical and dirty hand.
Rouse up revenge from ebon den with fell Alecto's
35   snake,
For Doll is in. Pistol speaks nought but truth.
Falstaff
I will deliver her.

[Shouts within, and the trumpets sound.]

Pistol
There roar'd the sea, and trumpet-clangor sounds.

[Enter the KING *and his Train, the* LORD CHIEF JUSTICE
among them.]

Falstaff

God save thy Grace, King Hal; my royal Hal!

Pistol

The heavens thee guard and keep, most royal imp of
fame!   45

Falstaff

God save thee, my sweet boy!

King

My Lord Chief Justice, speak to that vain man.

Chief Justice

Have you your wits? Know you what 'tis you speak?

Falstaff

My king! my Jove! I speak to thee, my heart!

King

I know thee not, old man. Fall to thy prayers.   50
How ill white hairs become a fool and jester!
I have long dreamt of such a kind of man,
So surfeit-swell'd, so old, and so profane,
But, being awak'd, I do despise my dream.
Make less thy body hence, and more thy grace;   55
Leave gormandizing; know the grave doth gape
For thee thrice wider than for other men –
Reply not to me with a fool-born jest;
Presume not that I am the thing I was,
For God doth know, so shall the world perceive,   60
That I have turn'd away my former self;
So will I those that kept me company.
When thou dost hear I am as I have been,
Approach me, and thou shalt be as thou wast,
The tutor and the feeder of my riots.   65
Till then I banish thee, on pain of death,
As I have done the rest of my misleaders,
Not to come near our person by ten mile.
For competence of life I will allow you,
That lack of means enforce you not to evils;   70
And, as we hear you do reform yourselves,
We will, according to your strengths and qualities,

Give you advancement. Be it your charge, my lord,
To see perform'd the tenour of our word.
75   Set on. *[Exeunt the* KING *and his Train.]*
Falstaff
Master Shallow, I owe you a thousand pound.
Shallow
Yea, marry, Sir John; which I beseech you to let me
have home with me.
Falstaff
That can hardly be, Master Shallow. Do not you grieve
80   at this; I shall be sent for in private to him. Look you,
he must seem thus to the world. Fear not your advance-
ments; I will be the man yet that shall make you great.
Shallow
I cannot perceive how, unless you give me your doublet,
and stuff me out with straw. I beseech you, good Sir
85   John, let me have five hundred of my thousand.
Falstaff
Sir, I will be as good as my word. This that you heard
was but a colour.
Shallow
A colour that I fear you will die in, Sir John.
Falstaff
Fear no colours; go with me to dinner. Come,
90   Lieutenant Pistol; come, Bardolph. I shall be sent for
soon at night.

[Re-enter PRINCE JOHN, *the* LORD CHIEF JUSTICE, *with
Officers.]*

Chief Justice
Go, carry Sir John Falstaff to the Fleet;
Take all his company along with him.
Falstaff
My lord, my lord –
Chief Justice
95   I cannot now speak. I will hear you soon.
Take them away.

Pistol
    Si fortuna me tormenta, spero me contenta.

      [Exeunt all but PRINCE JOHN *and the* LORD CHIEF
                  JUSTICE.]*

Prince John
    I like this fair proceeding of the King's.
    He hath intent his wonted followers
    Shall all be very well provided for;   100
    But all are banish'd till their conversations
    Appear more wise and modest to the world.
Chief Justice
    And so they are.
Prince John
    The King hath call'd his parliament, my lord.
Chief Justice
    He hath.   105
Prince John
    I will lay odds that, ere this year expire,
    We bear our civil swords and native fire
    As far as France. I heard a bird so sing,
    Whose music, to my thinking, pleas'd the King.
    Come, will you hence?   110

                [Exeunt.]

EPILOGUE

First my fear, then my curtsy, last my speech. My fear,
is your displeasure; my curtsy, my duty; and my speech,
to beg your pardons. If you look for a good speech
now, you undo me; for what I have to say is of mine
own making; and what, indeed, I should say will, I
doubt, prove mine own marring. But to the purpose,
and so to the venture. Be it known to you, as it is very
well, I was lately here in the end of a displeasing play,
to pray your patience for it and to promise you a better.
I meant indeed, to pay you with this; which if like an
ill venture it come unluckily home, I break, and you,
my gentle creditors, lose. Here I promis'd you I would
be, and here I commit my body to your mercies. Bate
me some, and I will pay you some, and, as most debtors
do, promise you infinitely; and so I kneel down before
you – but, indeed, to pray for the Queen.

If my tongue cannot entreat you to acquit me, will
you command me to use my legs? And yet that were
but light payment – to dance out of your debt. But a
good conscience will make any possible satisfaction,
and so would I. All the gentlewomen here have forgiven
me. If the gentlemen will not, then the gentlemen do
not agree with the gentlewomen, which was never seen
before in such an assembly.

One word more, I beseech you. If you be not too much
cloy'd with fat meat, our humble author will continue
the story, with Sir John in it, and make you merry
with fair Katherine of France; where, for anything I
know, Falstaff shall die of a sweat, unless already 'a be
kill'd with your hard opinions; for Oldcastle died a
martyr and this is not the man. My tongue is weary;
when my legs are too, I will bid you good night.

Shakespeare: Words and Phrases

adapted from the Collins English Dictionary

abate 1 VERB to abate here means to lessen or diminish ❑ *There lives within the very flame of love/ A kind of wick or snuff that will abate it* (*Hamlet 4.7*) 2 VERB to abate here means to shorten ❑ *Abate thy hours* (*A Midsummer Night's Dream 3.2*) 3 VERB to abate here means to deprive ❑ *She hath abated me of half my train* (*King Lear 2.4*)

abjure VERB to abjure means to renounce or give up ❑ *this rough magic I here abjure* (*Tempest 5.1*)

abroad ADV abroad means elsewhere or everywhere ❑ *You have heard of the news abroad* (*King Lear 2.1*)

abrogate VERB to abrogate means to put an end to ❑ *so it shall praise you to abrogate scurrility* (*Love's Labours Lost 4.2*)

abuse 1 NOUN abuse in this context means deception or fraud ❑ *What should this mean? Are all the rest come back?/ Or is it some abuse, and no such thing?* (*Hamlet 4.7*) 2 NOUN an abuse in this context means insult or offence ❑ *I will be deaf to pleading and excuses/ Nor tears nor prayers shall purchase our abuses* (*Romeo and Juliet 3.1*) 3 NOUN an abuse in this context means using something improperly ❑ *we'll digest/ Th'abuse*

of distance (*Henry II Chorus*) 4 NOUN an abuse in this context means doing something which is corrupt or dishonest ❑ *Come, bring them away: if these be good people in a commonweal that do nothing but their abuses in common houses, I know no law: bring them away.* (*Measure for Measure 2.1*)

abuser NOUN the abuser here is someone who betrays, a betrayer ❑ *I ... do attach thee/ For an abuser of the world* (*Othello 1.2*)

accent NOUN accent here means language ❑ *In states unborn, and accents yet unknown* (*Julius Caesar 3.1*)

accident NOUN an accident in this context is an event or something that happened ❑ *think no more of this night's accidents* (*A Midsummer Night's Dream 4.1*)

accommodate VERB to accommodate in this context means to equip or to give someone the equipment to do something ❑ *The safer sense will ne'er accommodate/ His master thus.* (*King Lear 4.6*)

according ADJ according means sympathetic or ready to agree ❑ *within the scope of choice/ Lies* *my consent and fair according voice* (*Romeo and Juliet* 1.2)

account NOUN account often means judgement (by God) or reckoning ❑ *No reckoning made, but sent to my account/ With all my imperfections on my head* (*Hamlet* 1.5)

accountant ADJ accountant here means answerable or accountable ❑ *his offence is… /Accountant to the law* (*Measure for Measure* 2.4)

ace NOUN ace here means one or first referring to the lowest score on a dice ❑ *No die, but an ace, for him; for he is but one./ Less than an ace, man; for he is dead; he is nothing.* (*A Midsummer Night's Dream* 5.1)

acquit VERB here acquit means to be rid of or free of. It is related to the verb quit ❑ *I am glad I am so acquit of this tinderbox* (*The Merry Wives of Windsor* 1.3)

afeard ADJ afeard means afraid or frightened ❑ *Nothing afeard of what thyself didst make* (*Macbeth* 1.3)

affiance NOUN affiance means confidence or trust ❑ *O how hast thou with jealousy infected/ The sweetness of affiance* (*Henry V* 2.2)

affinity NOUN in this context, affinity means important connections, or relationships with important people ❑ *The Moor replies/ That he you hurt is of great fame in Cyprus,/ And great affinity* (*Othello* 3.1)

agnize VERB to agnize is an old word that means that you recognize or acknowledge something ❑ *I do agnize/ A natural and prompt alacrity I find in hardness* (*Othello* 1.3)

ague NOUN an ague is a fever in which the patient has hot and cold

shivers one after the other ❑ *This is some monster of the isle with four legs, who hath got … an ague* (*The Tempest* 2.2)

alarm, alarum NOUN an alarm or alarum is a call to arms or a signal for soldiers to prepare to fight ❑ *Whence cometh this alarum and the noise?* (*Henry VI part I* 1.4)

Albion NOUN Albion is another word for England ❑ *but I will sell my dukedom,/ To buy a slobbery and a dirty farm In that nook-shotten isle of Albion* (*Henry V* 3.5)

all of all PHRASE all of all means everything, or the sum of all things ❑ *The very all of all* (*Love's Labours Lost* 5.1)

amend VERB amend in this context means to get better or to heal ❑ *at his touch… They presently amend* (*Macbeth* 4.3)

anchor VERB if you anchor on something you concentrate on it or fix on it ❑ *My invention … Anchors on Isabel* (*Measure for Measure* 2.4)

anon ADV anon was a common word for soon ❑ *You shall see anon how the murderer gets the love of Gonzago's wife* (*Hamlet* 3.2)

antic 1 ADJ antic here means weird or strange ❑ *I'll charm the air to give a sound/ While you perform your antic round* (*Macbeth* 4.1) 2 NOUN in this context antic means a clown or a strange, unattractive creature ❑ *If black, why nature, drawing an antic,/ Made a foul blot* (*Much Ado About Nothing* 3.1)

apace ADV apace was a common word for quickly ❑ *Come apace* (*As You Like It* 3.3)

apparel NOUN apparel means clothes or clothing ❑ *one suit of apparel* (Hamlet 3.2)

appliance NOUN appliance here means cure ❑ *Diseases desperate grown/By desperate appliance are relieved* (Hamlet 4.3)

argument NOUN argument here means a topic of conversation or the subject ❑ *Why 'tis the rarest argument of wonder that hath shot out in our latter times* (All's Well That Ends Well 2.3)

arrant ADJ arrant means absolute, complete. It strengthens the meaning of a noun ❑ *Fortune, that arrant whore* (King Lear 2.4)

arras NOUN an arras is a tapestry, a large cloth with a picture sewn on it using coloured thread ❑ *Behind the arras I'll convey myself/To hear the process* (Hamlet 3.3)

art 1 NOUN art in this context means knowledge ❑ *Their malady convinces/The great essay of art* (Macbeth 4.3) It can also mean skill as it does here ❑ *He ... gave you such a masterly report/For art and exercise in your defence* (Hamlet 4.7) 3 NOUN art here means magic ❑ *Now I want/Spirits to enforce, art to enchant* (The Tempest 5 Epilogue)

assay 1 NOUN an assay was an attempt, a try ❑ *Make assay./Bow, stubborn knees* (Hamlet 3.3) 2 NOUN assay can also mean a test or a trial ❑ *he hath made assay of her virtue* (Measure for Measure 3.1)

attend (on/upon) VERB attend on means to wait for or to expect ❑ *Tarry I here, I but attend on death* (Two Gentlemen of Verona 3.1)

auditor NOUN an auditor was a member of an audience or someone who listens ❑ *I'll be an auditor* (A Midsummer Night's Dream 3.1)

aught NOUN aught was a common word which meant anything ❑ *if my love thou holdest at aught* (Hamlet 4.3)

aunt 1 NOUN an aunt was another word for an old woman and also means someone who talks a lot or a gossip ❑ *The wisest aunt telling the saddest tale* (A Midsummer Night's Dream 2.1) 2 NOUN aunt could also mean a mistress or a prostitute ❑ *the thrush and the jay/Are summer songs for me and my aunts/While we lie tumbling in the hay* (The Winter's Tale 4.3)

avaunt EXCLAM avaunt was a common word which meant go away ❑ *Avaunt, you curs!* (King Lear 3.6)

aye ADV here aye means always or ever ❑ *Whose state and honour I for aye allow* (Richard II 5.2)

baffle VERB baffle meant to be disgraced in public or humiliated ❑ *I am disgraced, impeached, and baffled here* (Richard II 1.1)

bald ADJ bald means trivial or silly ❑ *I knew 'twould be a bald conclusion* (The Comedy of Errors 2.2)

ban NOUN a ban was a curse or an evil spell ❑ *Sometimes with lunatic bans... Enforce their charity* (King Lear 2.3)

barren ADJ barren meant empty or hollow ❑ *now I let go your hand, I am barren.* (Twelfth Night 1.3)

base ADJ base is an adjective that means unworthy or dishonourable ❑ *civet is of a baser birth than tar* (As You Like It 3.2)

base 1 ADJ base can also mean of low social standing or someone who was not part of the ruling class ❏ *Why brand they us with 'base'?* (*King Lear 1.2*) 2 ADJ here base means poor quality ❏ *Base cousin,/ Darest thou break first?* (*Two Noble Kinsmen 3.3*)

bawdy NOUN bawdy means obscene or rude ❏ *Bloody, bawdy villain!* (*Hamlet 2.2*)

bear in hand PHRASE bear in hand means taken advantage of or fooled ❏ *This I made good to you In our last conference, passed in probation with you/How you were borne in hand* (*Macbeth 3.1*)

beard VERB to beard someone was to oppose or confront them ❏ *Com'st thou to beard me in Denmark?* (*Hamlet 2.2*)

beard, in one's PHRASE if you say something in someone's beard you say it to their face ❏ *I will verify as much in his beard* (*Henry V 3.2*)

beaver NOUN a beaver was a visor on a battle helmet ❏ *O yes, my lord, he wore his beaver up* (*Hamlet 1.2*)

become VERB if something becomes you it suits you or is appropriate to you ❏ *Nothing in his life became him like the leaving it* (*Macbeth 1.4*)

bed, brought to PHRASE to be brought to bed means to give birth ❏ *His wife but yesternight was brought to bed* (*Titus Andronicus 4.2*)

bedabbled ADJ if something is bedabbled it is sprinkled ❏ *Bedabbled with the dew, and torn with briers* (*A Midsummer Night's Dream 3.2*)

Bedlam NOUN Bedlam was a word used for Bethlehem Hospital which was a place the insane were sent to ❏ *The country give me proof and precedent/Of Bedlam beggars* (*King Lear 2.3*)

bed-swerver NOUN a bed-swerver was someone who was unfaithful in marriage, an adulterer ❏ *she's/A bed-swerver* (*Winter's Tale 2.1*)

befall 1 VERB to befall is to happen, occur or take place ❏ *In this same interlude it doth befall/That I present a wall* (*A Midsummer Night's Dream 5.1*) 2 VERB to befall can also mean to happen to someone or something ❏ *fair befall thee and thy noble house* (*Richard III 1.3*)

behoof NOUN behoof was an advantage or benefit ❏ *All our surgeons/Convent in their behoof* (*Two Noble Kinsmen 1.4*)

beldam NOUN a beldam was a witch or old woman ❏ *Have I not reason, beldams as you are?* (*Macbeth 3.5*)

belike ADV belike meant probably, perhaps or presumably ❏ *belike he likes it not* (*Hamlet 3.2*)

bent 1 NOUN bent means a preference or a direction ❏ *Let me work,/For I can give his humour true bent,/And I will bring him to the Capitol* (*Julius Caesar 2.1*) 2 ADJ if you are bent on something you are determined to do it ❏ *for now I am bent to know/By the worst means the worst.* (*Macbeth 3.4*)

beshrew VERB beshrew meant to curse or wish evil on someone ❏ *much beshrew my manners and my pride/If Hermia meant to say Lysander lied* (*A Midsummer Night's Dream 2.2*)

betime (s) ADV betime means early ❑ *To business that we love we rise betime (Antony and Cleopatra 4.4)*

bevy NOUN bevy meant type or sort, it was also used to mean company ❑ *many more of the same bevy (Hamlet 5.2)*

blazon VERB to blazon something meant to display or show it ❑ *that thy skill be more to blazon it (Romeo and Juliet 2.6)*

blind ADJ if you are blind when you do something you are reckless or do not care about the consequences ❑ *are you yet to your own souls so blind/ That two you will war with God by murdering me (Richard III 1.4)*

bombast NOUN bombast was wool stuffing (used in a cushion for example) and so it came to mean padded out or long-winded. Here it means someone who talks a lot about nothing in particular ❑ *How now my sweet creature of bombast (Henry IV part I 2.4)*

bond 1 NOUN a bond is a contract or legal deed ❑ *Well, then, your bond, and let me see (Merchant of Venice 1.3)* 2 NOUN bond could also mean duty or commitment ❑ *I love your majesty/ According to my bond (King Lear 1.1)*

bottom NOUN here bottom means essence, main point or intent ❑ *Now I see/ The bottom of your purpose (All's Well That Ends Well 3.7)*

bounteously ADV bounteously means plentifully, abundantly ❑ *I prithee, and I'll pay thee bounteously (Twelfth Night 1.2)*

brace 1 NOUN a brace is a couple or two ❑ *Have lost a brace of kinsmen*

(Romeo and Juliet 5.3) 2 NOUN if you are in a brace position it means you are ready ❑ *For that it stands not in such warlike brace (Othello 1.3)*

brand VERB to mark permanantly like the markings on cattle ❑ *the wheeled seat/ Of fortunate Caesar ... branded his baseness that ensued (Anthony and Cleopatra 4.14)*

brave ADJ brave meant fine, excellent or splendid ❑ *O brave new world/ That has such people in't (The Tempest 5.1)*

brine NOUN brine is sea-water ❑ *He shall drink nought brine, for I'll not show him/ Where the quick freshes are (The Tempest 3.2)*

brow NOUN brow in this context means appearance ❑ *doth hourly grow/ Out of his brows (Hamlet 3.3)*

burden 1 NOUN the burden here is a chorus ❑ *I would sing my song without a burden (As You Like It 3.2)* 2 NOUN burden means load or weight (this is the current meaning) ❑ *the scarfs and the bannerets about thee did manifoldly dissuade me from believing thee a vessel of too great a burden (All's Well that Ends Well 2.3)*

buttons, in one's PHRASE this is a phrase that means clear, easy to see ❑ *Tis in his buttons he will carry't (The Merry Wives of Windsor 3.2)*

cable NOUN cable here means scope or reach ❑ *The law ... Will give her cable (Othello 1.2)*

cadent ADJ if something is cadent it is falling or dropping ❑ *With cadent tears fret channels in her cheeks (King Lear 1.4)*

canker VERB to canker is to decay, become corrupt ❑ *And, as with age his body uglier grows,/ So his mind cankers* (The Tempest 4.1)

canon, from the PHRASE from the canon is an expression meaning out of order, improper ❑ *Twas from the canon* (Coriolanus 3.1)

cap-a-pie ADV cap-a-pie means from head to foot, completely ❑ *I am courtier cap-a-pie* (The Winter's Tale 4.4)

carbonadoed ADJ if something is carbonadoed it is cut or scored (scratched) with a knife ❑ *it is your carbonadoed* (All's Well That Ends Well 4.5)

carouse VERB to carouse is to drink at length, party ❑ *They cast their caps up and carouse together* (Anthony and Cleopatra 4.12)

carrack NOUN a carrack was a large old ship, a galleon ❑ *Faith, he tonight hath boarded a land-carrack* (Othello 1.2)

cassock NOUN a cassock here means a military cloak, long coat ❑ *half of the which dare not shake the snow from off their cassocks lest they shake themselves to pieces* (All's Well That Ends Well 4.3)

catastrophe NOUN catastrophe here means conclusion or end ❑ *pat he comes, like the catastrophe of the old comedy* (King Lear 1.2)

cautel NOUN a cautel was a trick or a deceptive act ❑ *Perhaps he loves you now/ And now no soil not cautel doth besmirch* (Hamlet 1.2)

celerity NOUN celerity was a common word for speed, swiftness ❑ *Hence hath offence his quick celerity/ When it is borne in high authority* (Measure for Measure 4.2)

chafe NOUN chafe meant anger or temper ❑ *this Herculean Roman does become/ The carriage of his chafe* (Anthony and Cleopatra 1.3)

chanson NOUN chanson was an old word for a song ❑ *The first row of the pious chanson will show you more* (Hamlet 2.2)

chapman NOUN a chapman was a trader or merchant ❑ *Not uttered by base sale of chapman's tongues* (Love's Labours Lost 2.1)

chaps, chops NOUN chaps (and chops) was a word for jaws ❑ *Which ne'er shook hands nor bade farewell to him/ Till he unseamed him from the nave to th' chops* (Macbeth 1.2)

chattels NOUN chattels were your moveable possessions. The word is used in the traditional marriage ceremony ❑ *She is my goods, my chattels* (The Taming of the Shrew 3.3)

chide VERB if you are chided by someone you are told off or reprimanded ❑ *Now I but chide, but I should use thee worse* (A Midsummer Night's Dream 3.2)

chinks NOUN chinks was a word for cash or money ❑ *he that can lay hold of her/ Shall have the chinks* (Romeo and Juliet 1.5)

choleric ADJ if something was called choleric it meant that they were quick to get angry ❑ *therewithal unruly waywardness that infirm and choleric years bring with them* (King Lear 1.1)

chuff NOUN a chuff was a miser,

someone who clings to his or her money ❏ *ye fat chuffs* (*Henry IV part I 2.2*)

cipher NOUN cipher here means nothing ❏ *Mine were the very cipher of a function* (*Measure for Measure 2.2*)

circummured ADJ circummured means that something is surrounded with a wall ❏ *He hath a garden circummured with brick* (*Measure for Measure 4.1*)

civet NOUN a civet is a type of scent or perfume ❏ *Give me an ounce of civet* (*King Lear 4.6*)

clamorous ADJ clamorous means noisy or boisterous ❏ *Be clamorous and leap all civil bounds* (*Twelfth Night 1.4*)

clangour, clangor NOUN clangour is a word that means ringing (the sound that bells make) ❏ *Like to a dismal clangour heard from far* (*Henry VI part III 2.3*)

cleave VERB if you cleave to something you stick to it or are faithful to it ❏ *Thy thoughts I cleave to* (*The Tempest 4.1*)

clock and clock, 'twixt PHRASE from hour to hour, without stopping or continuously ❏ *To weep 'twixt clock and clock* (*Cymbeline 3.4*)

close ADJ here close means hidden ❏ *Stand close; this is the same Athenian* (*A Midsummer Night's Dream 3.2*)

cloud NOUN a cloud on your face means that you have a troubled, unhappy expression ❏ *He has cloud in's face* (*Anthony and Cleopatra 3.2*)

cloy VERB if you cloy an appetite you satisfy it ❏ *Other women cloy/The appetites they feed* (*Anthony and Cleopatra 2.2*)

cock-a-hoop, set PHRASE if you set cock-a-hoop you become free of everything ❏ *You will set cock-a-hoop* (*Romeo and Juliet 1.5*)

colours NOUN colours is a word used to describe battle-flags or banners. Sometimes we still say that we nail our colours to the mast if we are stating which team or side of an argument we support ❏ *the approbation of those that weep this lamentable divorce under her colours* (*Cymbeline 1.5*)

combustion NOUN combustion was a word meaning disorder or chaos ❏ *prophesying ... Of dire combustion and confused events* (*Macbeth 2.3*)

comely ADJ if you are or something is comely you or it is lovely, beautiful, graceful ❏ *O, what a world is this, when what is comely/Envenoms him that bears it!* (*As You Like It 2.3*)

commend VERB if you commend yourself to someone you send greetings to them ❏ *Commend me to my brother* (*Measure for Measure 1.4*)

compact NOUN a compact is an agreement or a contract ❏ *what compact mean you to have with us?* (*Julius Caesar 3.1*)

compass 1 NOUN here compass means range or scope ❏ *you would sound me from my lowest note to the top of my compass* (*Hamlet 3.2*) 2 VERB to compass here means to achieve, bring about or make happen ❏ *How now shall this be compassed?/Canst thou bring me to the party?* (*Tempest 3.2*)

comptible ADJ comptible is an old word meaning sensitive ❏ *I am very comptible, even to the least sinister usage.* (*Twelfth Night 1.5*)

confederacy NOUN a confederacy is a group of people usually joined together to commit a crime. It is another word for a conspiracy ❏ *Lo, she is one of this confederacy!* (*A Midsummer Night's Dream 3.2*)

confound VERB if you confound something you confuse it or mix it up; it also means to stop or prevent ❏ *A million fail, confounding oath on oath.* (*A Midsummer Night's Dream 3.2*)

contagion NOUN contagion is an old word for disease or poison ❏ *hell itself breathes out / Contagion to this world* (*Hamlet 3.2*)

contumely NOUN contumely is an old word for an insult ❏ *the proud man's contumely* (*Hamlet 3.1*)

counterfeit 1 VERB if you counterfeit something you copy or imitate it ❏ *Meantime your cheeks do counterfeit our roses* (*Henry VI part I 2.4*) 2 VERB in this context counterfeit means to pretend or make believe ❏ *I will counterfeit the bewitchment of some popular man* (*Coriolanus*)

coz NOUN coz was a shortened form of the word cousin ❏ *sweet my coz, be merry* (*As You Like It 1.2*)

cozenage NOUN cozenage is an old word meaning cheating or a deception ❏ *Thrown out his angle for my proper life, / And with such coz'nage* (*Hamlet 5.2*)

crave VERB crave used to mean to beg or request ❏ *I crave your pardon* (*The Comedy of Errors 1.2*)

crotchet NOUN crotchets are strange ideas or whims ❏ *thou hast some strange crotchets in thy head now* (*The Merry Wives of Windsor 2.1*)

cuckold NOUN a cuckold is a man whose wife has been unfaithful to him ❏ *As there is no true cuckold but calamity* (*Twelfth Night 1.5*)

cuffs, go to PHRASE this phrase meant to fight ❏ *the player went to cuffs in the question* (*Hamlet 2.2*)

cup VERB in this context cup is a verb which means to pour drink or fill glasses with alcohol ❏ *cup us til the world go round* (*Anthony and Cleopatra 2.7*)

cur NOUN cur is an insult meaning dog and is also used to mean coward ❏ *Out, dog! out, cur! Thou drivest me past the bounds / Of maiden's patience* (*A Midsummer Night's Dream 3.2*)

curiously ADV in this context curiously means carefully or skilfully ❏ *The sleeves curiously cut* (*The Taming of the Shrew 4.3*)

curry VERB curry means to flatter or to praise someone more than they are worth ❏ *I would curry with Master Shallow that no man could better command his servants* (*Henry IV part II 5.1*)

custom NOUN custom is a habit or a usual practice ❏ *Hath not old custom made this life more sweet / Than that of painted pomp?* (*As You Like It 2.1*)

cutpurse NOUN a cutpurse is an old word for a thief. Men used to carry their money in small bags (purse) that hung from their belts; thieves would cut the purse from the belt and steal their money ❏ *A cutpurse of the empire and the rule* (*Hamlet 3.4*)

dainty ADJ dainty used to mean splendid, fine ❑ *Why, that's my dainty Ariel!* (*Tempest 5.1*)

dally VERB if you dally with something you play with it or tease it ❑ *They that dally nicely with words may quickly make them wanton* (*Twelfth Night 3.1*)

damask COLOUR damask is a light-red or pink colour ❑ *Twas just the difference/Betwixt the constant red and mingled damask* (*As You Like It 3.5*)

dare 1 VERB dare means to challenge or, confront ❑ *He goes before me, and still dares me on* (*A Midsummer Night's Dream 3.3*) 2 VERB dare in this context means to present, deliver or inflict ❑ *all that fortune, death, and danger dare* (*Hamlet 4.4*)

darkly ADV darkly was used in this context to mean secretly or cunningly ❑ *I will go darkly to work with her* (*Measure for Measure 5.1*)

daw NOUN a daw was a slang term for idiot or fool (after the bird jackdaw which was famous for its stupidity) ❑ *Yea, just so much as you may take upon a knife's point and choke a daw withal* (*Much Ado About Nothing 3.1*)

debile ADJ debile meant weak or feeble ❑ *And debile minister great power* (*All's Well That Ends Well 2.3*)

deboshed ADJ deboshed was another way of saying corrupted or debauched ❑ *Men so disordered, deboshed and bold* (*King Lear 1.4*)

decoct VERB to decoct was to heat up, warm something ❑ *Can sodden water,/A drench for sur-reained jades*

... Decoct their cold blood to such valiant heat? (*Henry V 3.5*)

deep-revolving ADJ deep-revolving here uses the idea that you turn something over in your mind when you are thinking hard about it and so means deep-thinking, meditating ❑ *The deep-revolving Buckingham/No more shall be the neighbour to my counsels* (*Richard III 4.2*)

defect NOUN defect here means shortcoming or something that is not right ❑ *Being unprepared/Our will became the servant to defect* (*Macbeth 2.1*)

degree 1 NOUN degree here means rank, standing or station ❑ *Should a like language use to all degrees,/ And mannerly distinguishment leave out/Betwixt the prince and beggar* (*The Winter's Tale 2.1*) 2 NOUN in this context, degree means extent or measure ❑ *her offence/Must be of such unnatural degree* (*King Lear 1.1*)

deify VERB if you deify something or someone you worship it or them as a God ❑ *all.. deifying the name of Rosalind* (*As You Like It 3.2*)

delated ADJ delated here means detailed ❑ *the scope/Of these delated articles* (*Hamlet 1.2*)

delicate ADJ if something was described as delicate it meant it was of fine quality or valuable ❑ *thou wast a spirit too delicate* (*The Tempest 1.2*)

demise VERB in this context demise means to transmit, give or convey ❑ *what state ... Canst thou demise to any child of mine?* (*Richard III 4.4*)

deplore VERB to deplore means to express with grief or sorrow ❑ *Never more/ Will I my master's tears to you deplore* (*Twelfth Night 3.1*)

depose VERB if you depose someone you make them take an oath, or swear something to be true ❑ *Depose him in the justice of his cause* (*Richard II 1.3*)

depositary NOUN a depositary is a trustee ❑ *Made you ... my depositary* (*King Lear 2.4*)

derive 1 VERB to derive means to comes from or to descend (it usually applies to people) ❑ *No part of it is mine,/ This shame derives itself from unknown loins.* (*Much Ado About Nothing 4.1*) 2 VERB if you derive something from someone you inherit it ❑ *Treason is not inherited ...Or, if we derive it from our friends/ What's that to me?* (*As You Like It 1.3*)

descry VERB to see or catch sight of ❑ *The news is true, my lord. He is descried* (*Anthony and Cleopatra 3.7*)

desert 1 NOUN desert means worth or merit ❑ *That dost in vile misproson shackle up/ My love and her desert* (*All's Well That Ends Well 2.3*) 2 ADJ desert is used here to mean lonely or isolated ❑ *if that love or gold/ Can in this desert place buy entertainment* (*As You LIke It 2.4*)

design 1 VERB to design means to indicate or point out ❑ *we shall see/ Justice design the victor's chivalry* (*Richard II 1.1*) 2 NOUN a design is a plan, an intention or an undertaking ❑ *hinder not the honour of his design* (*All's Well That Ends Well 3.6*)

designment NOUN a designment was a plan or undertaking ❑ *The desperate tempest hath so bang'd the Turks,/ That their designment halts* (*Othello 2.1*)

despite VERB despite here means to spite or attempt to thwart a plan ❑ *Only to despite them I will endeavour anything* (*Much Ado About Nothing 2.2*)

device NOUN a device is a plan, plot or trick ❑ *Excellent, I smell a device* (*Twelfth Night 2.3*)

disable VERB to disable here means to devalue or make little of ❑ *he disabled my judgement* (*As You Like It 5.4*)

discandy VERB here discandy means to melt away or dissolve ❑ *The hearts ... do discandy , melt their sweets* (*Anthony and Cleopatra 4.12*)

disciple VERB to disciple is to teach or train ❑ *He ...was/ Discipled of the bravest* (*All's Well That Ends Well 1.2*)

discommend VERB if you discommend something you criticize it ❑ *my dialect which you discommend so much* (*King Lear 2.2*)

discourse NOUN discourse means conversation, talk or chat ❑ *which part of it I'll waste/ With such discourse as I not doubt shall make it/ Go quick away* (*The Tempest 5.1*)

discover VERB discover used to mean to reveal or show ❑ *the Prince discovered to Claudio that he loved my niece* (*Much Ado About Nothing 1.2*)

disliken VERB disguise, make unlike ❑ *disliken/ The truth of your own seeming* (*The Winter's Tale 4.4*)

dismantle VERB to dismantle is to remove or take away ❑ *Commit a thing so monstrous to dismantle/*

So many folds of favour (*King Lear 1.1*)

disponge VERB disponge means to pour out or rain down ❑ *The poisonous damp of night disponge upon me* (*Anthony and Cleopatra 4.9*)

distrain VERB to distrain something is to confiscate it ❑ *My father's goods are all distrained and sold* (*Richard II 2.3*)

divers ADJ divers is an old word for various ❑ *I will give out divers schedules of my beauty* (*Twelfth Night 1.5*)

doff VERB to doff is to get rid of or dispose ❑ *make our women fight/ To doff their dire distresses* (*Macbeth 4.3*)

dog VERB if you dog someone or something you follow them or it closely ❑ *I will rather leave to see Hector than not to dog him* (*Troilus and Cressida 5.1*)

dotage NOUN dotage here means infatuation ❑ *Her dotage now I do begin to pity* (*A Midsummer NIght's Dream 4.1*)

dotard NOUN a dotard was an old fool ❑ *I speak not like a dotard nor a fool* (*Much Ado About Nothing 5.1*)

dote VERB to dote is to love, cherish, care without seeing any fault ❑ *And won her soul; and she, sweet lady, dotes,/ Devoutly dotes, dotes in idolatry* (*A Midsummer Night's Dream 1.1*)

doublet NOUN a doublet was a man's close-fitting jacket with short skirt ❑ *Lord Hamlet, with his doublet all unbraced* (*Hamlet 2.1*)

dowager NOUN a dowager is a widow ❑ *Like to a step-dame or a dowage* (*A Midsummer Night's Dream 1.1*)

dowdy NOUN a dowdy was an ugly woman ❑ *Dido was a dowdy* (*Romeo and Juliet 2.4*)

dower NOUN a dower (or dowery) is the riches or property given by the father of a bride to her husband-to-be ❑ *Thy truth then by they dower* (*King Lear 1.1*)

dram NOUN a dram is a tiny amount ❑ *Why, everything adheres together that no dram of a scruple* (*Twelfth Night 3.4*)

drift NOUN drift is a plan, scheme or intention ❑ *Shall Romeo by my letters know our drift* (*Romeo and Juliet 4.1*)

dropsied ADJ dropsied means pretentious ❑ *Where great additions swell's and virtues none/ It is a dropsied honour* (*All's Well That Ends Well 2.3*)

drudge NOUN a drudge was a slave, servant ❑ *If I be his cuckold, he's my drudge* (*All's Well That Ends Well 1.3*)

dwell VERB to dwell sometimes meant to exist, to be ❑ *I'd rather dwell in my necessity* (*Merchant of Venice 1.3*)

earnest ADJ an earnest was a pledge to pay or a payment in advance ❑ *for an earnest of a greater honour/ He bade me from him call thee Thane of Cawdor* (*Macbeth 1.3*)

ecstasy NOUN madness ❑ *This is the very ecstasy of love* (*Hamlet 2.1*)

edict NOUN law or declaration ❑ *It stands as an edict in destiny.* (*A Midsummer Night's Dream 1.1*)

egall ADJ egall is an old word meaning equal ❑ *companions/Whose souls do bear an egall yoke of love* (*Merchant of Venice 2.4*)

eisel NOUN eisel meant vinegar ❑ *Woo't drink up eisel?* (*Hamlet 5.1*)

eke, eke out VERB eke meant to add to, to increase. Eke out nowadays means to make something last as long as possible – particularly in the sense of making money last a long time ❑ *Still be kind/And eke out our performance with your mind* (*Henry V Chorus*)

elbow, out at PHRASE out at elbow is an old phrase meaning in poor condition – as when your jacket sleeves are worn at the elbow which shows that it is an old jacket ❑ *He cannot, sir. He's out at elbow* (*Measure for Measure 2.1*)

element NOUN elements were thought to be the things from which all things were made. They were: air, earth, water and fire ❑ *Does not our lives consist of the four elements?* (*Twelfth Night 2.3*)

elf VERB to elf was to tangle ❑ *I'll ... elf all my hairs in knots* (*King Lear 2.3*)

embassy NOUN an embassy was a message ❑ *We'll once more hear Orsino's embassy.* (*Twelfth Night 1.5*)

emphasis NOUN emphasis here means a forceful expression or strong statement ❑ *What is he whose grief/Bears such an emphasis* (*Hamlet 5.1*)

empiric NOUN an empiric was an untrained doctor sometimes called a quack ❑ *we must not ... prostitute our past-cure malady/ To empirics* (*All's Well That Ends Well 2.1*)

emulate ADJ emulate here means envious ❑ *pricked on by a most emulate pride* (*Hamlet 1.1*)

enchant VERB to enchant meant to put a magic spell on ❑ *Damn'd as thou art, thou hast enchanted her,/ For I'll refer me to all things of sense* (*Othello 1.2*)

enclog VERB to enclog was to hinder something or to provide an obstacle to it ❑ *Traitors enscarped to enclog the guitless keel* (*Othello 1.2*)

endure VERB to endure was to allow or to permit ❑ *and will endure/ Our setting down before't.* (*Macbeth 5.4*)

enfranchise VERB if you enfranchised something you set it free ❑ *Do this or this;/ Take in that kingdom and enfranchise that;/ Perform't, or else we damn thee.'* (*Anthony and Cleopatra 1.1*)

engage VERB to engage here means to pledge or to promise ❑ *This to be true I do engage my life* (*As You Like It 5.4*)

engaol VERB to lock up or put in prison ❑ *Within my mouth you have engaoled my tongue* (*Richard II 1.3*)

engine NOUN an engine was a plot, device or a machine ❑ *their promises, enticements, oaths, tokens, and all these engines, of lust, are not the things they go under* (*All's Well That Ends Well 3.5*)

englut VERB if you were engulfed you were swallowed up or eaten whole ❑ *For certainly thou art so near the gulf,/ Thou needs must be englutted.* (*Henry V 4.3*)

enjoined ADJ enjoined describes people joined together for the same reason ❑ *Of enjoined penitents/*

There's four or five (*All's Well That Ends Well 3.5*)

entertain 1 VERB to entertain here means to welcome or receive ❑ *Approach, rich Ceres, her to entertain.* (*The Tempest 4.1*) 2 VERB to entertain in this context means to cherish, hold in high regard or to respect ❑ *and I quake,/Lest thou a feverous life shouldst entertain/And six or seven winters more respect/Than a perpetual honour.* (*Measure for Measure 3.1*) 3 VERB to entertain means here to give something consideration ❑ *But entertain it,/And though you think me poor, I am the man/Will give thee all the world.* (*Anthony and Cleopatra 2.7*) 4 VERB to entertain here means to treat or handle ❑ *your highness is not entertained with that ceremonious affection as you were wont* (*King Lear 1.4*)

envious ADJ envious meant spiteful or vindictive ❑ *he shall appear to the envious a scholar* (*Measure for Measure 3.2*)

ere PREP ere was a common word for before ❑ *ere this I should ha' fatted all the region kites* (*Hamlet 2.2*)

err VERB to err means to go astray, to make a mistake ❑ *And as he errs, doting on Hermia's eyes* (*A Midsummer Night's Dream 1.1*)

erst ADV erst was a common word for once or before ❑ *that erst brought sweetly forth/The freckled cowslip* (*Henry V 5.2*)

eschew VERB if you eschew something you deliberately avoid doing it ❑ *What cannot be eschewed must be embraced* (*The Merry Wives of Windsor 5.5*)

escote VERB to escote meant to pay for, support ❑ *How are they escoted?* (*Hamlet 2.2*)

estimable ADJ estimable meant appreciative ❑ *I could not with such estimable wonder over-far believe that* (*Twelfth Night 2.1*)

extenuate VERB extenuate means to lessen ❑ *Which by no means we may extenuate* (*A Midsummer Night's Dream 1.1*)

fain ADV fain was a common word meaning gladly or willingly ❑ *I would fain prove so* (*Hamlet 2.2*)

fall NOUN in a voice or music fall meant going higher and lower ❑ *and so die/That strain again! it had a dying fall* (*Twelfth Night 1.1*)

false ADJ false was a common word for treacherous ❑ *this is counter, you false Danish dogs!* (*Hamlet 4.5*)

fare VERB fare means to get on or manage ❑ *I fare well* (*The Taming of the Shrew Introduction 2*)

feign VERB to feign was to make up, pretend or fake ❑ *It is the more like to be feigned* (*Twelfth Night 1.5*)

fie EXCLAM fie was an exclamation of disgust ❑ *Fie, that you'll say so!* (*Twelfth Night 1.3*)

figure VERB to figure was to symbolize or look like ❑ *Wings and no eyes, figure unheedy haste* (*A Midsummer Night's Dream 1.1*)

filch VERB if you filch something you steal it ❑ *With cunning hast thou filch'd my daughter's heart* (*A Midsummer Night's Dream 1.1*)

flout VERB to flout something meant to scorn it ❑ *Why will you suffer her to flout me thus?* (*A Midsummer Night's Dream 3.2*)

fond ADJ fond was a common word meaning foolish ❑ *Shall we their fond pageant see?* (*A Midsummer Night's Dream 3.2*)

footing 1 NOUN footing meant landing on shore, arrival, disembarkation ❑ *Whose footing here anticipates our thoughts/A se'nnight's speed.* (*Othello 2.1*) 2 NOUN footing also means support ❑ *there your charity would have lacked footing* (*Winter's Tale 3.3*)

forsooth ADV in truth, certainly, truly
❑ *I had rather, forsooth, go before you like a man* (*The Merry Wives of Windsor 3.2*)

forswear VERB if you forswear you lie, swear falsely or break your word ❑ *he swore a thing to me on Monday night, which he forswore on Tuesday morning* (*Much Ado About Nothing 5.1*)

freshes NOUN a fresh is a fresh water stream ❑ *He shall drink nought brine, for I'll not show him/Where the quick freshes are.* (*Tempest 3.2*)

furlong NOUN a furlong is a measure of distance. It is the equivalent on one eight of a mile ❑ *Now would I give a thousand furlongs of sea for an acre of barren ground* (*Tempest 1.1*)

gaberdine NOUN a gaberdine is a cloak ❑ *My best way is to creep under his gaberdine* (*Tempest 2.2*)

gage NOUN a gage was a challenge to duel or fight ❑ *There is my gage, Aumerle, in gage to thine* (*Richard II 4.1*)

gait NOUN your gait is your way of walking or step ❑ *I know her by her gait* (*Tempest 4.1*)

gall VERB to gall is to annoy or irritate ❑ *Let it not gall your patience, good Iago,/That I extend my manners* (*Othello 2.1*)

gambol NOUN frolic or play ❑ *Hop in his walks, and gambol in his eyes* (*A Midsummer Night's Dream 3.1*)

gaskins NOUN gaskins is an old word for trousers ❑ *or, if both break, your gaskins fall.* (*Twelfth Night 1.5*)

gentle ADJ gentle means noble or well-born ❑ *thrice-gentle Cassio!* (*Othello 3.4*)

glass NOUN a glass was another word for a mirror ❑ *no woman's face remember/Save from my glass, mine own* (*Tempest 3.1*)

gleek VERB to gleek means to make a joke or jibe ❑ *Nay, I can gleek upon occasion* (*A Midsummer Night's Dream 3.1*)

gust NOUN gust meant taste, desire or enjoyment. We still say that if you do something with gusto you do it with enjoyment or enthusiasm ❑ *the gust he hath in quarrelling* (*Twelfth Night 1.3*)

habit NOUN habit means clothes ❑ *You know me by my habit* (*Henry V 3.6*)

heaviness NOUN heaviness means sadness or grief ❑ *So sorrow's heaviness doth heavier grow/For debt that bankrupt sleep doth sorrow owe* (*A Midsummer Night's Dream 3.2*)

heavy ADJ if you are heavy you are said to be sad or sorrowful ❑ *Away from light steals home my heavy son* (*Romeo and Juliet 1.1*)

hie VERB to hie meant to hurry ❑ *My husband hies him home* (*All Well That Ends Well 4.4*)

hollowly ADV if you did something hollowly you did it insincerely ❑ *If hollowly invert/ What best is boded me to mischief!* (*Tempest 3.1*)

holy-water, court PHRASE if you court holy water you make empty promises, or make statements which sound good but have no real meaning ❑ *court holy-water in a dry house is better than this rain-water out o'door* (*King Lear 3.2*)

howsoever ADV howsoever was often used instead of however ❑ *But howsoever strange and admirable* (*A Midsummer Night's Dream 5.1*)

humour NOUN your humour was your mood, frame of mind or temperament ❑ *it fits my humour well* (*As You Like It 3.2*)

ill ADJ ill means bad ❑ *I must thank him only,/ Let my remembrance suffer ill report* (*Antony and Cleopatra 2.2*)

indistinct ADJ inseparable or unable to see a difference ❑ *Even till we make the main and the aerial blue/ An indistinct regard.* (*Othello 2.1*)

indulgence NOUN indulgence meant approval ❑ *As you from crimes would pardoned be,/ Let your indulgence set me free* (*The Tempest Epilogue*)

infirmity NOUN infirmity was weakness or fraility ❑ *Be not disturbed with my infirmity* (*The Tempest 4.1*)

intelligence NOUN here intelligence means information ❑ *Pursue her; and for this intelligence/ If I have thanks* (*A Midsummer Night's Dream 1.1*)

inwards NOUN inwards meant someone's internal organs ❑ *the thought whereof/ Doth like a poisonous mineral gnaw my inwards* (*Othello 2.1*)

issue 1 NOUN the issue of a marriage are the children ❑ *To thine and Albany's issues,/ Be this perpetual* (*King Lear 1.1*) 2 NOUN in this context issue means outcome or result ❑ *I am to pray you, not to strain my speech,/ To grosser issues* (*Othello*)

kind NOUN kind here means situation or case ❑ *But in this kind, wanting your father's voice,/ The other must be held the worthier.* (*A Midsummer Night's Dream 1.1*)

knave NOUN a knave was a common word for scoundrel ❑ *How absolute the knave is!* (*Hamlet 5.1*)

league NOUN A distance. A league was the distance a person could walk in one hour ❑ *From Athens is her house remote seven leagues* (*A Midsummer Night's Dream 1.1*)

lief, had as ADJ I had as lief means I should like just as much ❑ *I had as lief the town crier spoke my lines* (*Hamlet 1.2*)

livery NOUN livery was a costume, outfit, uniform usually worn by a servant ❑ *You can endure the livery of a nun* (*A Midsummer Night's Dream 1.1*)

loam NOUN loam is soil containing decayed vegetable matter and therefore good for growing crops and plants ❑ *and let him have some plaster, or some loam, or some rough-cast about him, to signify wall* (*A Midsummer Night's Dream 3.1*)

lusty ADJ lusty meant strong ❑ *and oared/ Himself with his good arms in lusty stroke/ To th' shore* (*The Tempest 2.1*)

maidenhead NOUN maidenhead means chastity or virginity ❑ *What I am, and what I would, are as secret as maidenhead* (*Twelfth Night 1.5*)

mark VERB mark means to note or pay attention to ❑ *Where sighs and groans,/ Are made not marked* (*Macbeth 4.3*)

marvellous ADJ very or extremely ❑ *here's a marvellous convenient place for our rehearsal* (*A Midsummer Night's Dream 3.1*)

meet ADJ right or proper ❑ *tis most meet you should* (*Macbeth 5.1*)

merely ADV completely or entirely ❑ *Love is merely a madness* (*As You Like It 3.2*)

misgraffed ADJ misgraffed is an old word for mismatched or unequal ❑ *Or else misgraffed in respect of years* (*A Midsummer Night's Dream 1.1*)

misprision NOUN a misprision meant an error or mistake ❑ *Misprision in the highest degree!* (*Twelfth Night 1.5*)

mollification NOUN mollification is appeasement or a way of preventing someone getting angry ❑ *I am to hull here a little longer. Some mollification for your giant* (*Twelfth Night 1.5*)

mouth, cold in the PHRASE a well-known saying of the time which meant to be dead ❑ *What, must our mouths be cold?* (*The Tempest 1.1*)

murmur NOUN murmur was another word for rumour or hearsay ❑ *and then 'twas fresh in murmur* (*Twelfth Night 1.2*)

murrain NOUN murrain was another word for plague, pestilence ❑ *A murrain on your monster, and*

the devil take your fingers! (*The Tempest 3.2*)

neaf NOUN neaf meant fist ❑ *Give me your neaf, Monsieur Mustardseed* (*A Midsummer Night's Dream 4.1*)

nice 1 ADJ nice had a number of meanings here it means fussy or particular ❑ *An therefore, goaded with most sharp occasions,/ Which lay nice manners by, I put you to/ The use of your own virtues* (*All's Well That Ends Well 5.1*) 2 ADJ nice here means critical or delicate ❑ *We're good… To set so rich a man/ On the nice hazard of one doubtful hour?* (*Henry IV part 1*) 3 ADJ nice in this context means carefully accurate, fastidious ❑ *O relation/ Too nice and yet too true!* (*Macbeth 4.3*) 4 ADJ trivial, unimportant ❑ *Romeo .. Bid him bethink/ How nice the quarrel was* (*Romeo and Juliet 3.1*)

nonpareil NOUN if you are nonpareil you are without equal, peerless ❑ *though you were crown'd/ The nonpareil of beauty!* (*Twelfth Night 1.5*)

office NOUN office here means business or work ❑ *Speak your office* (*Twelfth Night 1.5*)

outsport VERB outsport meant to overdo ❑ *Let's teach ourselves that honorable stop,/ Not to outsport discretion.* (*Othello 2.2*)

owe VERB owe meant own, possess ❑ *Lend less than thou owest* (*King Lear 1.4*)

paragon 1 VERB to paragon was to surpass or excede ❑ *he hath achieved a maid/ That paragons description and wild fame* (*Othello 2.1*) 2 VERB to paragon could also mean to compare with ❑ *I will give thee* *bloody teeth If thou with Caesar paragon again/My man of men (Anthony and Cleopatra 1.5)*

pate NOUN pate is another word for head ❑ *Back, slave, or I will break thy pate across (The Comedy of Errors 2.1)*

paunch VERB to paunch someone is to stab (usually in the stomach). Paunch is still a common word for a stomach ❑ *Batter his skull, or paunch him with a stake (The Tempest 3.2)*

peevish ADJ if you are peevish you are irritable or easily angered ❑ *Run after that same peevish messenger (Twelfth Night 1.5)*

peradventure ADV perhaps or maybe ❑ *Peradventure this is not Fortune's work (As You Like It 1.2)*

perforce 1 ADV by force or violently ❑ *my rights and royalties,/Plucked from my arms perforce (Richard II 2.3)* 2 ADV necessarily ❑ *The hearts of men, they must perforce have melted (Richard II 5.2)*

personage NOUN personage meant your appearance ❑ *Of what personage and years is he? (Twelfth Night 1.5)*

pestilence NOUN pestilence was a common word for plague or disease ❑ *Methought she purg'd the air of pestilence! (Twelfth Night 1.1)*

physic NOUN physic was medicine or a treatment ❑ *tis a physic/That's bitter to sweet end (Measure for Measure 4.6)*

place NOUN place means a person's position or rank ❑ *Sons, kinsmen, thanes,/And you whose places are the nearest (Macbeth 1.4)*

post NOUN here a post means a messenger ❑ *there are twenty weak and wearied posts/Come from the north (Henry IV part II 2.4)*

pox NOUN pox was a word for any disease during which the victim had blisters on the skin. It was also a curse, a swear word ❑ *The pox of such antic, lisping, affecting phantasims (Romeo and Juliet 2.4)*

prate VERB to prate means to chatter ❑ *if thou prate of mountains (Hamlet 5.1)*

prattle VERB to prattle is to chatter or talk without purpose ❑ *I prattle out of fashion, and I dote In mine own comforts (Othello 2.1)*

precept NOUN a precept was an order or command ❑ *and my father's precepts I therein do forget. (The Tempest 3.1)*

present ADJ present here means immediate ❑ *We'll put the matter to the present push (Hamlet 5.1)*

prithee EXCLAM prithee is the equivalent of please or may I ask – a polite request ❑ *I prithee, and I'll pay thee bounteously (Twelfth Night 1.2)*

prodigal NOUN a prodigal is someone who wastes or squanders money ❑ *he's a very fool, and a prodigal (Twelfth Night 1.3)*

purpose NOUN purpose is used here to mean intention ❑ *understand my purposes aright (King Lear 1.4)*

quaff VERB quaff was a common word which meant to drink heavily or take a big drink ❑ *That quaffing and drinking will undo you (Twelfth Night 1.3)*

quaint 1 ADJ clever, ingenious ❏ *with a quaint device* (*The Tempest 3.3*) 2 ADJ cunning ❏ *I'll… tell quaint lies* (*Merchant of Venice 3.4*) 3 ADJ pretty, attractive ❏ *The clamorous owl, that nightly hoots and wonders/At our quaint spirit* (*A Midsummer Night's Dream 2.2*)

quoth VERB an old word which means say ❏ *'Tis dinner time.' quoth I* (*The Comedy of Errors 2.1*)

rack NOUN a rack described clouds or a cloud formation ❏ *And, like this insubstantial pageant faded,/ Leave not a rack behind* (*The Tempest 4.1*)

rail VERB to rant or swear at. It is still used occasionally today ❏ *Why do I rail on thee* (*Richard II 5.5*)

rate NOUN rate meant estimate, opinion ❏ *My son is lost, and, in my rate, she too* (*The Tempest 2.1*)

recreant NOUN recreant is an old word which means coward ❏ *Come, recreant, come, thou child* (*A Midsummer Night's Dream 3.2*)

remembrance NOUN remembrance is used here to mean memory or recollection ❏ *our remembrances of days foregone* (*All's Well That Ends Well 1.3*)

resolute ADJ firm or not going to change your mind ❏ *You are resolute, then?* (*Twelfth Night 1.5*)

revels NOUN revels means celebrations or a party ❏ *Our revels now are ended* (*The Tempest 4.1*)

rough-cast NOUN a mixture of lime and gravel (sometimes shells too) for use on an outer wall ❏ *and let him have some plaster, or some loam, or some rough-cast about him, to signify wall* (*A Midsummer Night's Dream 3.1*)

sack NOUN sack was another word for wine ❏ *My man-monster hath drowned his tongue in sack.* (*The Tempest 3.2*)

sad ADJ in this context sad means serious, grave ❏ *comes me the Prince and Claudio… in sad conference* (*Much Ado About Nothing 1.3*)

sampler NOUN a piece of embroidery, which often showed the family tree ❏ *Both on one sampler, sitting on one cushion* (*A Midsummer Night's Dream 3.2*)

saucy ADJ saucy means rude ❏ *I heard you were saucy at my gates* (*Twelfth Night 1.5*)

schooling NOUN schooling means advice ❏ *I have some private schooling for you both.* (*A Midsummer Night's Dream 1.1*)

seething ADJ seething in this case means boiling – we now use seething when we are very angry ❏ *Lovers and madmen have such seething brains* (*A Midsummer Night's Dream 5.1*)

semblative ADJ semblative means resembling or looking like ❏ *And all is semblative a woman's part.* (*Twelfth Night 1.4*)

several ADJ several here means separate or different ❏ *twenty several messengers* (*Anthony and Cleopatra 1.5*)

shrew NOUN An annoying person or someone who makes you cross ❏ *Bless you, fair shrew.* (*Twelfth Night 1.3*)

shroud VERB to shroud is to hide or shelter ❑ *I will here, shroud till the dregs of the storm be past* (*The Tempest 2.2*)

sickleman NOUN a sickleman was someone who used a sickle to harvest crops ❑ *You sunburnt sicklemen, of August weary* (*The Tempest 4.1*)

soft ADV soft here means wait a moment or stop ❑ *But, soft, what nymphs are these* (*A Midsummer Night's Dream 4.1*)

something ADV something here means somewhat or rather ❑ *Be something scanter of your maiden presence* (*Hamlet 1.3*)

sooth NOUN truly ❑ *Yes, sooth; and so do you* (*A Midsummer Night's Dream 3.2*)

spleen NOUN spleen means fury or anger ❑ *That, in a spleen, unfolds both heaven and earth* (*A Midsummer Night's Dream 1.1*)

sport NOUN sport means recreation or entertainment ❑ *I see our wars/ Will turn unto a peaceful comic sport* (*Henry VI part I 2.2*)

strain NOUN a strain is a tune or a musical phrase ❑ *and so die/ That strain again! it had a dying fall* (*Twelfth Night 1.1*)

suffer VERB in this context suffer means perish or die ❑ *but an islander that hath lately suffered by a thunderbolt.* (*The Tempest 2.2*)

suit NOUN a suit is a petition, request or proposal (marriage) ❑ *Because she will admit no kind of suit* (*Twelfth Night 1.2*)

sup VERB to sup is to have supper ❑ *Go know of Cassio where he supped tonight* (*Othello 5.1*)

surfeit NOUN a surfeit is an amount which is too large ❑ *If music be the food of love, play on;/ Give me excess of it, that, surfeiting,/ The appetite may sicken* (*Twelfth Night 1.1*)

swain NOUN a swain is a suitor or person who wants to marry ❑ *take this transformed scalp/ From off the head of this Athenian swain* (*A Midsummer Night's Dream 4.1*)

thereto ADV thereto meant also ❑ *If she be black, and thereto have a wit* (*Othello 2.1*)

throstle NOUN a throstle was a name for a song-bird ❑ *The throstle with his note so true* (*A Midsummer Night's Dream 3.1*)

tidings NOUN tidings meant news ❑ *that upon certain tidings now arrived, importing the mere perdition of the Turkish fleet* (*Othello 2.2*)

transgress VERB if you transgress you break a moral law or rule of behaviour ❑ *Virtue that transgresses is but patched with sin* (*Twelfth Night 1.5*)

troth, by my PHRASE this phrase means I swear or in truth or on my word ❑ *By my troth, Sir Toby, you must come in earlier o' nights* (*Twelfth Night 1.3*)

trumpery NOUN trumpery means things that look expensive but are worth nothing (often clothing) ❑ *The trumpery in my house, go bring it hither/ For stale catch these thieves* (*The Tempest 4.1*)

twink NOUN In the wink of an eye or no time at all ❑ *Ay, with a twink* (*The Tempest 4.1*)

undone ADJ if something or someone is undone they are ruined, destroyed, brought down ❑ *You have undone a man of fourscore three* (*The Winter's Tale 4.4*)

varlets NOUN varlets were villains or ruffians ❑ *Say again: where didst thou leave these varlets?* (*The Tempest 4.1*)

vaward NOUN the vaward is an old word for the vanguard, front part or earliest ❑ *And since we have the vaward of the day* (*A Midsummer Night's Dream 4.1*)

visage NOUN face ❑ *when Phoebe doth behold/ Her silver visage in the watery glass* (*A Midsummer Night's Dream 1.1*)

voice NOUN voice means vote ❑ *He has our voices* (*Coriolanus 2.3*)

waggish ADJ waggish means playful ❑ *As waggish boys in game themselves forswear* (*A Midsummer Night's Dream 1.1*)

wane VERB to wane is to vanish, go down or get slighter. It is most often used to describe a phase of the moon ❑ *but, O, methinks, how slow/ This old moon wanes* (*A Midsummer Night's Dream 1.1*)

want VERB to want means to lack or to be without ❑ *a beast that wants discourse of reason/ Would have mourned longer* (*Hamlet 1.2*)

warrant VERB to assure, promise, guarantee ❑ *I warrant your grace* (*As You Like It 1.2*)

welkin NOUN welkin is an old word for the sky or the heavens ❑ *The starry welkin cover thou anon/ With drooping fog as black as Acheron* (*A Midsummer Night's Dream 3.2*)

wench NOUN wench is an old word for a girl ❑ *Well demanded, wench* (*The Tempest 1.2*)

whence ADV from where ❑ *Whence came you, sir?* (*Twelfth Night 1.5*)

wherefore ADV why ❑ *Wherefore, sweetheart? what's your metaphor?* (*Twelfth Night 1.3*)

wide-chopped ADJ if you were wide-chopped you were big-mouthed ❑ *This wide-chopped rascal* (*The Tempest 1.1*)

wight NOUN wight is an old word for person or human being ❑ *She was a wight, if ever such wight were* (*Othello 2.1*)

wit NOUN wit means intelligence or wisdom ❑ *thou didst conclude hairy men plain dealers, without wit* (*The Comedy of Errors 2.2*)

wits NOUN wits mean mental sharpness ❑ *we that have good wits have much to answer for* (*As You Like It 4.1*)

wont ADJ to wont is to be in the habit of doing something regularly ❑ *When were you wont to use my sister thus?* (*The Comedy of Errors 2.2*)

wooer NOUN a wooer is a suitor, someone who is hoping to marry ❑ *and of a foolish knight that you brought in one night here to be her wooer* (*Twelfth Night 1.3*)

wot VERB wot is an old word which means know or learn ❑ *for well I wot/ Thou runnest before me* (*A Midsummer Night's Dream 3.2*)